The Grolier Library
of
Women's Biographies

THE GROLIER LIBRARY
OF
WOMEN'S BIOGRAPHIES

VOLUME 10

Ulanova, Galina Sergeyevna – Zoë

Grolier Educational
Sherman Turnpike, Danbury, Connecticut 06816

Published 1998 by Grolier Educational
Sherman Turnpike
Danbury, CT 06816

Copyright © 1998 by Market House Books Ltd.
Published for the School and Library market exclusively
by Grolier Educational, 1998

ISBN: 0-7172-9124-3

For information address the publisher:
Grolier Educational, Sherman Turnpike, Danbury, CT 06816

Library of Congress Cataloging-in-Publication Data

The Grolier library of women's biographies.
   p. cm.
  Includes index.
  Summary: Presents biographical sketches of 1,700 women from around the world
throughout history.
  ISBN 0-7172-9124-3
  1. Women–Biography–Dictionaries–Juvenile literature.   2. Women–History–Juvenile
literature. [1. Women–Biography.]
  CT3207.G76 1997
  920. 72–dc21
  [B]   97-25792
                                                              CIP
                                                                  AC

COMPILED AND TYPESET BY
    Market House Books Ltd., Aylesbury, UK

GENERAL EDITORS
    Dr. Alan Isaacs
    Elizabeth Martin

MARKET HOUSE EDITORS
    Peter Blair
    Jonathan Law
    Anne Stibbs

PICTURE RESEARCH
    Linda Wells

CONTRIBUTORS
    Rachel Beckett
    Dr. John Daintith
    Rosalind Fergusson
    Dr. Elizabeth Harris
    Amanda Isaacs
    Dr. Saul Kelly
    Jane Langley
    Dr. Peter Lewis
    Rabbi Julia Neuberger
    Simon Phillips
    Sharada Sugirtharajah
    Richard Tames
    Dr. Robert Youngson

CONTENTS

ix

PREFACE

From biblical times until relatively late in the 20th century the physically stronger half of the human race has systematically oppressed the physically weaker half. In almost every human society of which we have records, law, custom, religion, and economics have conspired to keep women in an inferior position. The presumably male authors of the book of Genesis in the Old Testament saw woman as no more than a product of spare-part surgery:

> *And the rib which the Lord God had taken from man, made he a woman...* (Genesis 3:16)

Even in the New Testament St. Paul shows all the prejudices of his era and background when he writes:

> *Let your women keep silence in the churches: for it is not permitted unto them to speak...* (I Corinthians 14:34)

In these matters, at least, the God of the Muslims appeared to be in agreement with the Judaeo-Christian Jehovah:

> *Men are in charge of women, because Allah hath made the one of them to excel...* (Koran, Ch. 4)

The ancient Greeks even doubted the role of women in procreation. According to Aeschylus:

> *The mother is not the parent of that which is called her child...*
> *The parent is he who mounts.* (*Eumenides*; 485 BC)

Against this background it is hardly surprising that the heroes and villains of the ancient world were almost exclusively men. Most women – deprived of the right to education – had no access to power or influence. Only a few women of exalted royal status succeeded in making an impact on the world stage: NEFERTITI in the 14th century BC, the queen of SHEBA in the 10th century BC, TAMIRIS in the 6th century BC, and CLEOPATRA in the 1st century BC. Shockingly, from some 14 centuries of history only a handful of women's names are remembered at all.

For the next 1,900 years the status of women improved only very gradually. Toward the end of the 19th century the American woman-suffrage leader Elizabeth Cady STANTON was justified in writing:

> *We still wonder at the stolid incapacity of all men to understand that woman feels the insidious distinctions of sex exactly as the black man does those of color...*
> (*History of Woman Suffrage*; 1880)

By the end of World War I most women in America and Europe were entitled to a vote and had some access to education – although some professions remained no-go areas for women. Only since the end of World War II, and then only in Western societies, have women achieved anything like full equality; most Western women now have the chance to follow an active professional life, if they choose, and to enjoy relationships in which both partners share the human experience, rather than the woman being merely a possession of the man.

Many of the biographies in this library of books provide an account of the struggles of the women who forced men to accept them as equals. Many others record the exceptional achievements of women who succeeded in making an impact in a man's world. Since World War II the growing number of women prime ministers – BANDARANAIKE in Sri Lanka, MEIR in Israel, GANDHI in India, THATCHER in the UK, BHUTTO in Pakistan, and ÇILLER in Turkey – has proved that women can compete with men for the highest political offices. In these pages will be found accounts of the achievements of the politicians, scientists, doctors, lawyers, writers, artists, educators, and sportswomen who have shown that women are in all respects the equals of men.

The justification for celebrating these lives and achievements in a set of books devoted exclusively to women is that for so much of human history women have been excluded or pushed to the margins. If this set can help redress the cruel prejudices and injustices of the past, its editors will be well satisfied. And if these biographies can provide an inspiration to help in the liberation of the women who are still oppressed in the less sophisticated parts of the contemporary world, the editors will be even better pleased.

The ten volumes in the set form one alphabetical sequence, and each volume contains a complete index of the whole set. In addition to some 1,850 biographies of women, the reader will also find dispersed throughout the set 20 short essay articles exploring the role of women in the world's main religions, in the professions, and in the arts. These essays can be located from the Table of Contents, which appears at the front of each volume. In both the biographies and the essays (and also in this Preface) the names of some women are printed in SMALL CAPITALS. This indicates that full biographies for these women can be found in the set. In Volume 10 an additional index of the literary, artistic, and scientific works of women will be found. If a noted woman does not appear in her alphabetical position in the text, the index should be checked to ensure that she does not appear under another name (maiden name, married name, pen name).

September 1997

Ulanova, Galina Sergeyevna

(1910–   )

RUSSIAN BALLERINA

Ulanova was one of the great figures of classical ballet in the 20th century. A poetic dancer, she had a magical ability to live her roles instead of merely acting them.

Galina Sergeyevna Ulanova was born in St. Petersburg, Russia, to parents who were both dancers and dance teachers. Her mother became her first teacher at the city dance school, and Professor Agrippina Vaganova taught her for the remaining four years that she studied there.

Ulanova spent the first half of her career at the Kirov Ballet (1928–44), where she created the role of Marie, a tragic Polish aristocrat, in *The Fountain of Bakhchisarai* in 1934. She also performed many principal roles in classic ballets. Delicate and pale, Ulanova brought something almost spiritual to her roles, using her body with great expression to create each character.

After dancing as a guest with the Bolshoi Ballet in Moscow, Ulanova joined the company in 1944 and remained with it until her retirement in 1962. With the Bolshoi Ulanova danced in the premieres of the ballets *The Red Poppy* (1950) and *The Stone Flower* (1954). She became well known for her performances in *Swan Lake, Raymonda, Don Quixote*, and especially *Giselle*. Many people view her portrayal of Giselle as the most perfectly danced and best acted of the 20th century.

In addition to her stage performances Ulanova danced in numerous movies, including *Stars of the Ballet* (1946), *Ballerina* (1947), *Trio Ballet* (1953), *Romeo and Juliet* (1954), and *The Bolshoi Ballet* (1957). Her famous interpretation of Giselle has also been recorded on film. After her retirement Ulanova was chairman of the jury in the International Ballet Competitions from 1964 to 1972. She also continued her association with the Bolshoi by coaching young dancers in important roles.

BIBLIOGRAPHY
Kahn, Albert, *Days with Ulanova* (1962).
L'vov-Anokhin, B., *Galina Ulanova* (1984).

Ullman, Tracey

(1959–   )

BRITISH ACTRESS, SINGER, AND DANCER

I can't bear being called a wacky, zany comedienne. I'm not a comedienne. I'm a character actress. I couldn't get up and tell a joke to save my life.

—Interview, 1988

Whether she thinks of herself as a comedienne or not, Tracey Ullman knows how to entertain people. Her diverse talents as an actress, singer, and dancer won her parts in various movies and ultimately her own TV show on the Fox Broadcasting Network (FBN).

Tracey Ullman was born in Slough, England. Her father died when she was six, and she and her sister were raised by their mother in a London suburb. Encouraged by her mother, Ullman developed a talent for performing and won a scholarship to London's Italia Conti Stage School. "Other girls wanted to be Joan COLLINS," said Ullman. "I wanted to be real." When she was 16, Ullman won a place in the chorus of *Gigi* in Berlin, Germany. On returning to London, she joined a dance troupe and played parts in several London musicals, including *Elvis*, *Grease*, and *The Rocky Horror Show*.

Ullman's first break came in 1981, when she appeared in the play *Four in a Million* and won an award for her performance. After this she starred in three British television series: *Three of a Kind*, *A Kick Up the Eighties*, and *Girls on Top*. It was *Three of a Kind* that made Ullman a household name in Britain, and in 1983 she won the British equivalent of an Emmy Award.

In 1984 Ullman branched out into recording and movies. She appeared with ex-Beatle Paul McCartney in *Give My Regards to*

Broad Street, and the same year four singles from her album *You Broke My Heart in Seventeen Places* reached the British top-ten list. The video of her single "They Don't Know" was one of MTV's most popular videos of 1984 and led to her appearance on talk shows, especially *The David Letterman Show*. Ullman's next movie role was in *Plenty* (1985), with Meryl STREEP. After that she appeared with Whoopi GOLDBERG in *Jumpin' Jack Flash* (1986) but became dissatisfied with the film work available. Then her agent sent a selection of her videotapes to one of television's most highly regarded producers, James Brooks.

Brooks was very impressed with Ullman's talent. *The Tracey Ullman Show* premiered on FBN that year and was nominated for five Emmy Awards. It featured Ullman playing an endless variety of characters and performing songs, dances, and sketches. The show ran for three seasons and made Ullman a national star.

In 1990 Ullman decided to leave the show to pursue her film and stage career. Although she was nominated for a Drama Desk Award for her one-woman play *The Big Love* (1991) and starred in the film *I Love You to Death* (1991), Ullman has yet to live up to the sensation she created on television. She has two children from her marriage (1984) with Allan McKeown.

Ullmann, Liv

(1939–)

NORWEGIAN ACTRESS AND
FILM DIRECTOR

Ullman was the most brilliant actress to come out of Swedish director Ingmar Bergman's acting company. She had her greatest successes in Bergman's films, making much less of an impact in Hollywood.

Liv Johanne Ullmann was born in Tokyo, Japan, where her Norwegian father was working as an engineer. During the Nazi occupation of Norway her family lived in Canada. After the war and her father's death Ullman returned to Norway with her mother and sister. Missing her father, she found comfort in reading and religion. She decided to become an actress and, after leaving school, studied drama for eight months in London, England.

On returning to Norway, Ullmann made her first stage appearance at Stavanger in the title role of *The Diary of Anne Frank*. After three years with the same company she joined the National Theater and the Norwegian Theater in Oslo, where she played Juliet in *Romeo and Juliet*, Ophelia in *Hamlet*, Nora in *A Doll's House*, and other classic roles.

Ullmann made her Norwegian film debut in 1957. In the early 1960s she began a relationship with the director Ingmar Bergman, who cast her in his movie *Persona* (1966). Ullmann demonstrated her remarkable acting ability by playing a character unable to speak and won great praise for her performance. Costarring with the Swedish actor Max von Sydow, Ullmann then appeared in Bergman's movies *Hour of the Wolf* (1968), *Shame* (1968), and *The Passion of Anna* (1969). In 1971 she received the New York Film Critics Award for her performance in Bergman's masterpiece *Cries* and *Whispers*. Bergman wrote the television film *The Six Faces of a Woman* especially for her in 1972.

After breaking her link with Bergman, Ullmann starred with von Sydow in Jan Troell's *The Emigrants* (1972). A success in America, the film won Ullmann an Oscar nomination and a Golden Globe Award. She then went to Hollywood, but the movies she made there – for example, *Lost Horizon* and *Forty Carats* (both 1973) – were unsuccessful.

Ullmann returned to Bergman's guidance to star in the brilliant *Scenes from a Marriage* (1974) and *Autumn Sonata* (1979). In the late 1970s she appeared on Broadway as Nora in *A Doll's House*, in the title role of *Anna Christie*, and in the musical *I Remember Mama*. She has also directed the films *Sofie* (1993) and *Private Confessions* (1997). Married twice, Ullmann has written two autobiographies, *Changing* (1978) and *Choices* (1984).

Undset, Sigrid

(1882–1949)

NORWEGIAN NOVELIST

Undset's work was at its finest when she combined a concern for the experiences of women with a colorful interpretation of history, most notably in *Kristin Lavransdatter* (1929). It earned her the Nobel Prize for literature.

Born in Kallundborg, Denmark, Undset had a Danish mother. Her father, a noted Norwegian archeologist, died when she was 11. There was no money to pay for a college education, and Sigrid had to earn her living. While she was working in a law office, she began to write. Her first success was *Jenny* (1911), a story of art students in Rome. In 1912 Undset married an artist, Anders C. Svarstad.

Undset was received into the Roman Catholic Church in 1924. Two years later she was separated from her husband. Undset's interest in the Middle Ages led to the writing of her most famous work, *Kristin Lavransdatter*. A study of a medieval woman's life from girlhood to old age, it was originally published in three volumes: *The Bridal Wreath* (1920), *The Mistress of Husaby* (1921), and *The Cross* (1922). It was widely praised and translated into many languages. In 1928 it won Undset the Nobel Prize for literature. Her religious and historical preoccupations were reflected in further novels, which included the two-part *Master of Hestviken* (1934), *The Faithful Wife* (1937), and *Madame Dorthea* (1940). She also wrote *Saga of the Saints* (1934), a religious history of Norway.

When the Germans invaded Norway, Undset escaped to the United States and spent several years there, returning to Norway in 1945. Her experiences are told in *Return to the Future* (1942). Other notable works include the children's tale *Sigurd and His Brave Companions* (1943) as well as short stories, essays, and poems. Undset died in Lillehammer, Norway.

Upshaw, Dawn

(1960–   )

AMERICAN SINGER

Dawn Upshaw combines great stylistic gifts with a pleasant if not spectacular soprano voice. Her intelligent, appealing interpretations have helped win audiences for relatively obscure modern works, and she has breathed fresh life into some of the standard light operatic roles.

Upshaw was born in Nashville, Tennessee, and was raised near Chicago. She graduated from Illinois Wesleyan University in 1982 and obtained a master's degree from the Manhattan School of Music in 1984. Later studies at the Aspen Music School focused on the performance of contemporary music. In 1984 Upshaw was chosen for the Metropolitan Opera's Young Artists program, leading to her Metropolitan Opera debut in a small role later that year. In 1989 Upshaw won a Grammy Award for *Knoxville, Summer of 1915*, a recording of a collection of American works.

By the 1991–92 season Upshaw was well established at the "Met," appearing that year in four Mozart roles (Despina in *Così fan tutte*, Pamina in *The Magic Flute*, Susanna in *The Marriage of Figaro*, and Ilia in *Idomeneo*). In 1992 she won her second Grammy for her recording *The Girl with Orange Lips*, a collection of songs by Ravel, Stravinsky, Delage, and Kim. That summer she also received excellent reviews in Messiaen's *Saint Francis of Assisi* at the Salzburg Festival and performed in Stravinsky's *Rake's Progress* at the festival of Aix-en-Provence in France.

Upshaw's large, enthusiastic following owes much to the fact that she has recorded popular and Broadway songs in addition to making extensive concert and opera appearances in the United States and abroad. She typifies the new-era prima donna with her emphasis on musical and linguistic versatility rather than on sensationalism. She is equally at home in popular and classical music. Though successful in light operatic roles, Upshaw is considered by some critics as better suited to concert work than to the opera house because of her subtle, intimate style.

Ursins, Princess des

(1642–1722)

FRENCH NOBLEWOMAN

As lady-in-waiting to Queen María Luisa, Ursins became the most influential member of the Spanish court during the first 14 years of Philip V's reign.

The daughter of a French duke, Marie-Anne de la Tremoille was born in Paris. She moved to Italy after her marriage, and when her first husband died, she married Flavio Orsini, Duke of Bracciano. They lived in Rome until Orsini's death in 1698, when his widow adopted the French form of his family name, Ursins.

After Philip V ascended the Spanish throne in 1700, the Princess des Ursins helped arrange his marriage to María Luisa of Savoy. Philip's grandfather, Louis XIV of France, then sent the princess to Spain as María Luisa's chief lady-in-waiting. A sharp-witted woman, the princess began to have great influence over the royal couple. With the French economist Jean Orry she also carried out important reforms in Spain's administration. It was the princess who chose ELIZABETH FARNESE as Philip's second wife after María Luisa's death in 1714, but this was her undoing. The new queen took an immediate dislike to her and banished her from Spain. She died in Rome.

Ursula, Saint

(late 3rd or early 4th century)

CHRISTIAN MARTYR

According to a 9th-century legend, Ursula, a British king's daughter, made a pilgrimage to Rome accompanied by 11,000 virgins. All of them were massacred by Huns on the way home.

Casting aside later myths, very little is known about Ursula. She may have been one of 11 (rather than 11,000) girls martyred near Cologne. Her feast, October 21, was removed from the church calendar in 1969 because of the uncertainty about her life. The 15th-century painter Carpaccio produced a series of panels, now in the Accademia, Venice, depicting the Saint Ursula legend.

Valadon, Suzanne

(1867–1938)

FRENCH PAINTER

Suzanne Valadon's career as an artist and model typifies the bohemian life associated with Paris in the late 19th and early 20th centuries, when it was the artistic capital of Europe.

Marie Clémentine Valadon was born in Bessines, near Limoges, France, to working-class parents – her mother was a laundress. First, she became a circus acrobat and then, at 15, an artists' model, posing for Toulouse-Lautrec, Puvis de Chavannes, Renoir, and Degas. At 16 she gave birth to an illegitimate son, who became the well-known painter Maurice Utrillo (1883–1955). About this time Suzanne began to draw and was encouraged by Toulouse-Lautrec – who advised her to change her name to Suzanne – and, especially, by Degas, who was amazed that a person of her background, without training, had such a masterly touch. After a while she gave up modeling altogether and turned to painting – landscapes, still lifes, and nudes.

Valadon's work shows some influence of Gauguin, but in general it is very personal, displaying simplicity and an earthy realism. She painted with a strong line, but her color was heavy and sometimes crude. At their best her paintings are vigorous and reflect her keen observation. Valadon died in Paris.

Vanderbilt, Gloria

(1924–)

AMERICAN ARTIST AND ACTRESS

If she has not yet made of herself a living work of art, she's come...as close as anyone I'd ever want to meet.
—Wyatt Cooper, Introduction to *Gloria Vanderbilt Book of Collage* (1970)

Rich, beautiful, and four times married, Gloria Vanderbilt also became famous as a painter, actress, writer, and designer.

The great-great-granddaughter of the multimillionaire Cornelius Vanderbilt, Gloria was born in New York City. A year later, on her father's death, she inherited $4,000,000, and her mother took her to live in Europe. After her return to America, the ten-year-old Gloria was nicknamed "poor little rich girl" when her paternal aunt fought her mother for custody and won. Gloria was sent to expensive schools but left at 17 to marry the actors' agent Pasquale di Cicco. Three years later she ran off with the conductor Leopold Stokowski, who was then over 60.

Vanderbilt married Stokowski in 1945 and had two sons. Based in New York City, she took up painting and writing poems. She gave her first one-woman show of oil paintings and pastels in 1948, and other successful shows followed.

In 1954 Vanderbilt ventured into acting. She appeared in various productions, including Noël Coward's *Tonight at 8:30* on television (1954) and *The Time of Your Life* on Broadway (1955). By this time she and Stokowski had agreed to divorce, and in 1956 Vanderbilt married the film director Sidney Lumet. A fourth marriage (in 1963), to Wyatt Cooper, produced two more sons.

In the late 1960s Vanderbilt turned to designing greetings cards and other items. By the time of Cooper's death in 1978 she had moved on to fabrics and fashion design, giving her name to a famous brand of jeans. Vanderbilt's published writings include poems, stories, articles, and an autobiography.

Van Duyn, Mona

(1921–)

AMERICAN POET

> Love and art...are compassionate.
> —*Valentines to the Wide World* (1959)

In 1992 Mona Van Duyn became the first woman poet laureate of the United States. Traditional in approach, her poetry tackles everyday experience with insight and gentle humor.

The daughter of a businessman, Mona Van Duyn was born in Waterloo, Iowa. After graduating from a teacher's course in 1942, she took an MA at the University of Iowa. That same year (1943) she married Jarvis Thurston. Van Duyn then established herself as a university English teacher, holding posts first in Iowa and later in Kentucky and Missouri.

In 1947 Van Duyn and her husband set up the journal *Perspective: A Quarterly of Literature*, which ran until 1967. In 1959 she published her first collection of poems, *Valentines to the Wide World*; this was followed by *A Time of Bees* (1964) and *To See, To Take* (1970). She also contributed poems, stories, and articles to a number of journals. Personal sorrows, including the deaths of parents and friends, were dealt with in some of her subsequent collections, *Bedtime Stories* (1972), *Letters from a Father* (1982), and *Firefall* (1993). *If It Be Not I: Collected Poems, 1959–1982* was published in 1993.

Van Duyn's work shows an awareness of both the cruelty and the beauty of life. She has won many awards, including the National Book Award (1971) and the Pulitzer Prize (1991), and has been chancellor of the Academy of American Poets (1985). In 1992 she was made not only poet laureate (an annual appointment) but also poetry consultant to the Library of Congress.

Varda, Agnès

(1928–)

FRENCH FILM DIRECTOR

Women have to make jokes about themselves, laugh about themselves, because they have nothing to lose.
—Interview, *Saturday Review*, 1972

Varda's work belongs to the "New Wave" of French cinema that emerged in the late 1950s. An original director with an eye for detail, she has written the screenplays for all her movies.

Born in Belgium to a French mother and a Greek father, Varda was raised and educated in the south of France. After World War II she studied in Paris at the Sorbonne and the Louvre and took a diploma in photography. From 1951 to 1961 Varda was a professional photographer. Her first movie, *La Pointe courte* (1954), was named after its setting, a fishing village she had known as a child. Despite her lack of experience as a director, the film's innovative technique (it had two interwoven plots) made it influential in the "New Wave" movement.

Varda's next feature, *Cleo from 5 to 7* (1962), was released in the year she married the film director Jacques Demy. It focuses on a singer whose outlook on life changes as she waits to find out whether or not she has cancer. More controversial was *Le Bonheur* (1965; Happiness). This story of marital infidelity and suicide, set in the idyllic France of the impressionist painters and accompanied by Mozart's music, was seen by many as tasteless and immoral, though it was pronounced Best Film at the Cannes Festival. A few years later Varda made three movies in America, including the feature *Lions Love* (1969). Her later works include the feminist movie *One Sings, the Other Does Not* (1977); *Vagabond* (1985), which won the Golden Lion at the Venice festival; *Jacquot of Nantes* (1991), a tribute to her late husband; and *The Hundred and One Nights* (1995).

Vaughan, Dame Janet

(1899–1993)

BRITISH MEDICAL DOCTOR
AND ACADEMIC

Janet Vaughan's most important contribution to medicine was in the field of hematology – the study of medical conditions relating to the blood.

Born and raised in southwest England, Vaughan studied medicine at Somerville College, Oxford, and completed her clinical training at University College Hospital, London (1927–29). The scenes of poverty she witnessed in London made her a socialist.

After taking up a scholarship to study in Boston, Massachusetts, for a year, Vaughan married David Gourlay in 1930, and they had two daughters. She held several academic posts in the early 1930s and in 1934 published a book on anemias – deficiencies in red blood cells or hemoglobin (the red, iron-rich substance that carries oxygen in the blood). In the late 1930s she set up an emergency blood transfusion service in London, based on techniques developed during the Spanish Civil War. During World War II Vaughan directed a blood-supply unit in northwest London, and after the war she was given the difficult task of rehabilitating half-starved victims of German concentration camps.

As principal of Somerville, her old Oxford college, from 1945 to 1967, Vaughan was popular for her strong character, energy, organizing skills, and warm personality. She was also a member of a number of public committees, including one promoting equal pay for women (1944–46). Continuing her own research, she wrote several books and articles on the medical effects of radiation. Vaughan received many honors from Oxford, Cambridge, and other universities. She was made a Dame Commander of the British Empire in 1957.

Vaughan, Sarah

(1924–1990)

AMERICAN JAZZ SINGER

> Is that child singing or am I crazy?
> —Earl Hines, on first hearing Vaughan,
> *c.* 1942

Sarah Vaughan had a deep, rich voice with a wide range, and although she could hit any note right on, she was always varying and embellishing what she sang. Her many popular recordings include "It's Magic," "Banana Boat Song," "Broken-Hearted Melody," and "Send in the Clowns."

Vaughan grew up in her birthplace, Newark, New Jersey. Her parents were both musical, and at the age of seven Sarah joined her mother in their local church choir. She also learned piano and organ and helped out locally as an accompanist.

Sneak visits to a local bar taught Vaughan to love jazz, and at 18 she won a talent contest at the Apollo Theater, Harlem, New York. Spotted by Billy Eckstine, she was recruited into the band of Earl Hines (1943). A year later she joined Eckstine's own breakaway band. With her fluid, vocal variations Vaughan made a big contribution to Eckstine's pioneering "bebop" style, which emphasized the importance of improvising melodies, before she left to pursue a solo career.

Vaughan married George Treadwell, the first of her four husbands, in 1947. He became her manager and spent his savings on making her a star. She began to make recordings and in 1949 signed with Columbia. A year later her records were selling in huge numbers.

In the 1950s and 1960s Vaughan enjoyed international fame. Nicknamed "Sassy," she traveled widely and made numerous recordings (from 1953 with Mercury). Her popularity suffered during the rock 'n' roll era, but in the 1970s she reemerged as a pop star, usually accompanied by a backup group or band. After signing up with Mainstream records in 1972, she made further albums and in 1982 won a Grammy Award.

Veil, Simone

(1927–)

FRENCH STATESWOMAN

If this [European] parliament has a Jew, a woman, for its president, it means everyone has the same rights.
—Remark, 1979

A survivor of the German concentration camps, in 1979 Simone Veil was voted president of the first directly elected European parliament.

The fourth child of a Jewish architect, Simone Jacob was born in Nice, southern France. In 1944, when Simone had just left school, she and her mother and sister were deported to Auschwitz concentration camp. Her mother died there, and Simone and her sister were moved to another camp at Belsen. When the camp was liberated by the Allies in 1945, the sisters found no trace of the rest of their family. Picking up the pieces of her life, Simone studied law and political science at the Paris Institute for Political Studies, where she met Antoine Veil; they married in 1946.

For the next ten years Simone Veil was busy with her family of three sons, but in 1956 she became a magistrate. Soon afterward she joined the French ministry of justice, where she dealt with issues concerning prisoners and children. She rose within the ranks and became the first female French secretary of state in 1970.

In 1974 Veil was chosen as the minister for health in Giscard d'Estaing's government. In a Catholic country she was a controversial minister, passing legislation to promote contraception and legalize abortion. Nevertheless, she was admired for her courage, self-control, and sincerity.

In 1979 Veil ran for the European parliament and was not only elected but also voted its president. After serving for three years, she decided not to run for reelection. Instead, she became chair of the parliament's legal affairs committee and, later, of the Liberal and Democratic Reformist Group. After leaving the European parliament, Veil served as the French minister of social affairs from 1993 to 1995. She has won many prizes and awards.

Verchères, Marie Madeleine Jarret de

(1678–1747)

FRENCH-CANADIAN HEROINE

Verchères's fame rests on her courage and leadership in mounting a defense during a week-long siege from Iroquois tribesmen.

Marie Madeleine was born in Verchères, Quebec, Canada. The event that made her famous occurred at her father's farm on the St. Lawrence River, about 20 miles (32 km) northeast of Quebec City. In October 1692, when her parents were away, Iroquois attacked the settlement. Most of the male settlers were ambushed and killed where they worked in the fields. The 14-year-old Madeleine escaped to the local fort, which was occupied by two soldiers, an old man, several women with young children, and the girl's two younger brothers. She gave out guns to all who were able to handle them, directed the defense of the fort, and resisted the attacks of the Iroquois until relief arrived from Montreal a week later. For this act of heroism she was awarded a pension by the French crown.

Verchères married Pierre Thomas Tarieu de la Pérade in 1706 and is said to have saved his life in 1722 when he was assaulted by a Native American. She died in Ste. Anne de la Pérade, Quebec.

Verdy, Violette

(1933–)

FRENCH BALLET DANCER AND
DANCE DIRECTOR

A significant figure in 20th-century ballet, Verdy has performed widely, notably with the American Ballet Theater and the New York City Ballet, and has directed the Paris Opéra Ballet.

Born Nelly Guillerm in Pont-l'Abbé, Brittany, Verdy studied dance with Madame Rousanne and Victor Gsovsky in Paris. A child prodigy, she first appeared with the Ballets of the Champs-Elysées before she was 12, and she remained with the company until 1949. In that year she appeared in the movie *Ballerina* and changed her name to Verdy. In 1950 and again in 1953–54 she danced with Roland Petit's Ballets de Paris. Her most famous role with the company – and one that was specially created for her – was the bride in *Le Loup* (1953; The Wolf). In 1954 she was again on screen in *The Glass Slipper*. Verdy performed with the London Festival Ballet (1954–55) before moving to New York City, where she became a leading dancer with the American Ballet Theater (1957–58) and appeared in the title role of *Miss Julie*.

From 1958 until 1977 Verdy was principal dancer with the New York City Ballet, where she danced lead roles created for her by George Balanchine. Some of her other important ballet roles were in *Romeo and Juliet* (1955), *Cinderella* (1955), *Episodes* (1959), *Jewels* (1967), *Dances at a Gathering* (1969), and *Pulcinella* (1972).

From 1977 until 1980 Verdy was director of the Paris Opéra Ballet, where she added a number of modern works to the repertoire. She was then associate artistic director of the Boston Ballet until 1984. While there she staged Nureyev's *La Sylphide*, introduced new ballets, choreographed several works, and improved the classical training at the ballet school.

In 1984 Verdy became a teaching associate with the New York City Ballet. She has served as a guest teacher with the Paris Opéra Ballet and other companies, a guest choreographer for regional and college companies, and an artistic consultant for the Royal and San Francisco ballet companies, among others. She has also won several awards and honors, and is the author of *Giselle: A Role for a Lifetime* (1977) and *Of Swans, Sugarplums, and Satin Slippers: Ballet Stories for Children* (1991).

Vestris, Madame

(1797–1856)

BRITISH ACTRESS AND SINGER

Famed for such songs as "Cherry Ripe" and "I've Been Roaming" and for her excellence in light comedy, Madame Vestris may also have been the first woman in the history of the stage to lease and run a theater.

Born Lucia Elizabeth Bartolozzi in London, she married Auguste-Armand Vestris in 1813 but separated from him a few years later. She began her 40-year stage career as Proserpina in an opera by Peter von Winter and might have had a great future in opera if she had troubled to train her contralto voice. As an actress, she scored great successes as Phoebe in *Paul Pry* and, in male costume, as Macheath in *The Beggar's Opera*. She also appeared as Cherubino in *The Marriage of Figaro*. Having become rich by 1830, Madame Vestris leased the Olympic Theatre, London, which she managed until 1837. She later managed Covent Garden (1839–42) and the Lyceum (1847–55), both in London. Despite constant financial difficulties, she was an excellent manager and improved scenery, costume, and staging. In 1838 she married Charles James Mathews, a noted actor.

Viardot-García, Pauline

(1821–1910)

FRENCH OPERA SINGER

A mezzo-soprano, Pauline Viardot-García was one of the most famous and distinguished operatic singers of the 19th century.

Michelle Ferdinande Pauline García was born in Paris, a daughter of the famous tenor Manuel García. Her sister was the great contralto Maria MALIBRAN. Having sung at concerts in Belgium, Germany, and France, she gave her first operatic performance as Desdemona in Rossini's *Otello* in London in 1839. In 1841 she married Louis Viardot, a journalist and director of the Italian Theater in Paris. After this she toured Europe with her husband.

At the Paris Opéra, Pauline Viardot created the role of Fidès in Meyerbeer's *The Prophet* (1849) and the title role in Gounod's *Sappho* (1851). In 1859 she appeared in a revival of Gluck's *Orpheus and Eurydice*, prepared for the Paris Opéra by Berlioz. She sang the role of Orpheus more than 150 times.

Pauline Viardot had a wide vocal range, taking both soprano and contralto roles. She was also known for her dramatic skill and intellectual distinction. After retiring from the stage in 1863, she took up composing and teaching. Her opera *Le Dernier Sorcier* (The Last Sorcerer), to a libretto by her close friend (and possible lover) Ivan Turgenev, was performed at Weimar in 1869. Viardot died in Paris. The autographed score of Mozart's *Don Giovanni*, which she owned, was willed to the library of the Paris Conservatory.

Victoria

(1819–1901)

QUEEN OF THE UNITED KINGDOM

It is impossible to imagine a *politer* little woman [than Victoria].
—Thomas Carlyle, letter, 1869

Nowadays a parlour-maid as ignorant as Queen Victoria was when she came to the throne would be classed as mentally defective.
—George Bernard Shaw

Spanning 63½ years, Queen Victoria's reign was the longest in British history and saw greater change than had ever previously been known. It was an age of industrialization, invention, scientific advancement, and imperialist expansion. But it was also a time when the problems of a "modern" society first became evident. Urbanization, unemployment, and pollution are among the 20th-century problems with roots in the Victorian era.

Known in infancy as Drina, Alexandrina Victoria was the only child of Edward Augustus (1767–1820), Duke of Kent, and his wife Victoria Mary Louisa (1786–1861). Her father, the fourth son of King George III, had married her mother (the daughter of the Duke of Saxe-Coburg-Saalfeld and the widow of the Prince of Leiningen-Dachsburg-Hardenburg) to produce an heir. Shortly before her birth the future queen's parents left their home in Franconia, Germany, so that she could be born in London, in the royal palace at Kensington. However, her father died in debt before she was a year old, and there were few luxuries during her lonely childhood at Kensington Palace. The young princess was distressed by quarrels between her mother and the English royal family. She became greatly attached to her governess, the Hanoverian baroness Louise Lehzen, who provided her with a somewhat limited education. When she was 13, Victoria started to keep a journal, which she maintained to the end of her life. In it she recalled that she had not been allowed to walk downstairs without someone holding her hand until she came to the throne.

Victoria became queen on the death of her uncle, William IV, in 1837 and was crowned in Westminster Abbey the following year. Almost unknown by the official world, the young girl impressed everyone with her poise and grace. She took a liking to her prime minister, the Whig (liberal) Lord Melbourne, who tutored her in politics and worldly wisdom. Having become a faithful Whig herself, Victoria obstructed Sir Robert Peel's attempt to form a Conservative government in 1839 when she refused to replace the ladies of her bedchamber appointed during the Whig administration. Another rumor that she had been unkind to the Tory lady-in-waiting Lady Flora Hastings began to make the queen unpopular.

Victoria's popularity was restored through marriage. Her mother and her uncle, King Leopold of the Belgians, had long thought of her cousin, Prince Albert of Saxe-Coburg-Gotha, as a suitable consort. The handsome prince captured Victoria's heart, and she proposed to him at Windsor Castle in 1839. They were married the next year. Albert was a popular choice, and the marriage was a very happy one. Victoria was greatly influenced by her husband in all aspects of her life. The couple had nine children: Victoria, the Princess Royal, later Empress of Germany (1840–1901); Albert Edward, Prince of Wales, later Edward VII (1841–1910); Alice, later Grand Duchess of Hesse-Darmstadt (1843–78); Alfred, Duke of Edinburgh, later Duke of Saxe-Coburg-Gotha (1844–1900); Helena, later Princess of Schleswig-Holstein (1846–1923); Louise, later Duchess of Argyll (1848–1939); Arthur, Duke of Connaught (1850–1942); Leopold, Duke of Albany (1853–84); and Beatrice, later Princess of Battenberg (1857–1944).

The responsibilities of a large family allowed the queen little time for society. Under her husband's influence she grew to dislike fashionable life and to enjoy country pursuits. There was no shortage of money. In addition to the £385,000 per year paid by Parliament throughout her reign, Victoria received from the

Duchy of Lancaster £60,000 per year, and in 1852 she also gained £500,000 in a bequest from the eccentric John Camden Neild. In 1845 Victoria acquired Osborne, a seaside estate on the Isle of Wight, and in 1848 she leased the estate of Balmoral in the Scottish highlands, which she purchased in 1852. New royal residences, largely designed by Prince Albert, were built on these estates, and Victoria afterward spent less time in her official residences, Buckingham Palace and Windsor Castle, both of which she disliked.

During Victoria's reign the monarchy developed a new ceremonial function in relation to the public and to state affairs. The queen paid several visits to the large industrial towns. In 1851 she opened the Great Exhibition, a showcase for Britain's technological supremacy planned by Prince Albert, and in 1855 she paid an official visit to Napoleon III of France. Guided by Albert, she also intervened in politics. She promoted the repeal of the Corn Laws (1846) to relieve the famine in Ireland (then part of the United Kingdom) but strongly opposed attempts by the foreign secretary, Lord Palmerston, to build up new democratic nationalistic forces in Europe. She and Albert were on friendly terms with the rulers of Belgium, Prussia, Portugal, and France and had a knowledge of foreign affairs that was in some ways better and more current than that of the government. Their disapproval of Palmerston was a major factor in his dismissal by the prime minister, Lord John Russell, in 1851. A year later Victoria welcomed Lord Aberdeen's formation of a coalition government, which she had helped to engineer. Although Victoria and Albert failed to prevent the outbreak of the Crimean War in 1853, Victoria won public approval by organizing relief for the wounded and visiting hospitals. She also distributed medals and instituted the Victoria Cross (VC), the highest British award for military bravery.

When Albert died from typhoid fever in 1861, the queen was devastated. She dressed in full mourning and used writing paper with a mourning band for the rest of her days. For years she lived in seclusion, appearing only to unveil memorials to her "prince consort," as she had named him in 1857, and in 1866 to open Parliament. She tried to continue her former involvement in public affairs but found it increasingly difficult.

Victoria had intense prejudices, which she never attempted to hide. In particular she loathed the liberal statesman William Gladstone; in 1880 she tried to prevent him becoming prime minister, and in 1885 she publicly blamed him for the death of General Charles Gordon at Khartoum in the Sudan. On the other hand, she doted on the Tory Benjamin Disraeli, who as prime minister in 1876 gave her the title Empress of India (India then being part of the British Empire). But despite her prejudices, the queen showed a devotion to duty that touched the public and helps to explain the almost frenzied celebrations that marked her golden jubilee of 1887, her diamond jubilee in 1897, her appearances during the Boer War from 1899, and her appearance in Dublin in 1900.

Victoria was a short, plain woman, though graceful and in her youth very fair. She had a beautiful speaking voice and spoke German, French, and late in her life even a little Hindustani. She was shy in public, especially in the presence of those she thought cleverer than herself. She enjoyed drama, music, dancing, poetry (especially Tennyson's *In Memoriam*, which comforted her during her widowhood) and writing journals and letters. Though hastily written and sometimes ungrammatical, her writings are among the most vivid materials for a study of the 19th century. Some extracts from her journals were published during her lifetime in *Leaves from the Journal of Our Life in the Highlands* (1868) and *More Leaves* (1883). After Albert's death she spent many months in the seclusion of Balmoral Castle, where she formed some kind of relationship with a manservant, John Brown, whom she promoted to a position enabling him to attend to her in London and the Isle of Wight. The exact nature of this relationship has never been discovered. After her death at Osborne House passages from her journals were burned by her youngest daughter, who was her literary executor.

BIBLIOGRAPHY
Charlot, Monica, *Victoria: The Young Queen* (1991).
Hibbert, Christopher, *Queen Victoria in her Letters* (1985).
Nevill, Barry St. John, ed., *Life at the Court of Queen Victoria* (1984).
Plowden, Alison, *The Young Victoria* (1981).
Shearman, Deirdre, *Queen Victoria* (1985).
Woodham-Smith, Cecil, *Queen Victoria* (1986).

Vieira da Silva, Maria Helena

(1908–1992)

PORTUGUESE-BORN FRENCH ABSTRACT PAINTER

Although she became a French citizen in 1956 and lived in Paris until her death, Vieira da Silva is generally considered Portugal's most important contemporary painter. Her paintings, often resembling mazes or mosaics, reflect the sense of confusion often experienced in modern cities.

Vieira da Silva was born in Lisbon, Portugal. From 1928 she studied sculpture in Paris with two followers of Auguste Rodin, Charles Despiau and Emile-Antoine Bourdelle, whose works had an abstract element. She also studied printmaking and painting with Othon Friesz and Fernand Léger. From Léger she gained an interest in the angular style known as cubism and in the theme of modern technology. In 1930 she married the Hungarian artist Arpad Szenés.

Vieira da Silva produced a controlled type of abstraction in her works, using mainly earth tones. Characteristic oil paintings, such as *The Dream* (1949; private collection, Finland) and *Invisible Walker* (1951; Museum of Modern Art, San Francisco), are made up of linear patterns that suggest perspective and space from different viewpoints. Two superb oils on canvas, *Chess Game* (1943; Pompidou Center, Paris) and *Card Players* (1947; private collection, Neuilly), include half-disguised figures that magically and playfully reveal themselves through wavy checkerboard patterns.

After 1946, the year she first exhibited in New York City, Vieira da Silva attracted the interest of the American abstract expressionist painters. In 1988 a major exhibition of her past work was held in Lisbon and Paris. Her paintings can be seen in many permanent collections, including the Guggenheim Museum, New York City; the Tate Gallery, London; and the National Museum, Amsterdam. She died in Paris.

Vigée-Lebrun, Marie Anne Elisabeth

(1755–1842)

FRENCH PORTRAIT PAINTER

One of the first women ever to become famous as an artist, Vigée-Lebrun specialized in portraits of royalty, painted in a somewhat sentimental style.

Born in Paris, Elisabeth Vigée was trained in painting by her father and encouraged by Gabriel François Doyen and Joseph Vernet. In 1776 she married the painter Jean Baptiste Pierre Lebrun; they had a daughter but later separated.

In 1779 Mme. Vigée-Lebrun painted Queen MARIE ANTOINETTE, marking the beginning of her lifelong career as a painter of royalty. Benefiting from the fashionable new idea that women should be taken seriously, she was elected to membership in the French Royal Academy in 1783.

At the outbreak of the French Revolution in 1789 Vigée-Lebrun fled to Rome with her daughter. The next year she went to Naples, where she painted the queen and her children, as well as Emma HAMILTON. She then traveled through Austria and Russia, receiving commissions from CATHERINE II (the Great) of Russia and other royal figures. She returned to France in 1801 and a year later went to England, where she painted the Prince of Wales (later George IV). Vigée-Lebrun returned to Paris from her long exile in 1805 and painted Napoleon's sister, Mme. Marie Murat.

Most of the large number of portraits that Vigée-Lebrun painted were of women. The aim was to make the sitters look as pretty as possible and to show off their fine costumes. But although she had to do what was fashionable and therefore profitable, Vigée-Lebrun had the talent of a great painter. Toward the end of her life she spent much of her time at her country house in Louveciennes, and in 1835 she wrote her memoirs. Some of her paintings are on display in the Metropolitan Museum, New York City; the Louvre, Paris; and the National Gallery and Wallace Collection, London. Portraits of Marie Antoinette and her children are in the Versailles Museum, and a self-portrait is in the Uffizi Gallery, Florence.

See also LABILLE-GUIARD, ADELAIDE.

Vionnet, Madeleine

(1876–1975)

FRENCH FASHION DESIGNER

Vionnet was responsible for a complete change in women's fashion that occurred after 1918 by replacing the 19th century's rigid clothing with the fluid, modern style of dress. Viewing clothes as a natural wrap, almost another skin, for the body, she liked to give them shape by means of their stretchable elements (bias, pleats, etc.) rather than by such features as darts.

Born in Aubervilliers, France, Vionnet was apprenticed at the age of 12 to a dressmaker and spent the rest of her life in the trade. She worked for the London dressmaker Kate Reilly from about 1896 to 1901, then returned to Paris to work for the house of Callot Soeurs and afterward Jacques Doucet. She opened her own fashion house in Paris in 1912.

Vionnet believed clothing should be comfortable and supple. Discarding boned structures and heavy undergarments, she cut clothes on the bias (diagonally), producing fluidity and style. This revolutionized clothing, since instead of being stiff, the fabric was able to stretch slightly to match the shape of the body. She introduced halter and cowl (hood-type) necklines; new lingerie finishes – a type of frilly pleating called crimping and a technique of embroidering over gathers called fagoting; hook-and-eye and wrap-over fastenings; soft fabrics, such as crêpe-de-chine; and such features as bouncy hems, pleating, and exposed seaming. Vionnet's dresses were daring, even in the liberal 1920s and 1930s, because the light, unstructured fabric would cling to the body, showing off the wearer's figure. Her dresses moved gently with the wearer's movements to create a dancelike effect.

Except for a brief interruption during World War I, Vionnet continued to design until she officially retired in 1940, becoming a legend in her long lifetime. Numerous American and European designers studied or were influenced by her work. She retained her interest in fashion almost until her death.

See also CHANEL, COCO.

BIBLIOGRAPHY
Demornex, Jacqueline, *Vionnet* (1991).

Von Stade, Frederica

(1945–   )

AMERICAN SINGER

Von Stade has been consistently successful in opera, concerts, and recordings thanks to her strong vocal technique and lively manner. Her light, agile singing and sunny personality have come across especially well in the comic operas of Mozart and Rossini, while her mastery of language and sense of style have served her well in performing subtle French art songs.

Frederica Von Stade was born in Somerville, New Jersey. After studying at the Mannes College of Music in New York City and the Mozart School in Paris, she reached the semifinals in the Metropolitan Opera Auditions and won a contract with the "Met" in 1969. She made her debut at the "Met" a year later and was soon performing leading roles there and in other prominent theaters. From 1973 Von Stade made many appearances as the boy Cherubino in Mozart's *The Marriage of Figaro* in both America and Europe. As well as singing at American venues, including performances with the Houston Grand Opera and the San Francisco and Boston operas, she appeared at Covent Garden (London), La Scala (Milan), the Spoleto in Italy, and the Vienna State Opera.

In addition to the standard roles for lighter mezzo-sopranos, Von Stade sang in several world premieres, starting in 1971 with a leading part in Heitor Villa-Lobos's *Yerma* at Santa Fe. She created the role of Nina in *The Seagull* by Thomas Pasatieri at the Houston Grand Opera in 1974; was the original Tina in *The Aspern Papers* by Dominick Argento at the Dallas Opera in 1988; and starred as the Marchioness of Merteuil in the world premiere of *The Dangerous Liaisons* by Conrad Susa at the San Francisco Opera in 1994. The Metropolitan Opera celebrated her 25th anniversary season by featuring her in a new production of Debussy's *Pelléas and Mélisande* in 1995.

In the latest phase of her career Von Stade has extended her concert and recital repertoire to include modern song cycles and other less familiar works. She has also ventured into operetta and has recorded Broadway musical comedies, including *Showboat* and *The Sound of Music.*

von Trotta, Margarethe

(1942–   )

GERMAN FILM DIRECTOR, SCREENWRITER, AND ACTRESS

Margarethe von Trotta's thoughtful films about the lives and relationships of women have made her one of Germany's most respected directors.

Born into an upper-class family in Berlin, Margarethe von Trotta studied German and Latin literature at universities in Munich and Paris. She subsequently trained as an actress and began to appear on the German stage from the mid-1960s.

In 1969, the year she made her film debut in Rainer Werner Fassbinder's *Gods of the Plague,* von Trotta married Volker Schlondorff, a young director who had recently emerged at the forefront of the so-called "New German Cinema." For the next five years the couple collaborated on a series of well-received films, including *The Sudden Fortune of the Poor People of Kombach* (1971) and *Summer Lightning* (1972), which were directed by Schlondorff but starred and were cowritten by von Trotta. In 1975 they codirected and cowrote one of the best-known German films of the 1970s, *The Lost Honor of Katherina Blum*; the film concerns an ordinary woman who is ruthlessly persecuted by the media after being falsely labeled a Communist conspirator.

Subsequently von Trotta chose to work independently of her husband. Her films, which she usually scripts as well as directing, include *The Second Awakening* (1977), *Sisters, or the Balance of Happiness* (1979), *The German Sisters* (1981), and *Rosa Luxemburg* (1986), a biography of the Polish-born German revolutionary. Admirers of von Trotta's work have praised the subtle way in which she explores political issues through the personal lives of her mainly female characters. In the 1990s she directed several films in Italy, including *Paura e amore* (1990; Fear and Love) and *I lungo silencio* (1992; The Long Silence).

Vreeland, Diana

(*c.* 1902–1989)

AMERICAN FASHION JOURNALIST

She [Vreeland] became news by creating an image so bizarre that it was instantly recognizable. She was "seen" wherever she went, listened to whenever she spoke, and quoted endlessly.

—Ingeborg Day, *Ms.*, 1975

A colorful personality and meticulous about her appearance, Diana Vreeland had an immense influence on 20th-century fashion as editor of two top American fashion magazines.

Born in Paris, France, the daughter of a stockbroker, Diana took her mother's surname, Dalziel. In 1914 she was taken to live in the United States, and after marrying the banker Thomas Vreeland in 1924, she took U.S. citizenship. By the time she became a journalist in the late 1920s, she already had two sons.

In 1936 Vreeland began writing the celebrated "Why Don't You...?" column for *Harper's Bazaar*, in which she made frivolous suggestions, such as "Why don't you cut your old ermine wrap into a bathrobe?" As fashion editor of the journal from 1937 to 1962, she was enormously influential.

In 1962 Vreeland went to work for *Vogue*, serving as chief editor from 1963 to 1971. Reshaping the magazine to reflect her own tastes and attitudes, she led the way in promoting such 1960s trends as see-through shirts and the bikini, which she called "the most important thing since the atom bomb." A distinctive figure, Vreeland was the embodiment of her editorial style – she loved red, dressed in chic clothes, and spoke in a manner described as "all capitals and italics."

From 1971 Vreeland served as consultant editor to *Vogue*. A year later she became the costume specialist at the Metropolitan Museum of Art, where she mounted a series of successful exhibitions. Vreeland contributed to various exhibition catalogs and books on fashion. She also invented the word "pizzazz."

Wade, (Sarah) Virginia

(1945–)

BRITISH TENNIS PLAYER

Virginia Wade dominated British women's tennis in the late 1960s and 1970s. She was inaugurated into the International Tennis Hall of Fame in 1989.

The daughter of Canon Eustace Wade, a former archdeacon of Durban in South Africa, Virginia Wade was born in the English coastal resort of Bournemouth. A dedicated amateur player from the age of 17, she turned professional after completing a science degree at the University of Sussex (1968).

While still an amateur, Virginia Wade was chosen to represent Britain in the Wightman Cup competition of 1965. She went on to make a record 20 appearances for her country, captaining both the Wightman Cup and the Federation Cup teams for most of the 1970s. As well as winning the British hard-court championships in 1967, 1968, 1973, and 1974, she scored international triumphs in the U.S. Open (1968) and the Australian Open (1972). However, the climax of her career came in 1977 when she won the ladies' singles championship at Wimbledon in the tournament's centenary year: her victory coincided with the silver jubilee celebrations of Queen ELIZABETH II and was greeted with a wave of patriotic euphoria.

Since her retirement from tennis in 1981 Virginia Wade has worked as a BBC sports commentator and a tennis administrator.

She was appointed a Member of the British Empire (MBE) in 1979 and an Officer of the Order of the British Empire (OBE) in 1986.

Wagner, Cosima

(1837–1930)

GERMAN WRITER AND MUSICAL DIRECTOR

Cosima Wagner devoted most of her adult life to her second husband, the German composer and conductor Richard Wagner, supporting and promoting his work through the annual Bayreuth Festival.

The daughter of the Hungarian composer and pianist Franz Liszt and the French writer Countess Marie d'AGOULT (who later used the pen name Daniel Stern), Francesca Gaetana Cosima Liszt was born at Bellaggio on Lake Como in Italy. Her parents' relationship ended in 1844, and Cosima had an unsettled childhood; she was educated in Paris and moved to Berlin in the 1850s to live with the family of the German musician Hans von Bülow. From an early age she showed signs of musical and literary talent inherited from her parents, particularly in playing the piano.

In 1857 Cosima married von Bülow, who was a great admirer of the work of Richard Wagner. During the years that followed Cosima found herself increasingly drawn to Wagner, despite the fact that he was nearly twice her age. They began a relationship that resulted in the birth of two daughters – Isolde in 1865 and Eva in 1867 – and a son, Siegfried, in 1869. Wagner's estranged wife, Minna, died in 1866, and in 1868 Cosima left her husband to live with her lover in Switzerland. Von Bülow agreed to a divorce, and the couple were finally married in 1870.

Cosima devoted the rest of her life to helping Wagner and his music gain the international recognition that she and many others – including her ex-husband – knew they deserved. An opera house was built at Bayreuth in Bavaria for the performance of Wagner's works, opening in 1876, and an annual festival was established. After the death of her husband in 1883 Cosima continued to direct all the productions at the Bayreuth Festival, insisting that her interpretation of the composer's wishes be followed in every detail. This often led to friction, but Cosima's strong will and dominant personality usually won the day. In 1906 her son Siegfried took over the organization of the festival.

Cosima also helped shape Wagner's public image through the publication of her diaries and his autobiography *Mein Leben* (1911; My Life). She kept a collection of his correspondence, and her own letters to the philosopher Nietzsche were published in 1940.

Waitz, Grete

(1953–   )

NORWEGIAN ATHLETE

In the 1970s and 1980s Grete Waitz was one of the fastest female distance runners in the world. Of the 19 marathons she entered between 1978 and 1990 she lost only six, and she won the World Cross-Country Championships a record five times between 1978 and 1983.

She was born Grete Andersen in Oslo, Norway, and changed her name to Grete Waitz on her marriage to Jack Nilsen in 1975. As a child she showed a talent for athletics, particularly running, and in 1971 she set a European junior record for the 1500 meters. She took part in the 1972 Olympic Games in Munich and went on to compete internationally in the 1500 meter- and 3000-meter events, breaking world records for the longer distance in 1975 and 1976.

Encouraged by her husband, who was also her coach, Waitz entered the New York marathon in 1978 and won, setting a new women's record at 2 hours, 32 minutes, and 30 seconds. In the following year's race she cut her winning time down by nearly five minutes, and in 1980 she finished in 2 hours, 25 minutes, and 41 seconds. She went on to shave a further 12 seconds off the world record in the 1983 London marathon. The 1984 Olympic Games at Los Angeles was the first to include a women's marathon, but Waitz managed only second place, losing to the American runner Joan Benoit SAMUELSON. In the 1986 London marathon she achieved a personal best time of 2 hours, 24 minutes, and 54 seconds.

Walburga, Saint

(710–779)

ENGLISH ABBESS

For the last 18 years of her life Walburga had sole charge of a double monastery of monks and nuns at Heidenheim in southern Germany.

Walburga, also known as Waldburg or Walpurgis, was born in Wessex, an Anglo-Saxon kingdom in southern England. Her brothers Willibald and Winebald were also destined to become saints, and all three took part in St. Boniface's mission to Germany in the 8th century. Willibald became the first bishop of Eichstätt in Bavaria, southern Germany, and Winebald and Walburga were made abbot and abbess of a new monastery at Heidenheim. A double monastery, with monks and nuns in adjoining buildings on the same site, it was the first of its kind in Germany, though there were many similar establishments in Anglo-Saxon England.

When Winebald died in 761, Walburga took charge of the whole monastery, which established a reputation as a center of education. She remained there until her death and was buried there, but her body was moved to Eichstätt in the second half of the 9th century. A miraculous oil with healing properties was said to flow from a rock at her new shrine, which became a place of pilgrimage.

St. Walburga's feast day is February 25, but the night of April 30 has also become associated with her name (possibly because her body was moved to Eichstätt on May 1). Known as Walpurgis Night, it is a time when witches are said to meet on the Brocken, the highest peak in the Harz mountains in central Germany. In other parts of Europe and elsewhere it is celebrated as a springtime festival with music and dancing.

Wald, Lillian D.

(1867–1940)

AMERICAN SOCIAL WORKER

Lillian D. Wald is best known as the founder of the Henry Street Settlement in New York City, the first nonsectarian, public-health nursing system in the world. By 1913 the service had 92 nurses making 200,000 visits annually.

Wald was born and raised in Cincinnati, Ohio, the third of four children. At the age of 22, after meeting a nurse who had been sent to care for her sister during childbirth, she decided to become a nurse herself. She studied medicine at the New York Hospital Training School for Nurses and the Women's Medical College in New York City. In 1893 she and another nurse, Mary Brewster, enlisted the financial support of several wealthy friends and established a small settlement on Rivington Street, New York City, before moving to the famous settlement at 265 Henry Street, which was Wald's home for nearly 40 years. In 1902 she set up in New York City the first municipal nursing service for schools in the world. Wald also originated the plan for town and country nursing adopted by the American Red Cross and the Federal Children's Bureau, which was created by Congress as part of the

Department of Labor in 1908. A bitter opponent of slums and child labor, she was a strong advocate of more parks and play areas.

In 1915 Wald became the first president of the American Union against Militarism. However, after the United States entered World War I, she became a subcommittee member of the Council of National Defense. After the war she represented the Children's Bureau at international conferences in Europe and founded the League of Free Nations Association; she was also chairman of the Nurses Emergency Council during the 1918 influenza epidemic. During the 1920s and 1930s Wald served on numerous state and city commissions in the interest of public health and became first president of the National Organization for Public Health Nursing. In 1933 she resigned as president of the Henry Street Settlement's board of directors.

In addition to a number of popular magazine articles and pamphlets, Wald also wrote two books: *The House on Henry Street* (1915) and *Windows on Henry Street* (1934).

Walker, Alice

(1944–   )

AMERICAN NOVELIST, POET, AND SOCIAL ACTIVIST

> We will be ourselves and free, or die in the attempt. Harriet Tubman was not our great-grandmother for nothing.
> —*You Can't Keep a Good Woman Down* (1981)

Underlying much of Alice Walker's fiction and poetry is the struggle of African-American women for self-fulfillment and public recognition.

The youngest of eight children in a family of sharecroppers, Alice Walker was born in Eatonton, Georgia, and attended Spelman College in Atlanta, where she took part in civil-rights demonstrations. A gifted student, she won a scholarship to Sarah

Lawrence College, from which she graduated in 1965. She then became a caseworker in the New York City Welfare Department and taught black studies at Jackson State College (1968–69) before becoming a full-time writer. Her marriage in 1967 to Melvyn Rosenman Leventhal, a white civil-rights attorney, ended in divorce in 1976.

Walker's first volume of poems, *Once* (1968), was inspired by a tour of Africa in 1964; it was praised for its penetrating treatment of African culture, racial politics, love, and despair. Subsequent collections, which were generally well received for their originality and lyrical grace, include *Revolutionary Petunias and Other Poems* (1973), *Goodnight, Willie, I'll See You in the Morning* (1979), and *Horses Make a Landscape More Beautiful* (1984).

In her first novel, *The Third Life of Grange Copeland* (1970), Walker analyzed the plight of African-American men who fail in their family relationships, partly because of social constraints but also because of their inability to treat women as equals. Her second novel, *Meridian* (1976), builds on her own experiences of the civil-rights movement. *The Color Purple* (1982), about a resolute African-American woman who finds success and happiness in her life despite physical and psychological abuse from the men around her, won the 1983 Pulitzer Prize and the American Book Award. The highly acclaimed 1985 film version starred Whoopi GOLDBERG, who won an Oscar nomination for her performance as the heroine.

Walker's collections of short stories include *Love and Trouble: Stories of Black Women* (1973) and *You Can't Keep a Good Woman Down* (1981). Her essays are represented in the collection *In Search of Our Mother's Gardens: Womanist Prose* (1983). Other works include *To Hell With Dying* (1980), and *Her Blue Body Everything We Know* (1991). *Possessing the Secret of Joy* (1992) is a controversial novel about an African-American woman who undergoes ritual female circumcision in a misguided attempt to get back to her African roots.

See also HURSTON, ZORA NEALE; TUBMAN, HARRIET.

Walker, Mary Edwards

(1832–1919)

AMERICAN PHYSICIAN

Noted for holding views on women's rights that were ahead of her time, Mary Walker became (in 1865) the first woman to receive the Congressional Medal of Honor for her medical work during the Civil War. The medal was withdrawn by the Board of Medal Awards in 1917 but restored by the Army in 1977.

Mary Walker was born in Oswego, New York, the daughter of a teacher and a physician. After graduating from the Syracuse Medical College in 1855, she practiced briefly in Columbus, Ohio, and in Rome, New York, before volunteering to serve in the Civil War as a nurse in the Union Army. In 1864 she was commissioned and made an assistant surgeon.

As a girl, she had begun to wear trousers, partly concealed by a skirt, and in the Army she wore the same uniform as the other officers. After leaving the Army in 1865, she worked briefly as a journalist in New York City, becoming one of the first woman journalists in the United States. She then took up medical practice in Washington, D.C. There she wore men's business clothes in the daytime and full evening dress, including a silk top hat, when she was lecturing on social reforms and women's rights. Despite wearing her hair in curls on these occasions to show that she was a woman, she was arrested several times for "masquerading in men's clothes." In 1897 she founded a colony for women called Adamless Eden.

Walter, Lucy

(*c.* 1630–1658)

ENGLISH COURTESAN

Mistress of the future King Charles II of England while he was in exile in Holland and France, Lucy Walter bore him a son, James Scott, Duke of Monmouth.

Lucy Walter (also known as Lucy Walters or Waters) was born at Roch Castle near Haverfordwest, in Wales, the daughter of a Welsh family who supported Charles I during the English Civil War. In 1648, after the Parliamentarians had captured and burned Roch Castle, Lucy traveled to The Hague in Holland. There she met the future Charles II, whose mistress she became for some three years. In 1649 she bore him a son, who was acknowledged by Charles and made Duke of Monmouth in 1663.

In 1651, after her liaison with Charles had ended, Lucy Walter turned to a life of promiscuity and bore a daughter, Mary, whose father was said to be Henry Bennet, Earl of Arlington. (Mary later married William Sarsfield, the brother of Patrick Sarsfield, Earl of Lucan.) In 1656 Lucy was briefly imprisoned in the Tower of London on suspicion of being a spy but was soon released and deported to France. She also used the alias of Mrs. Barlow (or Barlo) and was referred to by the contemporary diarist John Evelyn as "beautiful and bold." She died in Paris.

Shortly before the death of Charles II in 1685 Lucy's son, the Duke of Monmouth, became involved in an unsuccessful attempt by Whig (liberal) noblemen to put forward a Protestant claimant to the throne in order to exclude Charles's brother, the Catholic James, Duke of York (later James II), from the succession. It was said at the time that proof that Charles had married Lucy resided in a mysterious black box, but Charles himself always denied they were married. Monmouth was banished, but returned to lead a rebellion after James became king. He was defeated at the battle of Sedgemoor and beheaded.

Walters, Julie

(1950–   )

BRITISH ACTRESS AND COMEDIENNE

A versatile actress, Julie Walters excels in roles that blend comedy with drama or tragedy. She is also a talented comedienne, known for her long-standing partnership with Victoria WOOD on British television.

Julie Walters was born in Smethwick, near Birmingham in central England. She wanted to be an actress, but her mother persuaded her to go into nursing, a more secure profession. Still drawn to the stage, she took a teaching certificate in English and drama at Manchester Polytechnic and joined the Everyman Theatre in Liverpool. In 1980 she starred in the play *Educating Rita*, as a hairdresser determined to better herself by studying at the Open University, and won two best newcomer awards. In the 1983 film version she played the same role opposite Michael Caine, earning a British Academy of Film and Television Arts award and an Oscar nomination for her performance.

By this time Walters had made her name as a comic performer on British television, working with Victoria Wood in *Wood and Walters* (1980–82) and many subsequent series. In her other television appearances, and on stage and screen, she demonstrated her ability to play women of all ages and social backgrounds. Of her repertoire of accents she once remarked, "I can do Irish, Welsh, Manchester, Liverpool, Birmingham, Cockney, and New York Jewish lesbian." Her roles include a brothel-keeper in the movie *Personal Services* (1987), the wife of a train robber in *Buster* (1988), the aging mother of an ambitious local politician in the TV drama serial *GBH* (1991), and a dying woman in *Wide Eyed and Legless* (1993).

Among Walter's stage credits are *Macbeth* (1985), *Frankie and Johnny in the Clair de Lune* (1989), and *The Rose Tattoo* (1991). The birth of her daughter inspired the book *Baby Talk*, published in 1990. She has appeared most recently on the big screen in *Sister My Sister* (1995) and *Intimate Relations* (1996).

Ward, Dame Barbara

(1914–1981)

BRITISH ECONOMIST AND JOURNALIST

Barbara Ward was acknowledged in the United States and Europe as one of the most influential commentators on economic and political subjects after World War II.

Born at York in northern England, Barbara Ward was educated at Somerville College, Oxford, where she gained an honors degree in 1935 and was a lecturer from 1936 to 1939. In 1939 she joined the staff of *The Economist*, Britain's leading financial weekly, and became its foreign editor in 1940.

In 1942 she began lecturing in the United States and later became visiting scholar at Harvard (1957–68) and Schweitzer Professor of International Economic Development at Columbia University (1968–73). In 1967 she was appointed to the Vatican

Commission for Justice and Peace, becoming the first woman to address the Vatican Council in Rome in 1971. From 1973 until 1980 she was president of the International Institute for Environment and Development, remaining its chairman from 1980 to 1981. Her husband, Commander (later Sir) Robert Jackson, an Australian whom she married in 1950, was a UN official.

Barbara Ward's publications include *The International Share-Out* (1938), a study of the colonial system; *The West at Bay* (1948); *Faith and Freedom* (1954); *Five Ideas That Change the World* (1959); *India and the West* (1961); and *The Rich Nations and the Poor Nations* (1962). She was an early advocate of European economic union and urged the establishment of a broad Western policy to counter that of the Communist bloc in dealing with emergent nationalism in underdeveloped areas. Throughout her career she argued for a fairer balance between the developed nations and the Third World and for a more rational use of the world's natural resources. She wrote *Spaceship Earth* (1966) and *Only One Planet* (1972, with René Dubos), to bring these views to a wider public. She was also instrumental in instigating the UN's programs for clean water and sanitation.

Barbara Ward was created a Dame of the British Empire in 1974 and raised to the British peerage in 1976, taking the title Baroness Jackson of Lodsworth.

Ward, Mrs. Humphry

(1851–1920)

BRITISH NOVELIST AND
SOCIAL WORKER

Mrs. Humphry Ward is remembered for her best-selling novel *Robert Elsmere* (1888) and for her outstanding achievements as a social worker. In 1890 she founded a settlement house in a poor district of London, from which grew the famous Passmore Edwards Settlement.

Born Mary Augusta Arnold in Hobart, Tasmania, Australia, she was the granddaughter of Dr. Thomas Arnold, the founder of Rugby School, and a niece of the poet Matthew Arnold. Returning to England in 1856, soon after her father's conversion to Roman Catholicism, she was raised mostly in Oxford, where she became influenced by the liberal social philosophy of T. H. Green. In 1872 she married Thomas Humphry Ward, a fellow of Brasenose College, Oxford.

In 1881 the Wards moved to London, and Mrs. Ward began her career as a writer with the publication of a children's story, "Millie and Olly." Her first important literary work was a translation (1884) of Henri Frederic Amiel's *Journal Intime* (Intimate Journal). Her second novel, *Robert Elsmere*, dedicated to T. H. Green, was an instant success and was translated into several languages. It expressed her strongly held conviction that Christianity could best be served by minimizing its mystical qualities and striving toward fulfillment of the Gospel's social ideas.

Many of her novels of the next few years, namely *The History of David Grieve* (1892), *Marcella* (1894), *Sir George Tressaday* (1896), *Helbeck of Bannisdale* (1898), *Eleanor* (1900), and *Lady Rose's Daughter* (1903), are concerned with the need to help the poor. Sensitive to the plight of women, particularly poor ones, she pressed for women to become more involved in social work but nonetheless opposed the franchise movement, becoming in 1908 the first president of the Anti-Suffrage League. She criticized woman suffrage campaigners in several of her novels, notably *The Testing of Diana Mallory* (1908), *Delia Blanchflower* (1915), and *Cousin Philip* (1919). In 1911 she founded the Local Government Advancement Committee to promote the charitable activities of women.

After the death of her sister in 1908, Mrs. Ward devoted much of her time to the care of her nephews Julian Huxley (later Sir Julian Huxley, the well-known biologist and writer) and Aldous Huxley (who became a highly successful novelist). In 1918 she published *A Writer's Recollections*, which contains interesting accounts of her family and friends (including the novelist Henry James). She was appointed one of the first seven women magistrates in 1920. Altogether she wrote 25 novels, three plays, and nine nonfiction works. Her daughter, Janet Penrose Trevelyan, published *The Life of Mrs. Humphry Ward* in 1923.

Warner, Susan Bogert

(1819–1885)

AMERICAN NOVELIST

> The back is fitted to the burden, they say; and I always *did* pray that if I had work to do, I might be able to do it; and I always was, somehow.
> —*What She Could* (1870)

Susan Warner, who wrote under the pen name Elizabeth Wetherell, began her writing career with the publication of *The Wide, Wide World* in 1850. This became the first best-selling novel in the United States and a major influence on later novels by women.

Born in New York City, Susan Warner, like many other 19th-century women writers, wrote to support her family. Her highly successful first novel, which tells of the religious development of a 13-year-old orphan, was followed by a second novel, *Queechy*

(1852), which was almost as successful and also illustrates the spiritual growth of a young girl. Although she wrote many other novels, including *Daisy* (1868), *Diana* (1877), and *Nobody* (1882), she is remembered for the unusual popularity of these first books, which appealed to the age's sentimental piety. She also collaborated with her sister, Anna Bartlett Warner, on some of her later works.

Warner, Sylvia Townsend

(1893–1978)

BRITISH NOVELIST, SHORT-STORY WRITER, AND POET

Acclaimed as a subtle and imaginative writer, Sylvia Townsend Warner was also one of the editors of a ten-volume collection of Tudor church music and a well-known authority on supernatural matters. She took an active part in left-wing politics and served for a while in Spain during the Civil War (1936–39).

Born at Harrow-on-the-Hill, near London, Sylvia Townsend Warner was educated privately and began her writing career as a poet with the collection *The Espalier* in 1925. Her first novel, *Lolly Willowes*, which had the distinction of being the first Book of the Month Club selection, appeared the following year. Subsequent novels, such as *The Corner That Held Them* (1948), set in a medieval convent, and *The Flint Anchor* (1954), about a 19th-century English family, confirmed her critical reputation.

Warner's other novels include *Mr. Fortune's Maggot* (1927) and *Summer Will Show* (1936), while her collections of short stories include *A Garland of Straw* (1943), *A Spirit Rises* (1962), and *A Stranger with a Bag* (1966). *Sketches from Nature* (1963) are childhood reminiscences. She also wrote a biography of the British writer T. H. White (1967). Her *Collected Poems* appeared in 1982.

Warren, Mercy Otis

(1728–1814)

AMERICAN WRITER AND HISTORIAN

> Men rail at weakness themselves create,
> And boldly stigmatize the female mind,
> As though kind nature's just impartial hand
> Had form'd its features in a baser mold.
>
> *—The Ladies of Castille* (*c.* 1770)

> Maternal softness weakens my resolve,
> And wakes new fears – thou dearest,
> best of men,
> Torn from my side, I'm level'd with my sex.
> The wife – the mother – makes me less than woman.
>
> —As above

Mercy Otis Warren, sister of the Revolutionary leader James Otis, was one of early North America's most prolific and respected political writers. She led a literary salon in the pre-Revolutionary days, and her three-volume *History of the Rise, Progress, and Termination of the American Revolution* (1805) is still an important work for its factual information and its first-hand account of the personalities of the period.

Mercy Otis was born in Barnstable, Massachusetts, into a politically active family. Although she received no formal education, her writings reveal her wide reading of contemporary political and philosophical writers. In 1754 she married another Massachusetts patriotic leader, James Warren and in the years that followed became acquainted with many of the chief figures of the American Revolution, notably the members of the Adams family and Thomas Jefferson.

Warren wrote poems and plays in support of the patriot cause, including the dramatic satires *The Adulateur* (1773) and *The Group* (1775). Even such plays as *The Ladies of Castille*, which are not set in North America, put forward her ideas on democracy and acknowledge the role of women in the process of independence. Her *Poems Dramatic and Miscellaneous* was published in 1790.

Warwick, Dionne

(1940–)

AMERICAN POP AND SOUL
SINGER

Dionne Warwick made her name in the 1960s singing songs by Burt Bacharach and Hal David and was still producing successful albums three decades later.

Marie Dionne Warwick was born into a musical family in East Orange, New Jersey. Her aunt was the gospel singer Cissy Houston, whose daughter Whitney HOUSTON became a successful pop and soul singer in the late 1980s. At the age of six Warwick joined the choir of the New Hope Baptist Church in Newark, and in her teens she formed a group called the Gospelaires. She was working as a backup vocalist when her talent was discovered by the songwriting team Burt Bacharach and Hal David in the early 1960s. They became her producers and wrote numerous hits for her, including "Anyone Who Had a Heart," "Walk On By," and "I Say a Little Prayer". From 1964 to 1973 she released two or three albums every year, including *Here I Am* (1966) and *Windows of the World* (1968).

In the early 1970s she changed her name to Warwicke for a short time. She also changed her recording company and sang with the Spinners "Then Came You" (1974), which was the first of her singles to reach the top of the charts in the United States. After a major dispute with Bacharach and David in the mid-1970s her career declined for a time, but by 1979 she was back in form with the album *Dionne*, which earned her two Grammy Awards. Her success continued through the 1980s and into the 1990s with such albums as *Heartbreaker* (1982); *Friends* (1985), on which she was joined by Gladys Knight and Stevie Wonder, among others;

Reservations for Two (1987); and *Friends Can Be Lovers* (1993), which also featured her cousin Whitney Houston. In 1986 she joined 44 other singers to make the hit single "We Are the World," the proceeds of which were used to fight famine in Africa.

Warwick has appeared in a handful of movies, including *Slaves* (1969) and *Rent-a-Cop* (1988), and in a number of TV shows. In 1986 she launched a perfume called "Dionne."

Washington, Martha

(1731–1802)

WIFE OF GEORGE
WASHINGTON

As the wife of the first president of the United States, Martha Washington performed her social duties – which included entertaining distinguished visitors – with generous hospitality, dignity, and reserve.

Martha Dandridge was born in New Kent, Virginia, the daughter of John and Frances Jones Dandridge, who both belonged to respected New England families. In 1794 Martha, an attractive, capable girl, married Daniel Parke Custis, son of John Custis, a wealthy planter. The coupled lived in the "White House" on a plantation on the Pamunkey River and had four children, two of whom died in infancy. On the death of her husband on July 8, 1757, Martha inherited a sizable fortune.

This fortune enabled her to take her pick of many suitors, so by choosing George Washington, she was indicating her strong feelings for him. They were married on January 6, 1759, and in the following spring Washington took Martha and her children, John Parke Custis and Martha Parke Custis, to his estate, Mount Vernon, which they started to rebuild after its neglect during Washington's service in the French and Indian War.

Martha was a cheerful companion, good-natured and with abundant common sense. During the Revolution she spent her winters with General Washington and supervised Mount Vernon during the remainder of the year. They had no children of their own, and the death of Martha's daughter in 1773 was a grievous blow. Her son John had four children, Elizabeth, Martha, Eleanor, and George Washington, and after his death in 1781 George and Martha helped raise them. (The daughter of George Washington Parke Custis later married the Confederate general Robert E. Lee.)

After Washington died in 1799, Martha lived in seclusion at Mount Vernon until her death.

Waters, Ethel

(1896–1977)

AMERICAN ACTRESS AND JAZZ SINGER

Ethel Waters won acclaim for her performances on radio, television, stage, and screen and was still performing at the age of 80.

Born Ethel Howard in Chester, Pennsylvania, she spent her childhood in conditions of extreme poverty in the slums in and around Philadelphia. After working for a time as a hotel domestic, she began her career as a vocalist in a theater in Baltimore, Maryland. She made her first recordings in 1921, when she was backed by the Fletcher Henderson orchestra. She first appeared in New York City in 1925 at the Plantation Club in Harlem and later worked with Duke Ellington, Benny Goodman, and others.

After appearing on Broadway in 1927 in an African-American revue, *Africana*, Waters combined nightclub work with the theater. She appeared in the Irving Berlin success *As Thousands Cheer* (1933), costarred with Beatrice LILLIE in *At Home Abroad* (1935), and in 1938 gave a concert recital at Carnegie Hall.

Waters's first straight dramatic role, in *Mamba's Daughters* (1939), was a success; she went on to act and sing in the hit *Cabin in the Sky* (1940–41), also appearing in the film version (1943). Her greatest artistic success was as the wise and patient cook in Carson MCCULLERS's *The Member of the Wedding* (1950), which received the New York Drama Critics' Circle Award. She repeated this role in the film version of 1953. She also appeared extensively on radio and television.

In 1951 Ethel Waters brought out her autobiography (written with Charles Samuels), *His Eye Is on the Sparrow*, which was widely acclaimed for its candor and sensitivity. In it she describes how she was sustained by her religious faith through years of prejudice. Beginning in the late 1950s, she participated as a gospel singer in the crusades of the evangelist Billy Graham. She died in Chatsworth, California.

In both her acting and her singing Ethel Waters showed a freshness, exuberance, and warmth that captivated audiences. Popular songs with which she is identified include "Dinah," "Having a Heat Wave," and "Stormy Weather." The singer Ella FITZGERALD was greatly influenced by her vocal improvisations.

Weaver, Sigourney

(1949–)

AMERICAN ACTRESS

A tall, intelligent woman with a commanding presence on the screen, Sigourney Weaver rocketed to stardom as the astronaut Ellen Ripley in the movie *Alien* (1979) and its sequels. The $5 million she earned for *Alien³* (1992), which she also coproduced, made her one of the highest-paid actresses of the early 1990s.

She was born Susan Alexandra Weaver in New York City, the daughter of NBC president Sylvester ("Pat") Weaver. In the early 1960s she decided to adopt the name Sigourney, from F. Scott Fitzgerald's novel *The Great Gatsby*. After studying English at Stanford University and drama at Yale, she began acting in stage plays, making her debut in *Watergate Classics* (1973). She was first seen on the big screen – very briefly – in the Woody Allen film *Annie Hall* (1977).

In 1979 Weaver made her first appearance as Ellen Ripley, the tough heroine of the science-fiction classic *Alien*. Having made her name as such a strong character, there was a risk that she would be typecast, but she proved her versatility by playing a haunted cellist in the comedy *Ghostbusters* (1984), a double-dealing boss who gets her comeuppance in *Working Girl* (1988), and a nervous wreck in *Copycat* (1995). She took up the role of Ellen Ripley again in *Aliens* (1986), earning an Academy Award nomination for her performance. In *Alien³* (1992) Ripley finally met her death, but fans of what had become a cult series were relieved to hear that Weaver was to star in a fourth movie, *Alien Resurrection*, in 1997. Her other major film roles include that of the naturalist Dian

FOSSEY in *Gorillas in the Mist* (1988), which brought her a second Best Actress Oscar nomination.

Weaver continued to act on stage in her early career, appearing in such plays as *A Flea in Her Ear* (1978), *As You Like It, Beyond Therapy* (1981), and *Hurly Burly* (1984). After *The Merchant of Venice* (1986–87) she took a break from the theater, returning in 1996 to star in the Broadway play *Sex and Longing.* Having waited until her mid-thirties to marry and start a family, she once re-marked, "Whether it was work, marriage, or family, I've always been a late bloomer."

Webb, Beatrice

(1858–1943)

BRITISH ECONOMIST AND SOCIALIST

When a man said to Beatrice Webb, "Much of this talk about feminism is nonsense; any woman would rather be beautiful than clever," she replied, "Quite true. But that is be-cause so many men are stupid and so few are blind."
—*Daily Express*, October 14, 1947

If I ever felt inclined to be timid as I was going into a room full of people, I would say to myself, "You're the cleverest member of one of the cleverest families in the clever-est class of the cleverest nation in the world, why should you be frightened?"
—Quoted by Bertrand Russell in *Portraits from Memory* (1956)

In partnership with her husband, Sidney Webb, Beatrice Webb produced over 100 books and articles, and the Webbs became the leading researchers and propagandists for the Labour movement in Britain. Their first major works were *History of Trade Union-ism* (1894) and *Industrial Democracy* (1897). They were involved in the founding of the London School of Economics in 1895 and the left-wing journal *The New Statesman* in 1913.

Born Martha Beatrice Potter at Standish House near Gloucester, in southwest England, she was the eighth daughter of a railway and industrial magnate. Beatrice was educated privately and
became a close business associate of her father after her mother's
death in 1882. Moving in liberal, intellectual circles, she became
interested in reform and began to do social work in London. She
investigated working-class conditions as part of the survey *Life
and Labour of the People in London* (1891–1903), directed by her
cousin Charles Booth. In 1891 she published *The Co-operative
Movement in Great Britain*. It was while she was working on this
that she met Sidney Webb, a member of the socialist Fabian Society, whom she married in 1892.

Sidney and Beatrice Webb served on many royal commissions
and wrote widely on economic problems. After a tour of the
United States and the Dominions in 1898 they started their mas-
sive ten-volume work, *English Local Government* (1906–29). Mrs.
Webb also served on the Poor Law Commission (1906–09) and
was joint author of its minority report, which awakened public interest in the principles of social insurance. The Webbs' London
house became a socialist salon, and they played an increasingly influential role in guiding the intellectual development of the Labour
Party.

During World War I Beatrice Webb wrote *Wages of Men and
Women – Should They Be Equal?*. She was a member of the War
Cabinet Committee on Women in Industry (1918–19) and served
on the Lord Chancellor's Advisory Committee for Women Justices
(1919–20), being a justice of the peace herself from 1919 to 1927.
Her *Constitution for the Socialist Commonwealth of Great Britain*
was published in 1920. In 1922 Sidney Webb became a member of
Parliament and held ministerial office in both the early Labour
governments. In 1932, after he had left office, the Webbs visited
the USSR, where they were greatly impressed by the workings of
the socialist state. They recorded their views in *Soviet Communism:
A New Civilization* (1935). The Webbs retired to their home in
Hampshire, England, in 1928. Beatrice Webb wrote two volumes
of autobiography: *My Apprenticeship* (1926) and *Our Partnership*
(1948), which was published after her death.

BIBLIOGRAPHY
Seymour-Jones, Carole, *Beatrice Webb: A Life* (1992).
Webb, Beatrice, *Our Partnership* (1948; reprint, 1975).

Webb, Mary

(1881–1927)

BRITISH NOVELIST

Webb is remembered for the novel *Precious Bane* (1924), set in the rural county of Shropshire where she spent much of her life.

She was born Gladys Mary Meredith in Leighton, Shropshire, central England, the daughter of a schoolteacher. Through her mother she had family connections with the Scottish writer Sir Walter Scott; from her father she inherited a love of everything to do with nature and the countryside. She was educated at home and began writing poems and stories as a child. In 1912 she married Henry Webb, and together they worked as market gardeners, growing fruit and vegetables for sale at Shrewsbury market. The Webbs left Shropshire for London in 1921, but Mary, whose health had never been good, died six years later.

Her first novel, *The Golden Arrow*, was published in 1916. It was followed by *Gone to Earth* (1917), *The House in Dormer Forest* (1920), *Seven for a Secret* (1922), and *Precious Bane* (1924). In all her writings she painted a vivid picture of life in the Shropshire countryside, developing a passionate and melodramatic style of writing that was satirized by Stella Gibbons in *Cold Comfort Farm* (1932). Critical opinions of her work vary, but some have compared her novels with those of Thomas Hardy or D. H. Lawrence.

Webb found little fame in her lifetime, but a speech of praise made in 1928 by one of her admirers – the British prime minister Stanley Baldwin – led to a sudden demand for her work that the libraries and bookstores were unable to satisfy. Her novels were reprinted in 1928 with introductions by Baldwin and such noted writers as John Buchan and G. K. Chesterton. The following year saw new editions of Webb's poems and *The Spring of Joy* (a collection of nature essays originally published in 1917), as well as the first appearance of her unfinished historical novel, *Armour Wherein He Trusted*, and a number of short stories.

Webster, Margaret

(1905–1972)

BRITISH ACTRESS, DIRECTOR, AND PRODUCER

With Eva LE GALLIENNE and Cheryl CRAWFORD Margaret Webster was a cofounder of the American Repertory Company in 1946. In 1948 she formed the Margaret Webster Shakespeare Company, which brought exciting, swift-moving drama to most of the United States and many Canadian provinces.

Margaret Webster was the daughter of Ben Webster, a well-known English Shakespearean actor, and Dame May Whitty, a popular stage and film actress. Her great-grandfather was the British actor, manager, and playwright Benjamin Nottingham Webster. She was born in New York City, where her father was performing at the time, but the family soon returned to England. Margaret made her first professional appearance in the chorus of Euripides's *Trojan Women* in 1924. The following year she made her Shakespearean debut with John Barrymore in *Hamlet*. From 1929 she acted with John Gielgud's Old Vic company in London, appearing in such productions as *Musical Chairs* (1932) and *Richard of Bordeaux* (1933).

Webster's distinguished career as a director began in 1937, when the actor Maurice Evans invited her to stage his *Richard II* on Broadway. Paul Robeson's *Othello* (1943) was another of her major directorial successes. She continued to act and in 1944 also emerged as a producer as well as director. In 1950 she directed her first opera, *Don Carlos*, at the Metropolitan Opera House in New York City. Her acting successes of the 1950s included *An Evening with Will Shakespeare* (1952) and *Measure for Measure* (1957). She also worked in England during this period, directing *The Merchant of Venice* at Stratford-upon-Avon and *Measure for Measure* at the

Old Vic in London. In 1960 she directed Noël Coward's *Waiting in the Wings* at the Duke of York's Theatre in London.

Margaret Webster wrote the books *Shakespeare without Tears* (1942) and *The Same Only Different* (1969), which chronicled five generations of her theatrical family.

Wedgwood, Dame Veronica

(1910–1997)

BRITISH HISTORIAN

Wedgwood wrote about the 17th century, especially the period of the English Civil War (known also as the Great Rebellion), in a scholarly but readable style, with the aim of encouraging others to share her passion for the past.

Cicely Veronica Wedgwood was born in Northumberland in northeastern England, a direct descendant of the famous 18th-century potter Josiah Wedgwood. As a child, she was happier among her father's history books than playing with friends, and after a private education with a Swiss governess she went to Oxford University to study history. She graduated in 1931 with a first-class honors degree and joined the editorial staff of *Time and Tide*, a weekly review of arts and politics. She continued to work for the paper for many years, researching and writing her history books in her spare time.

In 1935 her first work, a biography of the Earl of Strafford, was published. Strafford was a 17th-century politician, adviser to King Charles I before the English Civil War, and this period of history became Wedgwood's specialty. Her books on the Great Rebellion include *Oliver Cromwell* (1939), *The King's Peace* (1955), *The King's War* (1958), and *The Trial of Charles I* (1964). She also produced historical and biographical works about other political figures and events of the 17th century, notably *The Thirty Years' War* (1938) and *Richelieu and the French Monarchy* (1949). For her biography of William the Silent (1944) she was awarded the James Tait Black Memorial Prize. In the latter part of her career she embarked on an ambitious new project – a history of the world – but completed only one volume, *The Spoils of Time* (1984).

Wedgwood was not an academic historian – she wrote for the general reader in an elegant narrative style, describing what happened rather than analyzing why it happened. Her biographies are well-rounded portraits of their subjects, not neglecting the human angle. She also wrote about art and literature and published three collections of essays: *Velvet Studies* (1946), *Truth and Opinion* (1960), and *History and Hope* (1987). In 1968 she was honored with the title Dame of the British Empire. The numerous awards and other honors she received during her lifetime included honorary degrees from universities in Britain and the United States.

Weil, Simone

(1909–1943)

FRENCH PHILOSPHER AND MYSTIC

> The word "revolution" is a word for which you kill, for which you die, for which you send the laboring masses to their death, but which does not possess any content.
> —*Oppression and Liberty* (1958)

> Learn to reject friendship, or rather the dream of friendship. To want friendship is a great fault. Friendship ought to be a gratuitous joy, like the joys afforded by art, or life (like aesthetic joys). I must refuse it in order to be worthy of it.
> —*First and Last Notebooks* (1970)

One of the first women to be admitted to the prestigious Ecole Normale Supérieure in Paris, where she studied philosophy, Simone Weil was an active socialist in the 1930s. After a mystical experience in 1938 she became a Roman Catholic, and during World War II she worked for the Free French Resistance in London.

Born in Paris into a well-to-do Jewish family, Simone Weil studied under the philosopher Alain (the pen name of Emile-Auguste Chartier) before attending the Ecole Normale Supérieure, from which she graduated in 1931. Although deeply influenced by the teachings of Karl Marx, she did not join the Communist Party. She taught philosophy at a girls' school at Le Puy, and later at Bourges and St. Quentin, but interspersed this work with periods of manual labor on farms and on the shop floor at the Renault motor works to experience the life of the working classes. In 1936 she joined the International Brigade to fight against General Franco in the Spanish Civil War.

After the first of her mystical experiences Weil embraced Roman Catholicism but was never baptized, preferring to identify herself with the powerless outside the Church. After the defeat of France by Nazi Germany Jews were forbidden to teach by the pro-German Vichy government, so Weil became a farm servant near Marseilles. In 1942 she and her family escaped to the United States, but after a few months she returned to Europe to work in London for the Free French Resistance. Never healthy, she refused to eat more than the official ration allotted to the citizens of occupied France. Ravaged by pleurisy, she was admitted to the Middlesex Hospital, London, and then to a sanatorium in Ashford, Kent, where she died at the age of 34.

Weil's writings were all collected and published after her death. They include *La Pesanteur et la grâce* (1948; English translation, *Gravity and Grace*, 1952), a collection of religious and philosphical guidelines; *L'Enracinement* (1949; English translation, *The Need for Roots*, 1952), an essay on the obligations of the individual and the state; *L'Attente de Dieu* (1950; English translation, *Waiting for God*, 1951), a spiritual autobiography; *La Source grecque* (1953; The Greek Source), translations and studies; *Oppression et liberté* (1955; English translation, *Oppression and Liberty*, 1958), political and social papers on war, factory work, and language; and three volumes of *Cahiers* (1951, 1955, 1956; translated as *Notebooks*, 2 vols., 1956). Her books have made her widely known as one of the great advocates for religion in our time, one of the subtlest psychologists of the spiritual quest, and a genuine analyzer of force, violence, terror, and death, who found in suffering a source of purity and grace.

Weir, Judith

(1954–)

BRITISH COMPOSER

Judith Weir has produced a wide range of compositions, including orchestral and choral works and many pieces for small groups of voices or instruments.

She was born in Cambridge, England, of Scottish parents and studied musical composition with John Tavener, Oliver Messiaen, and other famous composers. After graduating from Cambridge University in 1976, she spent three years as composer-in-residence at the Southern Arts Association before taking up a teaching fellowship at Glasgow University (1979–82). She returned to Cambridge in 1983, moving to London two years later. From 1988 to 1991 she was composer-in-residence at the Royal Scottish Academy of Music.

Weir's early works include a number of pieces for small instrumental groups, such as the wind quintet *Out of the Air* (1975), *Between Ourselves* (1978) for seven players, and *Music for 247 Strings* (1981) for violin and piano. In 1981 she also produced two orchestral compositions, *Isti Mirant Stella* and *Ballad*, and *Thread!*, a humorous piece for narrator and eight instruments inspired by the Bayeux Tapestry. *Spij döbrze* (*Pleasant Dreams*), for double bass with recorded electronic sound, had its first performance in 1983 as part of the International Society for Contemporary Music festival in Poland.

Her other compositions include the operas *The Black Spider* (1984), *A Night at the Chinese Opera* (1987), and *The Vanishing Bridegroom* (1990); choral works, such as *Heaven Ablaze in His Breast* (1989); and the piano pieces *Ardnamurchan Point* (1990) and *Roll off the Ragged Rocks of Sin* (1992). In 1994 she received the Critics' Circle Award for the most outstanding contribution to British musical life.

Welch, Raquel

(1940–   )

AMERICAN ACTRESS

Raquel Welch made her name as a voluptuous sex symbol in the 1960s, and in late middle age she was still considered to be one of the most beautiful women in the world. Rarely praised for her acting ability, she nevertheless won a Golden Globe Award for her performance in the movie *The Three Musketeers* (1973).

She was born Raquel Tejada in Chicago, Illinois. In her late teens and early twenties she worked as a model and cocktail waitress; by the age of 24 she had married and divorced her first husband, James Welch, and had given birth to two children. She made her film debut with a small part in *A House Is Not a Home* (1964). The press agent Patrick Curtis, who later became her second husband, marketed her as a sex symbol, and she gained international stardom with such films as *One Million Years B.C.* (1966), *Bedazzled* (1967), and *Lady in Cement* (1968). She also appeared in a number of European movies, including the French–German–Italian coproduction *The Oldest Profession* (1968), about prostitution in the past, present, and future.

Welch continued to make regular film appearances throughout the 1970s, ending with *Crossed Swords* (1978), based on Mark Twain's story *The Prince and the Pauper*. During the 1980s she concentrated on stage and television work, appearing in the

Broadway musical *Woman of the Year* (1982) and such TV movies as *Right to Die* (1987). She also produced exercise books and videos, notably *The Racquel Welch Total Beauty and Fitness Program* (1984). In 1994 she returned to the big screen in *Naked Gun 33⅓: The Final Insult*, and in 1997 she took over the title role in the Broadway production of *Victor/Victoria*.

Weldon, Fay

(1931–   )

BRITISH WRITER

The author of many novels and plays for the theater, radio, and television, Weldon is perhaps best known for the novel *The Life and Loves of a She-Devil* (1983), which she adapted for British television in 1985 and which was filmed in 1989 with Roseanne Arnold in the title role. It is the story of an unattractive wife's terrible revenge on her unfaithful husband and his beautiful lover, a best-selling writer.

Born Fay Birkinshaw in Worcestershire, England, she emigrated to New Zealand with her parents and was educated at Christchurch Girl's High School. After World War II the family returned to Britain, and Fay went on to study at the University of St. Andrews in Scotland. She subsequently worked as an advertising copywriter, creating such memorable slogans as "Go to work on an egg," used by the British Egg Marketing Board in 1958. In 1962 she married Ron Weldon, who died in 1994.

In the 1960s Weldon began writing for radio and television, and among her early credits is the first episode of the successful TV drama series *Upstairs Downstairs* (1970). Since then she has produced numerous plays, scripts, and adaptations, including a dramatization of Jane AUSTEN's *Pride and Prejudice* in 1980. Her first novel, *The Fat Woman's Joke* (1967), was followed by such works as *Down among the Women* (1971), *Female Friends* (1975), *Puffball* (1980), *The President's Child* (1982), *The Hearts and Lives of Men* (1987), *The Cloning of Joanna May* (1989), and *Affliction* (1994). *Praxis* (1978), about a woman who has killed a baby, was nominated for the Booker McConnell Prize for Fiction. She has also written short stories, published in *Watching Me, Watching You* (1981) and other collections. Weldon's writings show a feminist view of the world, centering on women's relationships with men, family members, and each other. But they are also relevant to society in general, skillfully blending realism with fantasy and tragedy with comedy. Her books are popular with readers of both sexes and all ages.

In the later part of her career Weldon has been an active campaigner for the rights of authors, supporting such causes as the Public Lending Right, by which novelists and other writers receive a small payment every time one of their books is borrowed from a public library. She has received awards from the Writers Guild and the Los Angeles *Times*, among others.

Wells-Barnett, Ida Bell

(1862–1931)

AMERICAN JOURNALIST AND CIVIL-RIGHTS ACTIVIST

Elected the first president of the Negro Fellowship League in 1900, Ida Wells-Barnett became a cofounder of the National Association for the Advancement of Colored People (NAACP) in 1909 and the chairman of the Chicago Equal Rights League in 1915.

The daughter of slaves, Ida Bell Wells was born in Holly Springs, Missouri. She was educated at the local freedmen's school and became a teacher at the age of 14 to support herself when her parents and three of her seven brothers and sisters died in a yellow fever epidemic. She briefly attended Fisk University in Nashville. In 1883 she moved to Memphis, Tennessee, where she continued to teach and started writing. She was dismissed from her teaching position in 1891, after she had brought an unsuccessful lawsuit challenging Tennessee's racist Jim Crow laws (1887) and, under the pen name "Iola," criticized the inadequate educational opportunities open to African Americans.

Wells became part-owner of an African-American weekly newspaper, the *Memphis Free Speech*, and in 1892 began an antilynching crusade by denouncing the lynching in Memphis of three of her friends. After the office of the *Memphis Free Speech* was destroyed by a white mob, she went to New York City, where she became a reporter on the newspaper *Age*. She wrote and lectured against lynching, both in northern U.S. cities and, between 1893 and 1894, in Britain. In 1895 she married Ferdinand Lee Barnett, a lawyer and editor, and settled in Chicago. They had four children.

Wells-Barnett organized antilynching societies and African-American women's clubs in Chicago and elsewhere and was active in the National Afro-American Council. She also organized protests against the exclusion of African Americans from the World Columbian Exposition. She generally supported the militant views of W. E. B. Du Bois and in 1895 published *A Red Record*, a statistical study of lynching. From 1913 until 1916 she was a probation officer for the Chicago city courts and organized legal aid for the victims of the 1918 Race Riots and similarly oppressed people. Wells-Barnett also organized and demonstrated on behalf of woman suffrage. Her autobiography, *Crusade for Justice*, was published in 1970.

Welty, Eudora

(1909–)

AMERICAN NOVELIST AND SHORT-STORY WRITER

One of the most distinguished American writers of the later 20th century, Eudora Welty explores the nuances of human behavior through a wide range of characters, rich and poor, black and white, from her native Mississippi delta. She was awarded the National Medal for Literature and the Presidential Medal of Freedom in 1980. In 1984 she received the Commonwealth Award for Distinguished Service in Literature.

Eudora Welty was born in Jackson, Mississippi, and attended Mississippi State College for Women before graduating in 1929 from the University of Wisconsin. From there she went to New York City, where she attended the Columbia School of Advertising (1930–31), but with the deepening Depression was unable to find work and returned to Jackson. She then took a job traveling throughout Mississippi as a publicity agent for the Works Progress Administration, a role that brought her into contact with many different kinds of people. (Arising from this work was her series of photographs of the people and places she encountered, a selection of which was published in 1971 as *One Time, One Place: Mississippi in the Depression: a Snapshot Album*.)

Welty published her first short story, "Death of a Traveling Salesman," in 1936; her first collection of stories, *A Curtain of Green*, followed in 1941. For one of these stories, "The Worn Path," Welty won the first of several O. Henry Memorial Contest Awards. *The Robber Bridegroom*, a fairytale novel set in Mississippi in 1798, appeared in 1942, and a second collection of stories, *The Wide Net*, in 1943. These and her first full-length novel, *Delta Wedding* (1946), were highly acclaimed by the critics.

Although Welty has lived virtually her entire life in Jackson, her themes are universal. She manages to capture the essential isolation of the individual and the way this can conflict with the responsibilities of family and community bonds. Her writing is distinguished by extensive use of monologue and dialogue and an unfailing ear for Southern dialect.

Eudora Welty won the William Dean Howells Medal of the American Academy in 1955 for her novel *The Ponder Heart* (1954). Both it and *The Robber Bridegroom* were produced on Broadway. In 1973 she received the Pulitzer Prize for *The Optimist's Daughter* (1972), another novel. Her other works include *The Golden Apples* (1943), a group of interrelated stories; the novel *Losing Battles* (1970); and *Collected Stories* (1981). *One Writer's Beginnings* (1984) is an autobiographical sketch based on a series of Harvard lectures.

Welty is also an accomplished reviewer and critic. During World War II she was on the staff of *The New York Times Book Review*. Her selected essays and reviews were reprinted in *The Eye of the Story* (1978). Two further collections of book reviews were published in 1994 as *A Writer's Eye* and *Monuments to Interruption*.

Wertmuller, Lina

(1928–)

ITALIAN FILM DIRECTOR AND SCREENWRITER

Wertmuller's films are often controversial, dealing with sexual relationships in an explicit manner. Her husband and business partner is the artist Enrico Job, who has worked as set designer on many of her productions.

Arcangela Felice Assunta Wertmuller von Elgg was born in Rome, Italy. After working as a teacher for a time, she studied at the Theater Academy in Rome and went on a tour of Europe with a puppet show. In the 1950s she worked as a stage actress, writer, and director. She broke into the world of Italian cinema when the actor Marcello Mastroianni introduced her to the director Federico Fellini, who gave her a job as assistant on his Oscar-winning movie *8½* (1963). In the same year Wertmuller wrote and directed *The Lizards*, her first film.

She gradually built up her reputation in Europe with such films as *The Seduction of Mimi* (1972), for which she was named Best Director at the Cannes Film Festival; *Love and Anarchy* (1973); and *Swept Away* (1974). Her fame spread to the United States and elsewhere with *Seven Beauties* (1976), set in a Nazi concentration camp, which earned her an Academy Award nomination and a contract with Warner Brothers for a series of films in English. Only one of these, *The End of the World in Our Usual Bed in a Night Full of Rain* (1977), was made. Starring Candice BERGEN as an American photographer and Giancarlo Giannini as her Italian lover, the movie received poor reviews, and the contract was terminated.

Wertmuller's subsequent films include *Revenge* (1979), *Softly, Softly* (1985), *Saturday, Sunday, and Monday* (1990), and *The Nymph* (1996). As well as writing the scripts for all her pictures – and often making drastic changes in the middle of shooting – she has also collaborated on the screenplays of other directors' movies. In 1993 she published her memoirs.

Wesley, Mary

(1912–   )

BRITISH NOVELIST

Success came to Mary Wesley relatively late in life: she was in her seventies when she began writing her novels about love and sex in the British upper middle classes, such as *The Camomile Lawn*.

She was born Mary Aline Mynors Farmar in Berkshire, England. The youngest of three children, she felt unloved and unwanted by her parents. Her father was an army officer, and the family frequently moved, so Mary had few friends of her own age. She married Lord Swinfen in 1936 and bore him two sons, but the relationship was not a happy one and ended in the early 1940s. During World War II she fell in love with the journalist Eric Siepmann and lived with him for several years before their marriage. Mary's parents showed their disapproval by cutting her out of their wills; when Eric died in 1970, she was left almost penniless, with a teenage son to support. Life was hard for the next 12 years, until Mary found her voice as a writer.

Wesley had written two books, *Speaking Terms* and *The Sixth Seal*, in the late 1960s, but she was 70 years old when her first major novel, *Jumping the Queue*, was published. It was followed by such works as *The Camomile Lawn* (1984), subsequently adapted for television; *Harnessing Peacocks* (1986), about a young unmarried mother who turns to prostitution to pay for her son's education; and *The Vacillations of Poppy Carew* (1986). Her stories often feature a female character who resembles the author's younger self – a shy misfit surrounded by self-assured and independent women.

Wesley's novels became best-sellers, and money was no longer a problem. By writing about the upper-middle-class world she had grown up in, she regained the wealth she had lost when she turned her back on it to "live in sin" with her lover. She continued writing well into the 1990s, producing such works as *A Sensible Life* (1990), *A Dubious Legacy* (1993), *An Imaginative Experience* (1994), and *Part of the Furniture* (1997).

West, Mae

(1893–1980)

AMERICAN ACTRESS

Mae West raised the spirits of cinemagoers during the Depression of the 1930s with her unique blend of comedy and sexuality. She is credited with a host of comic one-liners full of sexual innuendo, such as "Is that a gun in your pocket, or are you just glad to see me?," "It's not the men in my life that counts – it's the life in my men," and, most famously, "Come up and see me sometime." Her generous curves inspired U.S. airmen to nickname the inflatable life jacket issued to them during World War II a "Mae West."

Born in Brooklyn, New York, she began performing in vaudeville as a child, appearing as "The Baby Vamp" at the age of 14. Four years later she married the actor Frank Wallace and made her debut on Broadway. In 1926 she wrote, produced, directed, and starred in a Broadway show of her own. Its title was *Sex*, and it led to West's arrest and imprisonment for obscenity. Her next play, *Drag* (1927), was banned on Broadway because it dealt with the issue of homosexuality. She continued to write and perform on stage, returning to Broadway in triumph with the hugely success-ful *Diamond Lil* (1928).

In 1932 West made her first appearance on the big screen in *Night after Night*, in what should have been a supporting role. The star of the movie, George Raft, later remarked, "She stole every-thing but the cameras." The following year West starred in *She Done Him Wrong*, a film version of *Diamond Lil*, which broke box-office records. This was followed by starring roles in *I'm No Angel* (1933), *Belle of the Nineties* (1934), *Goin' to Town* (1935), and *Klondike Annie* (1936), all of which were written or cowritten by West, making her one of the highest paid women in the United States. However, censorship rules were being tightened, and she was forced to tone down the risqué style and content of her films to such an extent that they lost their appeal.

After retiring from the cinema in the early 1940s, West contin-ued to write and perform in plays and shows on stage, notably *Catherine Was Great* (1944), and went on tour with a cabaret act. Her autobiography, *Goodness Had Nothing to Do with It*, was published in 1959. (The title is a line from the film *Night after Night*, uttered by West in response to the remark "Goodness, what beautiful diamonds!") Having turned down the role of Norma Desmond in Billy Wilder's film *Sunset Boulevard* (1950), West was eventually lured back to the cinema for *Myra Breckin-ridge* (1970), after rewriting most of her dialogue. Her last ap-pearance on the big screen, in *Sextette* (1978), was not a great success. She suffered a serious stroke in 1980 and died three months later.

West, Dame Rebecca

(1892–1983)

BRITISH WRITER, JOURNALIST, AND CRITIC

She [West] regarded me as a piece of fiction – like one of her novels – that she could edit and improve.

—Her son, Anthony West, *Heritage*

God forbid that any book should be banned. The practice is as indefensible as infanticide.

—*The Strange Necessity* (1928)

One of the 20th century's most outspoken writers, Rebecca West found greater fame as a critic and a journalist than as a novelist.

She was born Cicily Isabel Fairfield in County Kerry, Ireland, the daughter of a soldier and war correspondent. After attending George Watson's Ladies College, Edinburgh, she appeared for a short time on the London stage, notably in Ibsen's *Rosmersholm*; she took her pen name from the heroine of this play. From 1911 West became involved in woman suffrage campaigns and turned to journalism; throughout her life she continued to contribute to important British and American periodicals, beginning with the feminist *Freewoman* (which her mother had forbidden her to read). She joined *The Clarion* the following year as a political writer and later reviewed novels for *The New Statesman* and contributed to *The Daily Telegraph*.

In about 1913 Rebecca began a ten-year affair with the British novelist H. G. Wells. Their son, Anthony West, who also became a writer, was born in 1914. In 1916 her first full-length book appeared, a critical study of the writer Henry James. Her first novels, *The Return of the Soldier* (1918), about the effects of shell shock, and *The Judge* (1922), a study of the Oedipus complex, show the impact of Freudian psychology on her thinking. All her later novels, which appeared at irregular intervals, have this psychological insight. They include *Harriet Hume* (1929), *The Harsh*

Voice (1935), *The Thinking Reed* (1936), and, after a gap of 20 years, *The Fountain Overflows* (1956) and *The Birds Fall Down* (1966). In 1923, after breaking with Wells, she went to the United States and began contributing to the prominent American journals *The New Republic* and *The New Yorker*.

After traveling in 1937 to Yugoslavia with her husband, Henry Maxwell Andrews, a banker whom she had married in 1930, West produced *Black Lamb and Grey Falcon* (1941). A controversial two-volume travel diary that expands into a cultural and political examination of Balkan history, it is generally considered her greatest work. During World War II she supervised BBC broadcasts to Yugoslavia. In 1945 she was highly acclaimed for her coverage for *The New Yorker* of the trial of William Joyce ("Lord Haw-Haw"), who was tried for treason for broadcasting Nazi propaganda in Britain and subsequently executed. This was later published as *The Meaning of Treason* (1949) and expanded and updated in 1965 to include material on the British Communist traitors Burgess, Maclean, Philby, and Blake. Her reports on the Nuremberg trials of German war criminals were collected in *A Train of Powder* (1955).

Rebecca West's other nonfictional works include *D. H. Lawrence* (1930), *St. Augustine* (1933), *The Modern Rake's Progress* (1934), *McLuhan and the Future of Literature* (1969), and *1900* (1982). She was created an Officer of the British Empire in 1949 and Dame Commander of the British Empire in 1959.

Westwood, Vivienne

(1941–)

BRITISH FASHION DESIGNER

> The English aristocracy is now only the middle class with knobs on.
> —Quoted in *The Guardian*,
> February 22, 1997

Considered one of the most influential fashion designers of the late 20th century, Vivienne Westwood is best known for her punk fashions of the 1970s but has continued to shock – and inspire – with her subsequent outrageous collections.

She was born Vivienne Isabel Swire in Glossop, central England. Her father came from a long line of cobblers, and her mother worked in the local cotton mills. When she was 17, the family moved to Harrow, a suburb of London, where they bought a post office. Vivienne worked in a factory for a while before attending a teacher-training college and becoming an elementary-school teacher for some years, during which time she married Derek Westwood.

Retaining her husband's surname after their divorce (the marriage lasted three years), Vivienne Westwood began her fashion career by designing jewelry, which she sold in a London street market. She did not begin designing clothes until 1971, when she met the entrepreneur Malcolm McLaren, who became her lover. In that year Westwood and McLaren opened Let It Rock, a shop in London on the King's Road, Chelsea, where they sold clothing designed in the style of the 1950s. By 1974 the shop was called Sex and emphasized themes of bondage, sadomasochism, and body fetishes. During the mid-1970s McLaren was the manager of the punk rock band the Sex Pistols, and Westwood became enthralled by the punk movement's anarchic style. Her designs gave commercial form to what was originally a wholly improvised street style, retaining the torn edges, safety pins, and combinations of fabrics popular in punk. Her shop was renamed Seditionaries in 1977 and World's End in the 1980s.

Westwood's early 1980s collections – Pirates (1981–82), Savages (1982), Buffalo Girls (1982–83), Punkature (1983), and Witches (1983) – helped create the fashionable "New Romantic" look of the era. In 1985 she showed hoop skirts – based on 19th-century crinolines – that critics immediately denounced as unwearable. Nevertheless, this "Mini Crini" collection (as Westwood called it) turned out to anticipate styles popular later in the 1980s. In 1991 Westwood added a made-to-order bridal line to her output, producing traditional white and ivory dresses but also an outrageous design (in the 1993–94 Anglomania collection) in her own tartan. This is now displayed with all the traditional tartans in the Lochcarron Museum of tartan in Scotland. It is called MacAndreas in honor of her second husband, Andreas Kronthaler, also a designer, whom she married in 1992. Her Café Society collection (1994) was inspired by turn-of-the-century Paris, notably the first couture house, Worth, and featured dresses with long trains and bustles.

Westwood continues to tease the British establishment: her trademark combines the orb, which is ceremonially held by the queen, with a satellite, Westwood's symbol of the future. Nevertheless, she supports the clothing industry in her homeland: her Gold Label clothes are produced in Britain and make ample use of such traditional regional fabrics as tartans, Harris tweeds, and Irish linen. (Her Red Label designs are made in Italy.) She has a longstanding interest in exposing "innerwear as outerwear" and bringing historical lingerie and corsets to street clothes, as in the 1990–91 Portrait collection, in which she created corsets that featured photo-printed details from old master paintings. After an absence of six years Vivienne Westwood returned to the London fashion shows in 1997 with her Vive La Bagatelle collection.

Westwood's forceful designs show her prodigious knowledge of fashion and social history and her equally acute awareness of contemporary trends. One of her ambitions has been to establish a "salon" in the spirit of the 19th-century establishments where artists, writers, and assorted intellectuals gathered. Her designs have inspired a host of younger designers, including Jean-Paul Gaultier, Alexander McQueen, John Galliano, and Helmut Lang.

Despite her refusal to conform to traditional standards in her designs, Westwood was the recipient of the British fashion industry's Designer of the Year Award an unprecedented two years in a row (1990, 1991). In his book *Chic Savages* (1989) John Fairchild, editor of *Women's Wear Daily*, named her one of the six best fashion designers in the world. From 1989 to 1991 Westwood was professor of fashion at the Vienna Academy of Applied Arts, and in 1993 she became professor of fashion at the Berlin Hochschule. In 1992 the Royal College of Art, London, named her an honorary senior fellow. She was created an Officer of the British Empire in 1997.

See also ASHLEY, LAURA; BENETTON, GIULIANA; CHANEL, COCO; KARAN, DONNA; QUANT, MARY.

Wexler, Nancy

(1946–)

AMERICAN CLINICAL PSYCHOLOGIST

Nancy Wexler was a professor of clinical psychology when the death of her mother from Huntington's disease caused her to devote most of her time to a search for the gene responsible for the disease.

Wexler was born in New York, the daughter of the well-known psychoanalyst Milton Wexler. She was educated at Harvard and the University of Michigan, where she completed her doctorate. In 1968 her mother developed Huntington's disease (HD), an untreatable and incurable hereditary condition that leads inevitably to the destruction of the mind. The disease usually appears between the ages of 35 and 50, and Nancy and her sister had a 50% chance of inheriting it. Milton Wexler's response was to set up the

Hereditary Disease Foundation to stimulate and organize research into Huntington's disease and other hereditary complaints.

After completing her doctorate, Nancy Wexler moved to Columbia University as professor of clinical psychology. Following the death of her mother in 1978, she began to devote more of her time to work on HD. In 1981 she heard from a Venezuelan biochemist, Americo Negrette, of an extended family on the shores of Lake Maracaibo in which HD was rife. Wexler sought to trace the gene through the family tree, which began with Maria Concepcion in about 1800. Of her 9,000 living descendants, Wexler traced 371 with HD and found 1,200 with a 50% chance of contracting the disease and a further 2,400 with a 25% chance. Wexler realized that the material she had gathered could be used to identify the gene responsible for HD.

The key step in this process had been the discovery by Ray White and his colleagues of isolated fragments of DNA that could be used as genetic markers. Blood samples were taken and sent immediately to James Gusella at Massachusetts General Hospital, and he began what he thought would be a lengthy search for the appropriate DNA fragment. But Gusella was extremely lucky and soon identified a fragment that seemed to be linked with HD. Further work established that the gene for HD was located on chromosome number 4.

Wexler and Gusella announced their results in 1983. They continued to home in on the gene and by 1992 had restricted it to a particular stretch of DNA in the chromosome in which a series of three particular bases (the chemicals making up DNA) was repeated. In people without HD there seem to be 11–34 copies of this series, while those affected by HD have 42–86 copies.

Wharton, Edith

(1862–1937)

AMERICAN NOVELIST

Edith Wharton's best-known works are her novels about the changing face of New York society at the turn of the century. These include *The House of Mirth* (1905), *Ethan Frome* (1911), and *The Age of Innocence* (1920), for which she won the Pulitzer Prize in 1921. In 1930 she was elected a member of the American Academy of Arts and Letters and in 1923 she became the first woman to receive an honorary LittD from Yale.

Born Edith Newbold Jones in New York City, a descendant of wealthy and socially prominent New York families, she was educated at home by governesses. In 1885, after her debut in society, she married Edward Wharton, a Boston banker. They spent much time in Europe, moving to France in 1907. The marriage was a disaster, and after her husband's mental breakdown the couple separated and were divorced in 1913. Wharton never remarried. She maintained a residence in the United States but continued to live in France, where she became an important figure in the American expatriate community. During World War I she organized American relief for refugees, running the Children of Flanders Rescue Committee, which helped 600 orphans to escape from Belgium. She received the Cross of the Legion of Honor in 1916 and the Order of Leopold in 1919.

Edith Wharton had written since her lonely and isolated childhood; a book of her verse appeared when she was 16. In the 1890s she began to contribute stories and poems to magazines and by the turn of the century she was publishing short-story collections and novels. Her first popular success came with *The House of Mirth*

(1905), which deals with the plight of a young woman who lacks the financial means to maintain her high position in New York society. It was followed by several other novels with similar themes, the most successful of which was *The Age of Innocence*. (In 1993 Martin Scorsese directed a film adaptation of this novel starring Daniel Day-Lewis, Winona RYDER, and Michelle PFEIFFER.) The moral hypocrisy of the New York social world is also explored in her novelette *Ethan Frome*, a stark and tragic story set in an imaginary New England town reminiscent of the region around Lenox, Massachusetts, where Wharton had often spent her summers. *Ethan Frome* achieved enormous popularity.

Wharton's other novels present a wide range of interest. The first, *The Valley of Decision* (1902), had an 18th-century European setting. *The Fruit of the Tree* (1907) treats an American executive's conflicts of love and business, while *Summer* (1917) returns to the New England realism of *Ethan Frome*. She explored Americans in France in *The Reef* (1912) and *The Custom of the Country* (1913); war themes in *The Marne* (1918) and *A Son at the Front* (1923); international manners in *The Glimpses of the Moon* (1922); parent and child relationships in *The Mother's Recompense* (1925), *Twilight Sleep* (1927), and *The Children* (1928); and Midwestern versus New York society in *Hudson River Bracketed* (1929) and its sequel *The Gods Arrive* (1932). Her final novel, *The Buccaneers* (1938), was left unfinished, but has since been adapted for a highly successful British TV series.

Wharton was also a master of the novelette and short story. Besides *Ethan Frome* her novelettes include *Sanctuary* (1903); *Madame de Treymes* (1907), contrasting French and American ideals; and her Old New York series (1924) comprising *False Dawn, The Old Maid, The Spark*, and *New Year's Day*. Her short-story collections include *The Greater Inclination* (1899), *Crucial Instances* (1924), *The Hermit and the Wild Woman* (1908), *Xingu and Other Stories* (1916), *Here and Beyond* (1926), *Human Nature* (1933), *The World Over* (1936), and *Ghosts* (1937).

Wharton is often compared to another expatriate writer, Henry James. Their work has much in common. Both depict an orderly, mannered world of delicate scruples and quiet heroism, but she pays more attention to the details of social gradation and custom. She was a close friend of James during the last 12 years of his life, a significant period in her own creative development, and sometimes read her work aloud to him for criticism. However, she was no slavish imitator of his and viewed with suspicion his preoccupation with pure artistic technique. At one point, hearing that he was in financial difficulties, she arranged for some of her own royalties to be transferred to his account, handling the transaction so that James never knew, a gesture befitting some of her fictional heroes.

Altogether Wharton wrote some 46 books, including travel books and a critical volume, *The Writing of Fiction* (1925). Her autobiography, *A Backward Glance*, appeared in 1934.

Wheatley, Phillis

(*c.* 1753–1784)

AFRICAN-AMERICAN POET

A slave, Phillis Wheatley was acclaimed as a poet in America and in England and even received a favorable mention from the French writer Voltaire. Nevertheless, her life ended in tragedy and poverty.

Phillis Wheatley was born in Africa, possibly Senegal, and was brought to Boston as a slave while still a child. There she was bought by John Wheatley, a tailor, as a servant for his wife. In the Wheatley household she learned to read English and the rudiments of Latin and became acquainted with mythology, ancient history, and the contemporary English poets. Beginning to write her first verses when she was 13 years old, she published her first poem in 1770. When she was about 20 years old, she was sent to England with the Wheatley's son Nathanial for her health. She was cordially received and became a popular figure in London society because of her personality and her easy conversation.

The first bound volume of her verse, published in 1773 and dedicated to Selina Hastings, Countess of HUNTINGDON, was *Poems on Various Subjects, Religious and Moral, by Phillis Wheatley, Negro Servant to Mr. John Wheatley of Boston, in New England.* After her return to America she published several poems, including an address to George Washington. In 1778, after the death of the Wheatleys and the granting of her freedom, she married John Peters, a free African American, but the marriage was an unhappy one. She lost touch with her old circle of friends, and two of her three children died. When her husband was imprisoned for debt, Phillis took work as a servant and died alone in poverty in Boston, her last child dying with her.

In 1834 Margaretta M. Odell published the *Memoir and Poems of Phillis Wheatley*, and *The Letters of Phillis Wheatley, the Negro Slave-Poet of Boston* appeared in 1864.

Whitbread, Fatima

(1961–)

BRITISH ATHLETE

Whitbread set new records for throwing the javelin in 1985 and 1986 and won the World Championship title the following year. A popular figure, she was voted BBC Sports Personality of the Year, British Sports Writers Sportswoman of the Year, and British Athletics Writers Woman Athlete of the Year in 1987.

Born Fatima Vedad in London, she was abandoned by her parents and raised in a children's home until the age of 12, when she was adopted by Margaret Whitbread, a former British athlete who had competed internationally in javelin throwing. Margaret felt that Fatima could do well in the same sport, despite her comparatively small stature, and trained her for international competition. Fatima's first major success came in 1979, when she won the javelin event at the European Junior Championships. She was voted Woman Athlete of the Year in 1983, after coming in second in the World Championships and first in the European Cup, and took the bronze medal in the Olympic Games the following year. Her teammate Tessa Sanderson, who was to become her closest rival, won the gold.

In 1985 Whitbread broke the women's 76-meter record for javelin throwing, and in 1986 she set a new record of 77.44 meters at the European Athletics Championships. She was consistent in her achievement, regularly exceeding the throw of 69.56 meters that had earned Sanderson the Olympic gold in 1984. After winning the 1987 World Championships, Whitbread had a second attempt at the Olympic title in 1988, but the coveted gold medal still eluded her, and she had to be content with the silver. A series of back and shoulder injuries brought her career in competition to an end, and in the 1990s she became involved with a variety of sporting and other organizations, including Thurrock Harriers Athletic Club and the Eastern Region Sports Council.

White, Antonia

(1899–1980)

BRITISH NOVELIST AND TRANSLATOR

Antonia White is best remembered for *Frost in May* (1933) and other autobiographical novels.

Antonia Botting was born in London, where her father taught at the prestigious St. Paul's Girls' School. Her parents, who were fervent Roman Catholics, sent Antonia to a strict convent school in Roehampton, London, where she displayed a precocious literary talent and a strong rebellious streak. When her secret writings about the school and its teachers were discovered, she was expelled. She finished her education at the more liberal St. Paul's Girls' School.

During her twenties Antonia worked variously as a teacher, an actress, and an advertising copywriter. She also made two disastrous short-lived marriages: in each case her husband turned out to be homosexual, and the marriage was annulled without having been consummated. It was during the earlier of these marriages that Antonia suffered the first of the mental breakdowns that would recur throughout her life; in 1920 she was certified insane and confined to an asylum for nine months. A third marriage, to the journalist H. T. Hopkinson, proved more satisfactory and provided the stability that enabled her to complete her first novel, *Frost in May*. This largely autobiographical work (published under the name Antonia White) was praised for its brilliant, bitter account of life at a Catholic girls' school in the 1910s. Despite this success, further literary work was held up by recurrent mental problems and the breakdown of her marriage to Hopkinson in 1938.

During the 1930s and 1940s Antonia White worked as a freelance journalist, as the fashion editor of a daily newspaper, and for the BBC. Her remaining novels appeared in the 1950s. Although the central character of these three works has a different name from the heroine of her first novel, *The Lost Traveller* (1950), *The Sugar House* (1952), and *Beyond the Glass* (1954) are effectively sequels to *Frost in May*. They describe the various mental and marital difficulties of "Clara Batchelor," who is clearly a stand-in for White herself.

In her later years White published books on subjects ranging from her pet cats to her reasons for returning to the Catholic faith of her youth (described in *The Hound and the Falcon*, 1966). She also translated prolifically from French authors, especially CO-LETTE.

After White's death her daughter Susan Chitty edited a selection from her diaries – writings that present a frank picture of her bohemian lifestyle and numerous love affairs. Chitty also caused controversy with *Now to My Mother*, a bitter memoir in which she accused her mother of neglect and emotional cruelty.

Whitlock, Elizabeth Kemble

(1761–1836)

BRITISH ACTRESS

Although somewhat overshadowed on the London stage by the brilliant success of her sister Sarah SIDDONS, Elizabeth Whitlock was herself an accomplished actress who was acclaimed in England and the United States.

Born Elizabeth Kemble in Warrington, northwest England, she was the fifth child of Roger and Sarah Kemble, who ran a well-known touring theater company. After gaining some stage experience in local towns, she went with her two elder sisters, Sarah Siddons and Frances KEMBLE, to London, where she first appeared at Drury Lane Theatre in 1783 as Portia in *The Merchant of Venice*. In 1785 she married Charles Edward Whitlock, a local theater manager and actor, and seven years later accompanied her husband to the United States, where they performed for many years in the principal cities. Elizabeth Whitlock became the most popular actress of the day in the United States and frequently performed before President Washington and other distinguished persons in Philadelphia.

She returned to England to an enthusiastic reception at the Drury Lane Theatre in 1807 but retired from the stage shortly afterward.

Whitman, Sarah Helen Power

(1803–1878)

AMERICAN POET

Sarah Helen Whitman is best known for her sequence of poems on her relationship with the American writer Edgar Allan Poe. His poem "To Helen" was written for her.

Sarah Helen Power was born in Providence, Rhode Island. In 1828 she married John W. Whitman, a Boston lawyer who died in 1833. She then returned to Providence and spent her time writing; her first poems were published in the *American Ladies' Magazine*. In 1848 she was engaged briefly to Edgar Allan Poe. She later wrote a literary and personal defense of him, *Edgar Poe and His Critics* (1860). Some of her verse was greatly influenced by his.

In addition to poems, Whitman contributed numerous articles on such topics as women's rights and suffrage to periodicals; she was also noted for her conversational powers. Her verse was in part collected in the volume *Hours of Life, and Other Poems* (1853); a complete edition of her poetic works, *Poems*, appeared in 1879. *Fairy Ballads* and some other works were written with her sister, Anna M. Power. "A Still Day in Autumn," probably her finest poem, was often included in anthologies. Whitman died in Providence. *The Last Letters of Edgar Allan Poe to Sarah Helen Whitman* was published in 1909.

Whitney, Anne

(1821–1915)

AMERICAN SCULPTOR

Anne Whitney received important public commissions for historical figures but is also remembered for works reflecting her lifelong interest in social justice. Notable examples of these include *Lady Godiva* (1864) and *Africa* (1865), which relate to the liberation of women and African Americans, respectively.

Whitney was born in Watertown, Massachusetts, the youngest of seven children. Educated mostly at home, she ran a school in Salem from 1847 to 1849. A keen abolitionist and feminist, she was also a writer, publishing her poems in 1859. Largely self-taught as an artist, she began to sculpt in her thirties. In 1858 she went to study art and sculpture in New York City and Philadelphia and anatomy in a Brooklyn hospital.

Whitney first began showing her work in 1860, when she exhibited a marble bust of a child at the National Academy of Design in New York City. In 1867 she went to Rome for four years, during which time she studied and traveled extensively, visiting (among other places) Munich and its noted bronze foundry. Her piece *Roma* (1989) personified Roman society as a beggar woman and caused such outrage at the papal court that it had to be moved to France.

On her return to Boston in 1873 Massachusetts commissioned Whitney to create a full-length figure of Samuel Adams for Statuary Hall in the U.S. Capitol, Washington, D.C. Her statues of Leif Ericsson (1887; Commonwealth Avenue, Boston) and Charles Sumner (1902; Harvard Square, Cambridge) are other major works, although the commission for the latter was initially withdrawn when it was realized that the sculptor was a woman. She also created a large marble statue of the famous English social reformer Harriet MARTINEAU, which the Boston abolitionist Maria Weston CHAPMAN commissioned in 1878 to represent the emancipation of women (it was on view at Wellesley College until 1914, when it was destroyed by a fire). Other important subjects were Lucy STONE, Harriet Beecher STOWE, and Frances WILLARD.

Whitney, Gertrude Vanderbilt

(1875–1942)

AMERICAN SCULPTOR AND PATRON OF THE ARTS

Gertrude Vanderbilt Whitney founded the Whitney Museum of American Art in 1930 in Greenwich Village, New York, where she had first opened a studio in 1907. It is now housed in a building on Madison Avenue designed by Marcel Breuer.

Gertrude Vanderbilt was born in New York City into a wealthy and socially prominent family. Her father was the financier and art patron Cornelius Vanderbilt (1843–99), and her great-grandfather was Commodore Cornelius Vanderbilt (1794–1877), the steamship and railway magnate and philanthropist. In 1896 Gertrude married the financier and sportsman Harry Payne Whitney, son of William Collins Whitney. She studied sculpture in New York City and Paris, where she was inspired by the French sculptor Auguste Rodin.

In 1908 she won her first prize, for a sculpture of *Pan*. During World War I she established a hospital and worked as a nurse. Her feelings of horror for war are expressed in many of her works, including *Victory Arch* (1918–20) and the *Washington Heights War Memorial* (1921), both in New York City. Among her other important works are the *Titanic Memorial* (1914–31), which symbolizes the words in Revelation 20:13: "The sea gave up its dead," and the terracotta *Aztec Fountain* (1912; Pan American Union building), both in Washington, D.C.; the *Peter Stuyvesant Memorial* (1936–39) in New York City; the *Columbus Memorial* (1928–33) in Palos, Spain; the *St.-Nazaire War Memorial* (1924) in St.-Nazaire, France; *Spirit of Flight*, for the 1939–40 New York World's Fair; and numerous equestrian statues. All her works are striking and inspired by a traditional simplicity. She was equally well known as a sponsor of aspiring artists, and much of her effort and wealth was directed toward developing and encouraging a national artistic taste.

In 1929 Gertrude Whitney offered to donate her collection of about 500 works of modern American artists to the Metropolitan

Museum of Art in the belief that such artists needed recognition. However, the museum's director, a traditionalist, turned her offer down, and she set about establishing her own institution, which was founded in 1930 and opened in November 1931. She also helped fund the Whitney Wing of the American Museum of Natural History in New York City.

BIBLIOGRAPHY
Berman, Avis, *Rebels on Eighth Street* (1990).
Friedman, Bernard H., *Gertrude Vanderbilt Whitney* (1978).

Wiggin, Kate Douglas

(1856–1923)

AMERICAN CHILDREN'S WRITER AND EDUCATOR

Kate Wiggin is perhaps best known for her story for girls, *Rebecca of Sunnybrook Farm*, which was published in 1903. She also organized the first free kindergarten in San Francisco in 1878.

Born Kate Smith in Philadelphia, Pennsylvania, she was educated at Abbott Academy, Andover, Massachusetts. In 1877 she and her sister Nora Archibald Smith (*c.* 1859–1934) became interested in the new art of kindergarten teaching. After studying under Emma J. C. Marwedel, a pioneer kindergarten worker, she helped to found the Silver Street Kindergarten in the slums of San Francisco in 1878. Two years later she and her sister established the California Kindergarten Training School for teachers to spread the educational principles of Friedrich Froebel. In 1881 she married Samuel B. Wiggin, a lawyer, who died in 1889.

Kate Wiggin began her literary career as a writer of stories for children to raise funds for kindergarten work. *The Story of Patsy*

(1883), *The Birds' Christmas Carol* (1887), *Timothy's Quest* (1890), and *Mother Carey's Chickens* (1911) were all very popular. She frequently visited England, and several of her books for adult readers grew out of these visits – among them the "Penelope" novels, which dealt lightly with the theme of the interaction of British and American cultures.

In 1895 Kate married a New York businessman, George Christopher Riggs. As well as her novels she also wrote educational texts, notably *Kindergarten Principles and Practice* (1896, with Nora A. Smith) and the three-volume *The Republic of Childhood* (1895–96). She died at Harrow, in England. Her autobiography, *My Garden of Memory*, was published in 1923, after her death.

Wightman, Hazel

(1886–1974)

AMERICAN TENNIS PLAYER

Hazel Wightman won 47 tennis titles between 1909 and 1954. She also donated a trophy for international women's team competition; the United States and Great Britain began competing for the Wightman Cup in 1923 and have continued ever since.

Hazel Hotchkiss was born near Healdsburg, California, and began playing tennis at the age of 16. She had to get up at dawn to play because the courts were reserved for men after 8 a.m. Entering her first major competition in 1909, she won the national singles title and played on the victorious doubles and mixed-doubles teams. She gained nationwide fame when she repeated this performance in 1910 and 1911. She and her women's doubles partner, Helen WILLS, were never beaten when they played together. They won the Wimbledon doubles in 1924 and the American title six times. In 1919 Hazel won her fourth national singles title.

She married George Wightman and had five children. Hazel Wightman continued to play competitively until she retired from the veterans' competitions at the age of 74. In her book *Better Tennis* (1934) she referred to the game as "a channel of intensified life." She died at Chestnut Hill, Massachusetts.

Wilcox, Ella Wheeler

(1850–1919)

AMERICAN POET

Laugh, and the world laughs with you.
Weep, and you weep alone.
—"Solitude"

Ella Wheeler Wilcox was probably the best-known poet of her day, writing verses of love and hope that appeared in more than 250 newspapers across the United States.

Ella Wheeler was born in Johnstown Center, Wisconsin, and claimed that she was a descendant of Princess POCAHONTAS. Encouraged by her mother, she began composing verses even before she could write. By the age of seven Ella was a "professional" poet, having received payment for her poems from the publishers of the magazines in which they appeared. She continued to write prolifically throughout her life, producing at least one or two poems every day, and was soon able to support her family on her income. In 1884 she married the journalist Robert M. Wilcox. The couple traveled widely, using their wealth to indulge their passion for collecting: she collected dolls and necklaces, and he collected musical instruments. Ella also made several visits to Britain, where she had almost as many fans as in the United

States; her hard work there during World War I may have contributed to her death from nervous exhaustion.

Wilcox's verses were first published in book form in the collection *Drops of Water* (1872). A later volume, *Poems of Passion* (1883), contained some mildly erotic verses that were condemned by the church but did not affect her popularity. Her simple, sentimental poetry, with its messages of wisdom and comfort, touched the hearts of readers of all ages and classes of society, though it failed to impress the literary critics. Wilcox also wrote novels, short stories, essays, and two autobiographical works: *Story of a Literary Career* (1905) and *The World and I* (1918).

Wilder, Laura Ingalls

(1867–1957)

AMERICAN WRITER

Laura Ingalls Wilder is best known as the author of the popular "Little House" series of novels for children, based mainly on her own pioneering experiences between the ages of five and 18.

She was born in Pepin, Wisconsin, and lived on a farm all her life. At 15 she became a teacher to pay for her blind sister's special schooling. A few years after her marriage in 1885 Laura moved to Florida with her husband and daughter, Rose Wilder Lane (who also became a writer). In 1894 the family settled in the Ozark country. There she began to write a newspaper column, "As a Farm Woman Thinks," and was the editor of the *Missouri Ruralist* for 12 years.

It was not until the age of 65, at the suggestion of her daughter, that she began to write her series of novels. The first of her "Little House" novels, *Little House in the Big Woods* (1932), is about the pioneering spirit and frontier life in Wisconsin. It was followed by *Farmer Boy* (1933), based on the early childhood experiences of her husband Almanzo. *Little House on the Prairie* (1935) continues her story into Kansas and is followed by five other novels in chronological sequence: *On the Banks of Plum Creek* (1937), in the Minnesota wheat country; *By the Shores of Silver Lake* (1939), in Dakota territory; *Long Winter* (1940), reintroducing the Wilder brothers of *Farmer Boy*; *Little Town on the Prairie* (1941), again in Dakota; *These Happy Golden Years* (1943), based on her experiences of pioneer schoolteaching, which she began at the age of 15, and marriage; and finally *The First Four Years* (1971), which covered the early years of Laura's marriage and was published after her death.

In 1954 the series won a special Newberg-Caldecot Award, and in the 1970s it was adapted for television as "The Little House on the Prairie," a show that also became extremely popular in Britain. In 1954 the American Library Association established the Laura Ingalls Wilder Award for lasting contributions to children's literature.

Wilhelmina

(1880–1962)

QUEEN OF THE NETHERLANDS

Queen Wilhelmina's reign, which lasted for 50 years, was characterized by her shrewd and practical judgment. Despite her wish to remain neutral during World War II (as she had during World War I), after the Netherlands was invaded by Germany, she headed the Dutch government in exile in England from May 1940 until July 1945.

Wilhelmina Helena Pauline Maria was born in The Hague, the daughter of King William III by his second wife, Emma of Waldeck. On her father's death in 1890 the ten-year-old Wilhelmina became queen under the regency of her mother until she was 18. On September 6, 1898, soon after her 18th birthday, she was crowned at Amsterdam. On February 7, 1901 she married

Henry Wladimir Albert Ernst, Duke of Mecklenburg-Schwerin, who died in 1934. Their only child, JULIANA, was born in 1909.

Queen Wilhelmina received popular support in her public activities and respected the powers of Parliament under the constitutional monarchy, maintaining the traditional peace and neutrality of her country until the outbreak of World War II. She oversaw a program of extensive social reform that was introduced to resolve an economic crisis resulting from World War I. At the same time, the development of industry and foreign trade under Wilhelmina's rule brought prosperity to an expanding population.

After Germany's invasion of the Netherlands on May 10, 1940, Queen Wilhelmina escaped to England with her family and leading government officials. She broadcast constantly to the Netherlands during her exile. In 1942 she visited Canada and the United States, where she addressed a joint meeting of Congress, and the following summer she visited President Franklin D. Roosevelt at Hyde Park.

After the invasion of France by Allied armies in 1944 Queen Wilhelmina remained in London until March 1945, when she visited liberated areas of her kingdom and began to apply herself to the problems of reconstruction. Her daughter, Crown Princess Juliana, had by then rejoined her in London after spending a few years in Canada. After the celebration of the 50th anniversary of the queen's reign in 1948 Wilhelmina, exhausted by illness and stress, abdicated in favor of Juliana. Her memoirs, *Lonely but Not Alone*, were published in 1958.

Wilkinson, Ellen

(1891–1947)

BRITISH POLITICAL LEADER

Known as "Red Ellen" (as much for her red hair as her politics), Ellen Wilkinson became the first woman Labour member of Parliament (MP) when she won a seat for Middlesborough East in 1924. Becoming the Labour MP for Jarrow in 1935, she was one of the leaders of the famous hunger march to London. She was appointed minister for education in 1945.

Ellen Cicely Wilkinson was born in Manchester, northwest England, the third of four children of a millworker. She was educated with the aid of secondary school scholarships and, after winning a history scholarship, graduated with an MA degree from Manchester University in 1913. Like her mother and grandmother before her, she became a member of the Manchester and Salford Co-operative Society. In 1912 she joined the Independent Labour Party, becoming an organizer of the National Union of Women's Suffrage Societies in 1913 and of the National Union of Distributive and Allied Workers in 1915. She was also a founder of the Communist Party of Great Britain in 1920. Failing to win a parliamentary seat in 1923, she was elected as a Communist to the Manchester City Council that same year.

After severing her Communist connection and joining the Labour Party, she was elected to Parliament in 1924, retaining her seat until 1931. In 1939, after the Jarrow hunger march, she published *The Town That Was Murdered*, describing the appalling conditions brought about by unemployment in Jarrow. Having criticized the Conservative government's policies on appeasement and unemployment, in 1938 she sponsored a bill (the Hire-Purchase Bill) protecting installment buyers.

Wilkinson joined Winston Churchill's wartime coalition government in 1940, first as parliamentary secretary to the Ministry of Pensions, then as parliamentary secretary to the Ministry of Home Security. After the sweeping Labour Party victory in the general election in 1945 she was appointed by the new prime minister, Clement Attlee, to the post of minister of education, with the job of translating the 1944 Education Act into practical reality. She was a member of the British delegation to the 1945 United Nations Conference at San Francisco. Her writings include *Why War?* (1934) and, with Edward Conze, *Why Fascism?* (1934).

Wilkinson, Jemima

(1752–1819)

AMERICAN RELIGIOUS LEADER

Jemima Wilkinson, who called herself the "Universal Public Friend," convinced her followers of her own resurrection.

Born into an affluent Quaker family in Cumberland, Rhode Island, Jemima Wilkinson was powerfully impressed as a girl by the sermons of the Methodist George Whitefield and later by Ann LEE, the founder of the Shakers. During her early twenties, after a severe attack of fever that was followed by a prolonged coma, Jemima claimed that she had been raised from the dead and that her body was occupied by the "Spirit of Life," sent by God to warn the world of his impending wrath. She preached widely throughout Rhode Island and Connecticut and pretended to work miracles. She induced many intelligent people to become her followers, and churches were established by her adherents in Greenwich, Rhode Island, and New Milford, Connecticut. However, she was forced to leave New England when she began to advocate the Shaker practice of celibacy, and some of her disciples claimed that she was the Messiah.

In 1790, accompanied by two "witnesses," Sarah Richards and Rachel Miller, Wilkinson established a colony of Universal Friends at Jerusalem Township in Yates County, New York, near Seneca Lake. She exacted from the group complete submission and the most menial services, her influence over them being practically supreme. When her rules were broken, the punishment that followed often gave rise to dissension. Wilkinson also taught mystical dream interpretation and professed that she was a divine messenger from God, even perhaps that she was Christ reincarnated.

Although she never abandoned her claims, after some years her influence began to wane, she lost her physical beauty, and the latter part of her life was embittered by illness, jealousies, annoyances, and controversies between herself and her followers. She ended her days living alone, away from the other houses in the community. The sect broke up after her death.

Wilkinson, Marguerite Ogden

(1883–1928)

CANADIAN-BORN AMERICAN POET AND ANTHOLOGIST

Marguerite Ogden Wilkinson, who was a popular poet and lecturer on poetry, was more widely known during the 1920s for her anthologies of verse, which include *Golden Songs of the Golden State* (1917).

Born Marguerite Bigelow in Halifax, Nova Scotia, Canada, she completed her education at Northwestern University and in 1909 married James G. Wilkinson, principal of the Roosevelt School, New Rochelle, New York. She began writing verse and also reviewed poetry for the *New York Times Book Review*, becoming a popular lecturer on poetry for school and club groups.

Her first collections, *In Vivid Gardens* and *By a Western Wayside*, were published in 1911 and 1912, respectively. *The Great Dream*, a long visionary poem, appeared in 1923, and *Citadels*, a collection of religious poems, in 1928. Her other anthologies include *New Voices* (1919), *Contemporary Poetry* (1923), and *Yule Fire* (1925). She drowned while swimming at Coney Island.

Willard, Emma

(1787–1870)

AMERICAN EDUCATIONALIST

The first woman to prove the value of higher education for women, Emma Willard provided the inspiration for the founding of many high schools for girls and colleges for women. The seminary that she herself founded in 1821 became the Emma Willard School in 1895. In 1854 she represented the United States at the World's Educational Convention in London.

Born Emma Hart in Berlin, Connecticut, into a large and influential family, she attended Berlin Academy from 1802 to 1803. In 1807 she took charge of the Female Academy at Middlebury, Vermont, but left in 1809 to marry Dr. John Willard. Continuing her own studies, she completed the curriculum at the all-male Middlebury College but was not allowed to attend classes or obtain a degree. In 1814 she opened a school for young ladies in her own home, introducing mathematics and philosophy, subjects previously not taught to women.

In 1818, anxious to further the cause of women's education, Willard sent the New York governor, DeWitt Clinton, her *Plan for Improving Female Education* (1819) and pleaded for it herself before the state legislature. She asked that state aid be provided for female seminaries and that women be given the same educational opportunities as men. In 1819 she moved her school to Waterford, New York, and in 1821, with the help of local citizens but without state aid, she established the Troy Female Seminary, effectively the first women's college. Here she continued her policy of teaching traditionally "male" subjects, including science. She evolved new methods of teaching geography and history, published many best-selling textbooks, and trained hundreds of teachers whom she sent into the South and West, making her seminary a model in the United States and Europe.

After a trip to Europe in 1830 Willard published a volume of poems (1831), which included "Rocked in the Cradle of the Deep," as well as her *Journal and Letters from France and Great Britain* (1833), the proceeds of which she used to help found a training school for teachers in liberated Greece in 1833. In 1838 she handed the seminary over to her son and his wife and devoted herself to campaigning for improved public schools, traveling widely to demand that women be given equal opportunities as teachers. That same year she married Dr. Christopher Yates (her first husband had died in 1825), but they were divorced in 1843. She continued to publish textbooks, among them *Last Leaves of American History* (1849).

Emma Willard's other published works include *Nineteen Beautiful Years* (1864), a life of her sister; *How to Win: A Book for Girls* (1886); and *Glimpse of Fifty Years* (1889).

See also AGASSIZ, ELIZABETH; LYON, MARY; THOMAS, MARTHA CAREY.

Willard, Frances

(1839–1898)

AMERICAN EDUCATOR, REFORMER, AND LECTURER

Frances Willard was a founder of the National Women's Christian Temperance Union (WCTU) and served as its first president from 1879 until her death. From 1891 she was also first president of the worldwide WCTU, an organization with a membership of two million women. Acclaimed as a brilliant speaker, she traveled widely to present her views and win recruits. By the end of the century she had also established a temperance hospital, a publishing association, a lecture bureau, and an office building in Chicago. Twenty states had by then enacted woman suffrage – another cause she campaigned for – in whole or in part.

Frances Elizabeth Caroline Willard was born in Churchville, New York, and grew up on a farm at Janesville, Wisconsin, where she lived a pioneer lifestyle with her school-teacher parents until she was 18. After graduating from Northwestern Female College, Evanston, Illinois, in 1859, she began teaching, first in a local school and then in colleges, before traveling to Europe and spending time at the Sorbonne and the Collège de France. In 1871 she became president of the Evanston College for Ladies and, when this institution became part of Northwestern University in 1873, dean of women.

In 1874 Willard resigned from teaching and, influenced by the revivalist crusade, became secretary of the National WCTU and later (1879) its president. Under her leadership it grew to 10,000 local units with a paying membership of 250,000 women, one of the great women's movement of the century. Her campaigns, which linked temperance to woman suffrage, attracted many women into politics for the first time. She also worked for women's legal rights and better working conditions, better schools, prison reform, improved nutrition, and the provision of kindergartens. The power and the prestige of the WCTU were enhanced by the support and encouragement it received from such important organizations as the Young Men's Christian Association, the Ministerial Alliance, and the Sunday School Association. Willard became president of the National Council of Women in 1890.

After her death Congress voted to place her statue in the rotunda of the Capitol in Washington, D.C., extolling Frances Willard as "the first woman of the 19th century, the most beloved character of her times."

See also SOMERSET, LADY ISABELLA CAROLINE.

Willebrandt, Mabel

(1896–1963)

AMERICAN LAWYER AND GOVERNMENT OFFICIAL

Famous during the 1920s for her relentless enforcement of prohibition, Mabel Willebrandt became the second woman to hold the post of assistant attorney general of the United States in 1921.

Born Mabel Walker in Woodsdale, Kansas, she graduated from Tempe (Arizona) Normal School in 1911. She then became the principal of a school in South Pasadena, California, while she studied law at the University of Southern California. In 1915 she began to practice law in California and was appointed a non-salaried public defender with special responsibility for women's cases for Los Angeles city and county. In this capacity she handled over 2,000 cases.

During her second term as assistant attorney general (she was the first woman to hold the post for an extended term) Willebrandt also supervised the federal Bureau of Prisons and was involved in tax programs. Resigning from her federal posts in 1929, she returned to private practice in California. In 1938 she became the first woman to serve as chairman of an important committee of the American Bar Association (the committee on aeronautical law). She died at Riverside, California.

Williams, Betty

(1943–   )

NORTHERN IRISH PEACE
ACTIVIST

With Mairéad Corrigan, Betty Williams founded the Northern Ireland Peace Movement and shared the Nobel Prize for Peace in 1976.

Born in Belfast, Northern Ireland, Betty Williams was living there with her husband and two children when she witnessed an incident that sparked off her campaign to end the violence between Catholics and Protestants in the province. In 1976 three children from the Maguire family were accidentally killed by a car whose driver had been involved in a terrorist shooting, and the horror-struck Williams immediately began to gather support among her neighbors for a peace movement. Mairéad Corrigan, aunt of the Maguire children, was one of the first to join the campaign, and the following week more than 10,000 Catholics and Protestants came together in a march for peace through Belfast.

The movement spread throughout Northern Ireland and gained support from far and wide, including the United States. A Peace Assembly was set up, with small local groups working within the community. Williams was on the Executive Committee until 1978 and remained involved with the movement until 1980, traveling around the British Isles and abroad to speak about the Troubles in Northern Ireland. She was awarded an honorary doctorate from Yale University in 1977. After her first marriage ended in divorce, she married James Perkins in 1982 and settled in Florida.

Williams, Esther

(1923–)

AMERICAN SWIMMER AND
FILM ACTRESS

A former swimming champion, Esther Williams was the star of numerous aquatic MGM musicals and other movies of the 1940s and 1950s.

Born in Inglewood, near Los Angeles, Esther Jane Williams showed an early talent for swimming. She would have competed in the 1940 Olympic Games if they had not been canceled (because of World War II); instead she joined an aquacade in San Francisco, where she was spotted by a Hollywood talent scout. Her first film appearance, with Mickey Rooney in *Andy Hardy's Double Life* (1942), was followed by a string of movies in which her swimming skills were exploited to the full. *Bathing Beauty* (1944) made her a star – and a major box-office attraction – in a story about a water pageant at a girls' school. Most of her films were romantic or spectacular musicals, such as *Neptune's Daughter* (1949), in which she and Ricardo Montalban sang the Oscar-winning song "Baby, It's Cold Outside," and *Dangerous When Wet* (1953). In the biopic *Million Dollar Mermaid* (1952) she took the part of Annette Kellerman, the Australian swimmer-turned-actress who pioneered the one-piece bathing suit.

Williams came out of the water to play a more serious role in *The Unguarded Moment* (1956). Her dramatic skills were limited – the comment "Wet she's a star, dry she ain't" has been attributed to various people, including the entertainer Fanny BRICE, who appeared with Williams in *Ziegfeld Follies* (1945), and the producer Joe Pasternak, who worked on some of her films. After retiring from the cinema in the early 1960s, Williams became a successful businesswoman, designing swimwear and marketing Esther Williams Swimming Pools. In 1967 she married her third husband, the actor Fernando Lamas, who died in 1982.

Williams, Shirley, Baroness

(1930–   )

BRITISH POLITICIAN

Shirley Williams was one of the founder members of the Social Democratic Party, a group of politicians who broke away from the British Labour Party in 1981, and remained its president until 1988, when it merged with the Liberal Party.

Shirley Vivien Teresa Brittain was born in Chelsea, London, England, the daughter of the writer and feminist Vera BRITTAIN and Sir George Catlin, a professor of political science. She was educated in London (apart from a period during World War II when she was evacuated to the United States) and went on to study at the University of Oxford. After a year in New York at Columbia University she returned to Britain and worked as a journalist while trying to gain a seat in Parliament. In 1955 she married her first husband, Bernard Williams, a professor of philosophy.

Shirley Williams had been involved with Labour politics since her teens, when she belonged to the Labour League of Youth. She was finally elected in 1964 as Labour member of Parliament for Hitchin and she remained in Parliament for the next 15 years. During that time she served in various ministerial positions, including minister of state for the Home Office (1969–70) and secretary of state for education and science (1976–79). She played an important role in the reorganization of the state secondary education system in Britain, campaigning for the replacement of selective grammar schools with comprehensive schools.

When the Conservative Party was returned to power in the general election of 1979, Williams lost her seat in Parliament. After a series of disagreements with the more left-wing elements of the Labour Party she left in 1981 to form the Social Democratic Party (SDP) with three other ex-Labour politicians. In a by-election later that year she became the new party's first member of Parliament, but she lost her seat in 1983. The SDP merged with the Liberal Party to form the Social and Liberal Democrats in 1988; in the same year Williams moved to the United States with her new husband, Harvard professor Richard Neustadt, to become professor of elective politics at the John F. Kennedy School of Government, Harvard. In 1993 she was raised to the British peerage as Baroness Williams of Crosby.

Wills, Helen Newington

(1905–   )

AMERICAN TENNIS PLAYER

Called the "Queen of the Nets" and the greatest woman tennis player of her time, she was known as Helen Wills Moody during the years of her marriage to Frederick S. Moody, Jr. She won 31 titles, a record only broken by the Australian player Margaret COURT in the early 1970s.

Helen Wills was born in Centerville, California, the daughter of a doctor who taught her to play tennis. She was educated at the

Anna Head School and the University of California and later studied art, exhibiting her work in New York City.

She joined the Berkeley Lawn Tennis Club at the age of 14 and entered the National Singles Championships for the first time when she was 16. Although unsuccessful that year, she went on to win the U.S. singles title seven times (1923–25, 1927–29, 1931), the Wimbledon singles eight times, the French singles four times, and the Wightman Cup singles 18 times.

Helen Wills retired from major tournament play in 1938 to spend her time painting. She wrote and illustrated *Tennis* (1928) and *Fifteen-Thirty* (1937). In 1939 she married Aidan Roark.

Winchilsea, Anne Finch, Countess of

(1660–1720)

BRITISH POET

Anne Finch, Countess of Winchilsea, is remembered for her nature poetry and satirical verses.

Born Anne Kingsmill near Southampton in southern England, she was the daughter of a country landowner. Although educated entirely at home, she was clearly a woman of some learning. In 1683 she became a maid of honor to MARY OF MODENA, the second wife of James, Duke of York, the future King James II (from 1685). Interestingly, Anne's fellow maids of honor included Anne Killigrew, another young woman who became known as a poet.

In 1684 Anne married Colonel Heneage Finch, who in 1712 became the Earl of Winchilsea. Following the Glorious Revolution of 1688, in which James II was forced to flee abroad, Anne Finch and her husband left court and settled on their estates in Kent. It was during this period that she began to write poems and verse dramas, which she circulated among friends.

In 1701 Anne Finch found a wider audience when her poem "The Spleen" was printed and received praise from several critics. The poem is a satirical ode describing the symptoms of melancholy, a condition to which she seems to have been prone. During the 1710s she mixed in literary circles, winning the friendship of such leading contemporary writers as Alexander Pope and Jonathan Swift. Her chief publication, *Miscellany Poems on Several Occasions*, appeared in 1713.

The Countess of Winchilsea's poems have interested later critics mainly because of their descriptions of nature, which are unusually observant and sensitive for their time. In particular, such poems as "A Nocturnal Reverie" show an awareness of how the observing mind projects its own moods onto the landscape. This aspect of her work was to win special praise from the English Romantic poet William Wordsworth. Her work also includes a number of lively satirical pieces in which she defends women's rights to education and literary expression and contrasts the liberties allowed to married men with the restrictions imposed on their spouses.

Windsor, Duchess of

(1896–1986)

AMERICAN SOCIALITE

As Mrs. Wallis Simpson, a divorcée, she was the woman for whom King Edward VIII gave up the British throne in 1936 with the historic announcement: "I have found it impossible...to discharge my duties as King as I would wish to do without the help and support of the woman I love."

Bessie Wallis Warfield was born at Blue Ridge Summit, Pennsylvania. Her father died when she was just a few months old, leaving the family with little money, but a wealthy uncle provided for Wallis's education and enabled her to enter Baltimore society in 1914. Although she was not a great beauty, her lively personality and her elegant sense of fashion won her many admirers. In 1916 she married Lieutenant Earl Winfield Spencer, but this first marriage was not a happy one and ended in divorce in 1927. The following year Wallis married Ernest Simpson, an American-born British subject, in England.

The couple set up home in London, and in 1931 Mrs. Simpson was introduced to Edward, Prince of Wales, at a country house party. During the following years the Simpsons were frequent weekend guests at the prince's home. In 1934 Wallis joined Edward and his friends on a Spanish vacation without her husband; it was probably at this time, in her own words, that she and the future king "crossed the line that marks the indefinable boundary between friendship and love." Her second marriage ended in divorce in 1936.

Earlier the same year the Prince of Wales had succeeded his father to the British throne as Edward VIII. His relationship with Wallis was condemned by the royal family and the British government: as a divorcée of common birth, Wallis was not considered to be a fit wife for the new king. Forced to choose between the crown and the woman he loved, Edward abdicated in December 1936 and married the former Mrs. Simpson six months later. They were given the titles Duke and Duchess of Windsor, but they were not welcome at Court.

The Windsors lived in France for most of their married life, apart from a period during World War II when the duke served as governor of the Bahamas. After the war they traveled widely in Europe and the United States, and in 1956 Wallis published her memoirs, *The Heart Has Its Reasons*. The Windsors' estrangement from the British royal family finally came to an official end in 1967, when they were invited by Queen ELIZABETH II to attend the unveiling of a memorial to Queen MARY (OF TECK), the duke's mother. Five years later, when Edward was seriously ill and close to death, the queen and the Duke of Edinburgh visited the couple at their Paris home. After Edward's death in 1972 the Duchess of Windsor lived as a recluse.

Winfrey, Oprah

(1954–)

AMERICAN TALK-SHOW HOST, ACTRESS, AND PRODUCER

With a television talk show watched by millions in more than a hundred countries, Oprah Winfrey was the highest paid entertainer in the United States in 1997. Such was her influence over the viewing public that most of the books she recommended on her book-club slot headed straight for the best-seller lists.

Oprah Winfrey was born in Kosciusko, Mississippi. Her teenage parents were unmarried, and she was raised in poverty by her grandmother. After moving to Milwaukee to live with her mother in the mid-1960s, she was sexually abused and raped by relatives and gave birth to a baby – her only child – at the age of 14. The baby did not live long, and Oprah moved on again, this time to her father's home in Nashville. He insisted that she have a proper education, and she went on to study at Tennessee State University, gaining a BA in speech and performing arts. During this time she began working as a broadcaster, first at a Nashville radio station and then on TV. At the age of 24 she hosted her first talk show at Baltimore's WJZ-TV station, and in 1984 she moved to *A.M. Chicago*. It was there that she discovered the secret of success as a talk-show host – by coming across as everybody's best friend and chatting freely about her own problems, she encouraged her guests to open up and talk about themselves.

In 1985 Winfrey made her first appearance on the big screen in the Steven Spielberg movie *The Color Purple*, based on Alice WALKER's novel of that name, and earned an Academy Award nomination for her performance. In the same year her TV talk show was relaunched nationally as *The Oprah Winfrey Show*, and her fame spread far and wide. She became a highly influential figure, debating controversial topics on daytime television, and established her own production company, Harpo Productions. One of the personal issues Oprah shared with her audience was her obesity: for many years she was seriously overweight, but with a combination of diet and exercise she managed to slim down from 200 pounds to around 120.

Winfrey's other acting credits include the films *Native Son* (1986) and *Throw Momma from the Train* (1987) and a starring role in the TV miniseries *The Women of Brewster Place* (1989). She has received numerous awards, including three Emmys for her talk show, and has used her great wealth to further the work of a number of charitable causes. Her attempt to help the poor in Chicago, which began in 1994 with the Families for a Better Life Foundation and swallowed nearly $1 million of her own money, ended in failure after two years.

Winterson, Jeanette

(1959–)

BRITISH NOVELIST AND WRITER

Jeanette Winterson is one of the most original and controversial writers to have emerged from Britain in recent decades. Her books combine fantasy with realism and are generally experimental in style.

An adopted child, Jeanette was brought up by a family of Pentecostal Evangelists in Lancashire, northern England. Her adolescence was largely dominated by two motives, her rejection of her narrowly religious upbringing and her discovery that she was a lesbian. After gaining an English degree from Oxford University in 1982, she went to live in London, where she concentrated on her writing.

Jeanette Winterson's first novel, *Oranges Are Not the Only Fruit*, attracted much praise when it appeared in 1985. The book, which received the Whitbread Prize for a first novel, is clearly autobiographical, drawing on Winterson's eccentric upbringing and her family's horrified reaction to her lesbianism. In 1990 Winterson's adaptation of the book for BBC television drew a large audience and won several international awards.

By contrast, Winterson's second novel, *Boating for Beginners* (1985), a comic fantasy based on the story of the Flood, received poor reviews and was quickly disowned by the author. Much more substantial were her novels of the late 1980s, *The Passion* (1987) and *Sexing the Cherry* (1989), which show an increasingly experimental approach to language and literary structure; both books won major literary awards. Winterson's experimentation reached a climax in *Written on the Body* (1992), a poetic meditation on love, sex, art, and post-Newtonian physics, and *Art and Lies* (1994). These novels sharply divided the critics, some of whom found them insufferably pretentious. Indeed, Winterson's unabashed belief in herself as the true heir to Virginia WOOLF and the great literary modernists of the early 20th century has raised many hackles. Her exalted view of art and the artist emerges clearly from her *Art Objects: Essays on Ecstasy and Effrontery* (1995).

Another novel, *Gut Symmetries*, was published in 1997.

Witt, Katerina

(1965–)

GERMAN ICE SKATER

After winning the gold medal at the 1984 Olympic Games in Sarajevo, Katerina Witt became the first female figure skater for 50 years to retain the Olympic title by winning a second gold at the Calgary Olympics in 1988.

Katarina Witt was born in Karl-Marx-Stadt, which was then in East Germany, and began skating at the age of five. Her talent was spotted in the mid-1970s by Jutta Mueller, who coached her for international competition. In 1979 Katarina entered the European championships for the first time and came in 14th; by 1983 she had worked her way up to first place, a position she held for six years. During the same period she also won the World Championships four times – in 1984, 1985, 1987, and 1988 – and took the gold medal at the 1984 and 1988 Olympic Games. At that time her career was dependent on her success – the Communist government would support her only as long as she continued winning.

Following the reunification of Germany in 1989, Witt took advantage of her greater freedom to perform professionally in ice shows and on television in the United States and elsewhere. She bought an apartment in New York City and won an Emmy Award for her performance in *Carmen on Ice* (1991). After a brief and disappointing return to international competition in the 1994 Olympics at Lillehammer, she went on tour with the ice show *Discover Card Stars on Ice.* In 1996 she took first place in the Legends Championship.

Woffington, Peg

(*c.* 1714–1760)

IRISH ACTRESS

Peg Woffington was renowned for her beauty and for her portrayal of "breeches parts" (male roles played by actresses). She dominated the stage in London and Dublin from 1740 to 1757. A woman of uncertain temper, she had tempestuous relationships with many other actresses, one of whom she stabbed during a performance.

Born Margaret Woffington in Dublin, she first appeared on the stage at the age of ten in a children's production of *The Beggar's Opera*. Her role in this play attracted attention and launched her career as an actress. She went on to appear in Dublin's Smock Alley Theatre, where she played Ophelia in *Hamlet* and Silvia in *The Recruiting Officer*. In 1740 she moved to London, where she took the part of Sir Harry Wildair in George Farquhar's *The Constant Couple* at Covent Garden. It was phenomenally successful. She also played opposite David Garrick in many famous roles there and was openly acknowledged as his mistress.

Peg Woffington was particularly admired in such comic roles as Millimant in William Congreve's *The Way of the World* and Lady Betty Modish in Colley Cibber's *The Careless Husband*, but the audiences preferred her male impersonations. She continued to star at Drury Lane until 1746, then spent seven years in Dublin (1747–54) before returning to London to perform at Covent Garden. On May 3, 1757, she collapsed during a performance of *As You Like It*, in which she was playing Rosalind. Amid thunderous applause she left the stage, never to return. She died three years later, the same year as her *Memoirs* were published.

Wolf, Christa

(1929–)

GERMAN WRITER

Many of Christa Wolf's novels and short stories were inspired by the political situation in East Germany and examine the effect that totalitarian systems of government have on the individual. In 1964 she received the National Prize for Art and Literature of the German Democratic Republic.

Christa Wolf was born in Landsberg, which is now in Poland. She grew up in Nazi Germany and studied at the universities of Leipzig and Jena. After graduation she worked as an editor and critic on various literary journals and other publications. She made her name as a writer in her homeland with such novels as *Moskauer Novelle* (1961; Moscow Novella); *Der geteilte Himmel* (1963; *Divided Heaven*, 1976), about an East German woman whose lover moves to West Berlin; and *Nachdenken über Christa T.* (1968; *The Quest for Christa T.*, 1982), which was initially banned because of its central theme of disillusionment. However, her work was little known in the outside world until the 1970s, when her novels began to be translated into English.

Wolf's other writings include a collection of critical essays, *Lesen und Schreiben* (1972; *The Reader and the Writer*, 1978), and several short-story collections, such as *Unter den Linden* (1974; Under the Linden) and the internationally successful *Kassandra* (1983; published in English as *Cassandra*, 1984), some of which have feminist themes. The novel *Kindheitsmuster* (1976), published in English as *A Model Childhood* (1982), is partly autobiographical, being inspired by her own early years.

Wood, Mrs. Henry

(1814–1887)

BRITISH NOVELIST

A prolific writer who was also a devout and deeply conservative Anglican Christian, Mrs. Henry Wood is now best remembered for her second novel, *East Lynne* (1861). It became a best-seller and by 1900 had sold more than 500,000 copies. Since then it has often been dramatized and has also been translated into many languages.

She was born Ellen Price in Worcester, central England, the daughter of a prosperous glove manufacturer. From her girlhood she suffered from curvature of the spine, which made her a partial invalid and required her to be educated at home. After she married Henry Wood, a banker and consular official, in 1836, she lived on the French Riviera for most of the following 20 years. She began her literary career by contributing stories to *Bentley's Miscellany* and the *New Monthly Magazine*.

In 1860 Mrs. Wood returned to England with her husband and settled in Norwood, south of London. She published almost 50 volumes of fiction; the most popular of her early novels were *East Lynne*, *Mrs. Halliburton's Troubles* (1862), and *The Channings* (1862). In 1867 she became editor and proprietor of *Argosy* magazine, in which her "Johnny Ludlow" stories appeared. Of her later novels *Within the Maze* (1872) and *Edina* (1876) were the most popular. Mrs. Wood's works owed their popularity to their ingeniously melodramatic plots and their vivid depiction of character.

Wood, Mary Elizabeth

(1861–1931)

AMERICAN LIBRARIAN

Mary Elizabeth Wood founded a library school at Boone College in Wuchang, China, in 1920 and spent the rest of her life enlarging the endowment of Boone and developing various humanitarian projects on behalf of the Chinese.

Wood was born in Elba, New York. While visiting her missionary brother in China in 1899, she became interested in Boone College and decided to remain there to work. She enlarged the college library, helped establish traveling libraries, and founded the library school. She also helped send young Chinese to the United States for education.

In 1923 she began campaigning for Chinese national libraries, working tirelessly in Washington to secure the passage of a bill designating the unassigned portion (about $6 million) of the Chinese Boxer Rebellion indemnity to educational and other cultural uses in China. She died in Wuchang.

Wood, Victoria

(1953–   )

BRITISH COMEDIENNE AND
WRITER

Victoria Wood's sharply observed humor and her lively, cheerful personality made her a popular figure on British television in the 1980s and 1990s. In 1995 she received a British Comedy Award as Top Female Comedy Performer.

Victoria Wood was born in Prestwich, in northern England. While she was a drama student at Birmingham University, she made her first broadcasts on local radio and television, singing comic songs she had written herself. In 1975 she appeared on a television talent show, *New Faces*, and the following year she was given a regular spot as one of the comic acts on Esther RANTZEN's consumer program *That's Life*. She teamed up with Julie WALTERS for the television comedy series *Wood and Walters* (1981–82), and in 1985 she made her first solo series, *Victoria Wood – As Seen on TV*. This was followed by a number of award-winning TV series and specials, such as *An Audience with Victoria Wood* (1988) and *Victoria Wood's All Day Breakfast* (Christmas, 1992). Most of her shows combine stand-up monologues and sketches (often featuring Walters and other regulars, such as the actresses Celia Imrie and Susie Blake) with the occasional comic song. The main targets of her humor are incidents from everyday life and such popular institutions as package holidays, health farms, talk shows, and soap operas.

As well as writing most of the material for her shows, Wood has also written stage plays and television screenplays, including *Talent* (1978) and *Happy Since I Met You* (1981). In 1994 she wrote and costarred with Julie Walters in a film for television, *Pat and*

Margaret. Her books include *Up to You, Porky* (1985), *Barmy* (1987), *Mens Sana in Thingummy Doodah* (1990), and *Chunky* (1996). In 1980 she married the magician Geoffrey Durham. She was appointed an Officer of the Order of the British Empire in 1997.

Woodward, Joanne

(1930–)

AMERICAN ACTRESS

Woodward starred in many films of the 1950s and 1960s, sometimes with her husband Paul Newman, and remained a familiar face in the cinema and on television in subsequent years. She also became known as a social and political activist, campaigning for a variety of causes. In 1990 she received the New York Critics' Award for Best Actress, as well as an Oscar nomination, for her portrayal of a discontented lawyer's wife in the movie *Mr. & Mrs. Bridge.*

Joanne Woodward was born in Thomasville, Georgia, and began her career as a stage and television actress. In 1955 she made her movie debut in the western *Count Three and Pray.* Her performance in *The Three Faces of Eve* (1957), as a woman suffering from a multiple personality disorder, earned her an Academy Award for Best Actress. In *The Long Hot Summer* (1958), based on a story by William Faulkner, she costarred with Paul Newman, whom she married the same year. Their marriage was to become one of the most durable in show-business history, spanning four decades during which they frequently appeared on screen together.

Woodward's films of the 1960s include *The Stripper* (1963), *A Fine Madness* (1966), and *Rachel Rachel* (1968). In the last of these, directed by her husband, she gave a moving, Oscar-nominated performance as an unmarried schoolteacher. *Summer Wishes, Winter Dreams* (1973), in which she played a middle-aged housewife devastated by the sudden death of her mother, brought her another Academy Award nomination. This was followed by four more films with Newman: *The Drowning Pool* (1975), *Harry and Son* (1984), *The Glass Menagerie* (1987) – in which her husband remained on the director's side of the camera – and *Mr. & Mrs. Bridge* (1990), with the famous couple in the title roles. From the mid-1970s onward Woodward was also seen in a number of TV movies, winning Emmys for *See How She Runs* (1978) and *Do You Remember Love* (1985).

Woolf, Virginia

(1882–1941)

BRITISH WRITER

I do not believe that she [Woolf] wrote one word of fiction which does not put out boundaries a little way; one book which does not break new ground and form part of the total experiment.
—Susan Hill, *The Daily Telegraph*, May 5, 1974

It would be a thousand pities if women wrote like men, or lived like men, or looked like men, for if two sexes are quite inadequate, considering the vastness and variety of the world, how should we manage with one only? Ought not education to bring out and fortify the differences rather than the similarities?
—*A Room of One's Own* (1929)

If you do not tell the truth about yourself you cannot tell it about other people.
—*The Moment and Other Essays* (1947)

Virginia Woolf was a central figure in the Bloomsbury Group – a group of writers and artists who met during the 1910s and 1920s in London's Bloomsbury district to explore new freedoms both in personal relationships and in art. In 1917 she and her husband, the writer Leonard Woolf, a fellow member of the Bloomsbury Group, founded the Hogarth Press. Her own novels, notably *Mrs. Dalloway* (1925), *To the Lighthouse* (1927), and *The Waves* (1931), are highly innovative.

Born Adeline Virginia Stephen in London, the second daughter of the writer Sir Leslie Stephen and Julia Duckworth, she was only 13 when her mother died. She was educated through "the free run of a large and unexpurgated library," owned by her father. When he died in 1904, she moved, together with her sister Vanessa, a painter (see BELL, VANESSA), and her brothers Adrian and Thoby, to Gordon Square, Bloomsbury, London. The first of her many reviews for the *Times Literary Supplement* appeared in 1905. The death of her brother Thoby in 1906 was a further shock to her delicate health, already affected by the death of her parents. In 1907 she settled in Fitzroy Square, London, with her brother Adrian after her sister had married the art critic Clive Bell. The meetings of the Bloomsbury Group began at this time. Its members included Clive and Vanessa Bell, the writers Lytton Strachey and E. M. Forster, the art critic Roger Fry, and the economist J. M. Keynes. It was in this environment that Virginia started to formulate the critical ideas and theories that so influenced her creative career. In 1912 she married Leonard Woolf, and together they launched the Hogarth Press, which was to publish some of the most interesting literature of the 20th century, including the works of T. S. Eliot and Katherine MANSFIELD as well as Virginia's own novels.

The Woolfs divided their time between London and the house they had bought at Rodmell in Sussex. Virginia's first novel, *The Voyage Out* (1915), is comparatively conventional and autobiographical. However, her second novel, *Night and Day* (1919), reveals her growing tendency to describe the "arrows of sensation striking strangely through the envelope of personality which shelters us so conveniently from our fellows." This approach is further developed in the impressionistic study of a talented young man's world, *Jacob's Room* (1922), and in *Mrs. Dalloway*, a complex image of life revealed through the thought and action of a single day in London. Virginia's next novel, *To the Lighthouse*, often considered her finest, is set on the Isle of Skye in Scotland but draws on her childhood memories of summers spent with her family in St. Ives in Cornwall, southwest England. In it she makes extensive use of a "stream of consciousness" technique – recording the flow of thoughts and feelings as they pass through her characters' minds. After the extravagant fantasy biography of *Orlando* (1928), a remarkable work deriving from her love for Vita SACKVILLE-WEST, and the symbolism of *The Waves* (1931) her creative urge declined. *The Years* (1937) is more traditional in technique.

In addition to her novels Virginia Woolf produced a great variety of other work – short stories, criticism, and biography – despite recurring bouts of depression, which had begun early in life after her mother's death. Her best critical essays are contained in *The Common Reader* (1925; second series, 1932). *A Room of One's Own* (1929) and *Three Guineas* (1938) are feminist classics. Her biographical works include *Flush* (1933), a fanciful biography of Elizabeth Barrett BROWNING's dog; and *Roger Fry* (1940), a friendly tribute.

In the end Virginia could no longer cope with her depression, made worse by the oppressive news of World War II. She committed suicide by drowning herself in the river running close to her Sussex home. Leonard Woolf, her widower, wrote movingly about his relationship with her in his autobiography and edited several volumes of her criticism, published after her death. He also printed her final novel, *Between the Acts* (1941), which was completed just before her death, and a collection of short stories, *A Haunted House* (1943), which included the major part of *Monday or Tuesday* (1921).

BIBLIOGRAPHY
Batchelor, John, *Virginia Woolf: The Major Novels* (1991).
Bell, Quentin, *Virginia Woolf: A Biography* (1972).
Daiches, D., *Virginia Woolf* (1963; reprint, 1979).
Gordon, Lyndall, *Virginia Woolf: A Writer's Life* (1984; reprint, 1993).
Homans, Margaret, *Virginia Woolf: A Collection of Critical Essays* (1992).
Leaska, Mitchell A., ed., *The Virginia Woolf Reader* (1984).
Lee, Hermione, *Virginia Woolf* (1996).

Woolley, Celia Parker

(1848–1918)

AMERICAN SETTLEMENT WORKER

Celia Parker Woolley worked tirelessly during her later life to improve race relations in Chicago.

Celia Parker was born in Toledo, Ohio. After graduating from the Coldwater Female Seminary in Michigan, she married Jefferson H. Woolley, a dentist, in 1868. In 1878 the couple moved to Chicago, where Celia began to take an interest in the cultural and civic life of the city and to develop a talent for writing. Having been interested all her life in religion, she studied for the ministry and at the age of 46 was ordained in the Unitarian Church. Between 1893 and 1898 she held pastorates in the church but subsequently resigned to return to writing and lecturing.

Led by her wish to help people, she was drawn into the field of social work, and in 1904 she established the Frederick Douglass Center on the south side of Chicago for work among the African-American population. Together with her husband, Woolley lived at the settlement for the rest of her life, working to improve race relations and winning over to her cause many of the important figures in the city.

Woolley, Mary Emma

(1863–1947)

AMERICAN EDUCATOR

In 1894 Mary Emma Woolley became the first woman to receive a BA degree from Brown University. From 1900 until her retirement in 1931 she was president of Mount Holyoke College, whose growth and development were in large part due to her efforts.

Born in South Norwalk, Connecticut, Mary Emma Woolley taught at Wheaton Seminary in Norton, Massachusetts, from 1886 to 1891. After receiving her BA degree from Brown University, she completed her MA there and taught biblical history and literature at Wellesley College (1895–1900); for her last two years at Wellesley she served as professor and head of the Department of Biblical History and Literature.

In addition to her academic work Woolley was active in many organizations concerned with education, religion, and world peace. In 1922 she made a six-month tour of China as a member of the Commission on Christian Education. Ten years later she was appointed the first woman delegate to the Disarmament Conference in Geneva in 1932. In a nationwide poll that same year, she was named one of the 12 greatest American women. In 1933 she was reappointed as a delegate to the Geneva conference by President Franklin D. Roosevelt. She also served on the board of electors of the Hall of Fame, the national board of the YWCA, and the international relations committee of the American Association of University Women. In 1944 she organized the Committee for the Participation of Women in Post-War Planning.

Woolley's publications include *Early History of the Colonial Post Office* (1894), *Internationalism and Disarmament* (1935), and numerous articles on education and international affairs.

Woolsey, Sarah Chauncey

(1835–1905)

AMERICAN WRITER

Sarah Chauncey Woolsey is best known under her pen name, Susan Coolidge, as the author of popular stories for girls, notably *What Katy Did* (1872) and its sequels *What Katy Did at School* and *What Katy Did Next*. These books describe the adventures and trials of their heroine in a natural, unsentimental style.

Born in Cleveland, Ohio, she grew up in a comfortable home there before moving with her family to New Haven, Connecticut, where her uncle, Theodore Dwight Woolsey, was president of Yale. After her father's death in 1870, she began to write verse and prose under her pen name. Her first girls' novel, *The New Year's Bargain* (1871), was followed over the next two decades by the "Katy" series and other popular stories.

In addition to her girls' story books Woolsey published three volumes of verse (1880, 1889, 1906), wrote *A Short History of the City of Philadelphia* (1887), and edited numerous literary papers and letters. She died in Newport, Rhode Island.

Woolson, Constance Fenimore

(1840–1894)

AMERICAN WRITER

Constance Woolson's fame rests chiefly on her pioneer work in the "local color" movement, which flourished, notably among female writers, in the late 19th century in the United States. In this movement writers used themes and subject matter that had strong links with a particular place or region. Woolson was particuarly acclaimed for her stories about the South.

Constance Fenimore Woolson, the grandniece of the novelist James Fenimore Cooper, was born in Claremont, New Hampshire. She grew up in Cleveland, Ohio, only deciding to become a professional writer after her father's death in 1869. During the 1870s she lived mainly in the Carolinas and Florida. Following the death of her mother in 1879, she traveled to Europe, living in England (at Oxford) and Italy (in Florence and Venice).

Woolson's early writings include reminiscences of life in Ohio published as *The Old Stone House* (1873) and numerous stories published in magazines (especially *Appleton's Journal*), some of which were collected in *Castle Nowhere: Lake Country Sketches* (1875). Sympathetic observations of Southern postwar conditions are found in *Rodman the Keeper: Southern Sketches* (1880). Her five novels have special interest for their regional settings: *Anne* (1882) and *Mackinac Island; For the Major* (1883) are set in western North Carolina; *East Angels* (1886) in St. Augustine, Florida; *Jupiter Lights* (1889) in Georgia and the Great Lakes country; and

Horace Chase (1894) in Carolina and Florida. Her *Dorothy and Other Italian Stories* (1896) deals interestingly with Americans in Italy.

Woolson became a friend of the writer Henry James, whom she idolized, and a sketch of her appears in his *The Aspern Papers*. She died in Venice, Italy.

See also JEWETT, SARAH ORNE.

Wootton, Barbara, Baroness

(1897–1988)

BRITISH SOCIAL SCIENTIST

Barbara Wootton made major contributions to academic life at a time when there were few openings for gifted, intelligent women like herself; she went on to become a prominent public figure.

Barbara Frances Adam was born into an intellectual family in Cambridge, England. Her father, the son of a Scottish farm worker, had graduated in classics from Cambridge University and was a tutor there until his death in 1907. Her mother was also a classicist and encouraged Barbara to embark on a university course in the same subject. Barbara dutifully followed her mother's wishes but eventually abandoned Greek and Latin to take a degree in economics. In 1917 she married Jack Wootton, a research student, but he died in World War I just five weeks after their wedding. The early loss of her father and her husband, as well as a schoolfriend and a brother, contributed to Barbara's rejection of religion in later life.

Having graduated from Girton College, Cambridge, in 1919, Wootton returned to Cambridge the following year as director of social studies and lecturer in economics. In 1922 she joined the research department of the Labour Party and the Trades Union Congress, and from 1927 to 1944 she was director of studies for adult education at the University of London. Her second husband, George Percival Wright, whom she married in 1935, was persistently unfaithful to her, but they remained together for nearly 30 years until he died from cancer.

In 1948 Wootton became professor of social studies at the University of London, and from 1950 to 1956 she was a governor of the British Broadcasting Corporation. In 1958 she was raised to the British peerage as Baroness Wootton of Abinger and took her place in the House of Lords. As a socialist, she disagreed in principle with the existence of this upper chamber in the British parliamentary system, but she respected the antiquity of the institution, commenting: "no one in his senses would invent the present house if it did not already exist...but...ancient monuments are not light-heartedly to be destroyed."

Wootton wrote or contributed to many academic texts, notably *Lament for Economics* (1938), *Freedom under Planning* (1945), *Social Science and Social Pathology* (1959), and *Crime and the Criminal Law* (1963). Toward the end of her career she was regarded as expert in criminal justice and social work, and in her seventies she served on advisory councils for the penal system (1966–74) and the misuse of drugs (1971–74).

Wordsworth, Dorothy

(1771–1855)

BRITISH DIARIST

Devoted to her brother, the poet William Wordsworth, Dorothy Wordsworth was his housekeeper-companion both before and after his marriage to Mary Hutchinson in 1802. He called her the "sister of my soul" (in *The Prelude*, XIII), and her *Grasmere Journal* was a direct inspiration to him for such poems as "Daffodils" and "The Leech-Gatherer."

Dorothy Wordsworth was born in Cockermouth, northwest England, but was sent away to live with a succession of relatives after her mother's death in 1778. In 1795 a legacy enabled William to take a house at Racedown in Dorset, which he shared with Dorothy. There they met the poet Samuel Taylor Coleridge and in 1797 moved to live nearer to him, beginning a long and close friendship. The period between 1798 and 1799 was spent in Germany before they finally settled at Grasmere in the Lake District of northwest England.

Dorothy is a prominent figure in many of William's poems, including "Tintern Abbey" and *The Prelude*, and is the probable original of his "Lucy" and "Emma." It was she who sustained him during his period of breakdown following the failure of his hopes for political revolution, which he writes about in *The Prelude*, X.

Although William printed a few of Dorothy's poems with his own, her talent found its fullest expression in her journals. The most elaborate is *Recollections of a Tour Made in Scotland* (1874), which she started soon after returning from a tour with her brother and Coleridge in September 1803 and finished in May

1805. Her miscellaneous diaries kept at Alfoxden (January to May 1798) and Grasmere (May to December 1800, October 1801 to January 1803) range from mere trivia to exquisite descriptions of light, lakewater, and the wild flowers growing on the hillsides; these are interspersed with lively observations of country life and country people and poignant personal comments. Dorothy's journals were first published 30 years after her death. She was also an excellent letter writer.

In April 1829 she became ill (it is possible she had a nervous breakdown) and never quite recovered, gradually becoming increasingly confused and agitated. The shock of William's death in 1850 brought about a period of relative calm before her own death five years later.

Workman, Fanny

(1859–1925)

AMERICAN EXPLORER AND MOUNTAINEER

With her cycling, her sensible clothes, and her belief in woman suffrage, Fanny Workman personified the "New Woman" at the turn of the 20th century. In 1906 she established an altitude record for women of 23,300 feet on one of the peaks of Nunkun in Kashmir.

Born Fanny Bullock, in Worcester, Massachusetts, the daughter of Governor Alexander Hamilton Bullock of Massachusetts, she married a prominent physician, William Hunter Workman, in 1881. Between 1895 and 1899 they undertook several cycling tours in Europe, North Africa, and the Far East, which they then wrote about in such books as *Sketches Awheel in Fin de Siècle Iberia*

(1897) and *Through Town and Jungle: 14,000 Miles Awheel among the Temples and Peoples of the Indian Plain* (1904), which were illustrated with their photographs. From 1899 to 1912 they explored and mapped parts of the Himalaya and Karakoram ranges, making several first ascents of peaks over 20,000 feet.

The Workmans collaborated on other books describing their travels, notably *Ice-Bound Heights of the Mustagh* (1908), *Peaks and Glaciers of Nun Kun* (1909), *The Call of the Snowy Hispar* (1910), and *Two Summers in the Ice Wilds of Eastern Karakoram* (1917). Fanny Workman also gave many lectures about her travels and in November 1905 was the first woman to address the Royal Geographical Society since Isabella BISHOP, the British explorer, in 1897.

Wray, Fay

(1907–)

AMERICAN FILM ACTRESS

Chiefly remembered as the screaming heroine of *King Kong* (1933), Fay Wray starred in a number of other films of the 1930s and made a brief comeback as a character actress in the 1950s.

Fay Wray was born in Alberta, Canada, grew up in Los Angeles, and made her screen debut in 1919. After playing minor roles for several years, she costarred with director Erich Von Stroheim in the silent movie *The Wedding March* (1928). This was followed by an early silent version of *The Four Feathers* (1929) and a western, *The Texan* (1930), with Gary Cooper. In the early 1930s Wray began to be cast in horror movies, such as *Doctor X* (1931), *The Most Dangerous Game* (1932), and *The Vampire Bat* (1933). Most of these films are long forgotten, but the classic original version of *King Kong* (1933) has lived on (even after the inferior 1976 re-make). Its spectacular special effects included shots of Wray screaming and writhing in the hand of the giant ape at the top of the Empire State Building, and this image was to remain with her forevermore: "At the premiere of *King Kong* I wasn't too impressed...I didn't realize then that King Kong and I were going to be together for the rest of our lives, and longer."

Wray's other films of the 1930s include the costume drama *The Affairs of Cellini* (1934), *The Clairvoyant* (1935), with Claude Rains, and *Murder in Greenwich Village* (1937). She retired from the cinema in 1942 but returned in the 1950s to appear in such movies as *Small Town Girl* (1953), *Queen Bee* (1955), and *Crime of Passion* (1956). After her second retirement in 1958 she made just one television appearance, in the TV movie *Gideon's Trumpet* (1980). In 1989 she published her autobiography, *On the Other Hand*. She also wrote a number of plays and stories.

Wright, Frances

(1795–1852)

SCOTTISH-BORN AMERICAN SOCIAL REFORMER

> The prejudices still to be found in Europe...which would confine...female conversation to the last new publication, new bonnet, and *pas seul* are entirely unknown here. The women are assuming their places as thinking beings.
> —*Views of Society and Manners in America* (1821)

Following the publication of her book *Views of Society and Manners in America* (1821), Frances Wright became a close friend of the French general, the Marquis de Lafayette, who fought against the British in the American Revolutionary War, and she and her sister Camilla accompanied him on his triumphal tour of the

United States in 1824–25. Afterward Frances was determined to work at the problem of slavery in the United States; she was also active in the causes of women's rights, education, and reform.

Frances (known as Fanny) Wright was born in Dundee, Scotland. Her parents died when she was two years old, and she became heir to a substantial fortune. She was educated in London and then returned to Scotland. Wright first visited the United States with her sister in 1818–20; having decided to settle there, she bought a few slaves and 2,000 acres of woodland, which she called Nashoba, in western Tennessee. She was not an abolitionist but hoped to demonstrate that slaves could use their labor to buy their freedom and finance their colonization outside the United States, while their children were being schooled for freedom. Her *Plan for the Gradual Abolition of Slavery* (1825) won the approval of Thomas Jefferson and James Madison. She was also impressed by the socialist community in New Harmony, Indiana, started by Robert Owen and his son Robert Dale Owen; she therefore resolved to make Nashoba a cooperative community. One of her radical recruits published a report that Nashoba advocated free love and racial interbreeding. The scandal had little basis, but it destroyed Nashoba. Wright eventually settled her slaves in Haiti.

Meanwhile, she had become America's first woman lecturer, denouncing the influence of the church in politics and demanding rights for women and workers. With Robert Dale Owen she edited the *Free Enquirer* in New York City (1829–30), which opposed imprisonment for debt and proposed free public education. In this paper Wright also advocated birth control, which the public found particularly scandalous; mobs threatened her, and the newspapers attacked her. Nevertheless, the "Fanny Wrighters" polled 6,000 votes in the New York election of 1829. She also published her *Course of Popular Lectures* and joined the Working Men's Club.

From 1829 to 1835 Fanny Wright lived in Europe. After Camilla's death in 1831 she married Guillaume Phiquepal D'Arusmont, a Frenchman who had worked with her in the United States. Her return to lecturing in the United States in 1835 led to the breakup of her marriage, but she nevertheless embarked on a lecture tour, speaking out against monopolies, the banking system, and slavery. She also wrote for the Boston *Investigator* and became the editor of the *Manual of American Principles*. After 1838 she became still more controversial, returning to the subject of birth control as well as advocating equal distribution of property and the social and legal emancipation of women. She died in Cincinnati, Ohio, after breaking her hip in a fall.

BIBLIOGRAPHY

Eckhardt, Celia M., *Fanny Wright: Rebel in America* (1894).
Kissel, Susan S., *In Common Cause: The "Conservative" Frances Trollope and the "Radical" Frances Wright* (1993).
Perkins, A. J. G., and Theresa Wolfson, *Frances Wright, Free Enquirer* (1939).

Wright, Judith

(1915–)

AUSTRALIAN POET

> Brought up in a landscape once of extraordinary beauty, but despised by its settlers because of its unfamiliarity, I have I suppose been trying to expiate a deep sense of guilt over what we have done to the country, to its first inhabitants of all kinds, and are still and increasingly doing.
>   —Describing an important source of inspiration for her work

Judith Wright's love and concern for the natural heritage of Australia is reflected in her poems, essays, and other writings. In 1993 she was awarded the Queen's Medal for Poetry.

Judith Arundell Wright was born in New South Wales, Australia, and grew up in a rural sheep-farming area. After studying at Sydney University, she traveled around Europe for a year, returning to Australia in 1938 to work as a secretary. In the early 1940s she moved to the mountains of Queensland, where she found inspiration for her poetry. Her first collection, *The Moving Image*, was published in 1946. She continued to write poetry and essays, occasionally lecturing at Australian universities, and became an active conservationist. Her subsequent volumes of poetry include *Woman to Man* (1949), *The Gateway* (1955), *Birds* (1962), *The Other Half* (1966), *Alive* (1973), *The Double Tree* (1978), *Journeys* (1982), *A Human Pattern* (1990), and *Collected Poems 1942–1985* (1994). She also wrote about other poets and their verse in such works as *Charles Harpur* (1963) and *Preoccupations in Australian*

Poetry (1965). In 1956 she edited *A Book of Australian Verse* for Oxford University Press; a revised edition was published in 1968.

Wright's research into Australian history, including her own family background and the effect that her pioneering ancestors had on the Aboriginal way of life, is contained in such works as *The Generations of Men* (1959), *The Cry for the Dead* (1981), *We Call for a Treaty* (1985), and *Born of the Conquerors* (1991). Among her other writings are the collection of short stories *The Nature of Love* (1966), essays on environmental issues, and four books for children. In the 1970s she was president of the Wildlife Preservation Society of Queensland, and in the 1980s she became involved with the peace movement and with organizations supporting the rights of Australian Aborigines.

Wrinch, Dorothy

(1894–1976)

AMERICAN MATHEMATICIAN AND BIOCHEMIST

Dorothy Wrinch was one of the many scientists who, in the 1930s, sought to find a chemical model for the passing on of genetic information from one generation to the next. Although the model she devised was not correct, it was a positive step toward the discovery of genetics.

Wrinch was born at Rosario in Argentina of British parents and educated at Cambridge University, England, where she held a research fellowship from 1920 to 1924. She then taught physics at Oxford until 1939, when she moved to America to take up an appointment as lecturer in chemistry at Johns Hopkins University, Baltimore, Maryland. In 1942 she moved to Smith College,

Northampton, Massachusetts, where she remained until her retirement in 1959.

In 1934 Wrinch tackled the important problem of identifying the chemical carriers of genetic information. In common with other scientists at that time, she argued that chromosomes consisted of sequences of amino acids; these were the only molecules thought to possess sufficient variety to permit the construction of complex molecules. She proposed a model of the gene in the form of a T-like structure with a nucleic-acid stem and a sequence of amino acids as the cross bar.

In fact many such models were proposed in the 1930s. If it was not accepted that genes consisted of specific sequences of amino acids, then it became very difficult to visualize what they could consist of. The trouble with all these models was that the experimentalists quickly found serious defects in them. Thus W. Schmidt in 1936 was able to show that Wrinch's model was incompatible with the known optical properties of nucleic acid and the chromosomes. The first suggestion that there might be an alternative to the protein structure of the gene came with the famous experiment of Oswald Avery in 1944.

Wu, Chien-Shiung

(1912–1997)

CHINESE-BORN AMERICAN
PHYSICIST

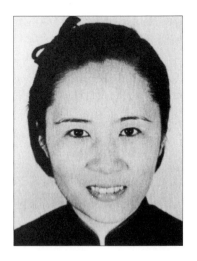

An outstanding experimental physicist, Chien-Shiung Wu over-came the traditional Chinese reluctance to permit women to take part in higher education. She was greatly respected by many of the leading American physicists of the 20th century.

Wu, who was born in Shanghai, China, gained her BS from the National Central University of China before moving to America in 1936. There she studied under Ernest O. Lawrence at the University of California, Berkeley. She gained her PhD in 1940 then went on to teach at Smith College, Northampton, Massachusetts, and later at Princeton University. In 1946 she became a staff member at Columbia University, advancing to become professor of physics in 1957.

Her first significant research work was on the mechanism of beta disintegration (electron emission in radioactive decay). In particular, she demonstrated in 1956 that the direction of emission of the electrons is strongly correlated with the direction of spin of the emitting nucleus, showing that parity is not conserved in beta disintegration (i.e., more than half the electrons can spin in one direction). This experiment confirmed the theories advanced by Tsung Dao Lee of Columbia and Chen Ning Yang of Princeton that in the so-called "weak" nuclear interactions the previously held "law of symmetry" was violated. Yang and Lee later received the Nobel prize for physics for their theory, and the discovery overturned many central ideas in physics.

In 1958 Richard Feynman and Murray Gell-Mann proposed the theory of conservation of vector current in beta decay. This theory was experimentally confirmed in 1967 by Wu, in collaboration with two other Columbia University physicists.

Wu's other contributions to particle physics include her demonstration that the electromagnetic radiation from the annihilation of positrons and electrons is polarized – a finding in accordance with Dirac's theory, proving that the electron and positron have opposite parity. She also undertook a study of the x-ray spectra of muonic atoms. Later in her life she became interested in biological problems, especially the structure of hemoglobin, the pigment of red blood cells.

Chien-Shiung Wu was married to another Chinese physicist who had emigrated to America, Yuang Chia-liu (who later Americanized his name to Luke Yuan).

Wu Zhao

(625–705)

CHINESE EMPRESS

Wu Zhao ruled the vast Chinese empire for 50 years, first as Emperor Gao Zong's wife and then as China's first female sovereign. During this period she brought peace, prosperity, and unity to the country.

Wu Zhao was just 13 or 14 years old when she was called to the palace of Emperor Tai Zong and became one of his young concubines. When Tai Zong died in 649, the new emperor, Gao Zong, allowed Wu Zhao to remain at the palace because he had fallen in love with her. After giving birth to Gao Zong's son, Wu Zhao took the place of his chief wife, who had no children, and became empress. Throughout the remainder of Gao Zong's reign she was a powerful influence at court, and all those who opposed her or stood in the path of her ambition were either removed from office or killed. The emperor, weakened by illness in 660, gave her a free hand in running the country, and she played a major role in the conquest of Korea.

In 683 Gao Zong died and was succeeded by his eldest son, Zhong Zong. Fearing that her authority would be weakened, Wu Zhao deposed Zhong and made his younger brother Rui Zong the official emperor. After continuing to govern through Rui for some years, she finally claimed the throne for herself in 690 and ruled the country until her death. Her long reign saw the introduction of a number of social reforms, including greater freedom for women and better care for the sick. She was also a patron of the arts and literature and was responsible for the building of many magnificent pagodas and temples.

Wylie, Elinor Morton

(1885–1928)

AMERICAN POET AND NOVELIST

During the 1920s Elinor Wylie established herself as a poet and novelist of sensitivity and elegance.

Born Elinor Hoyt in Somerville, New Jersey, she was educated at the Baldwin Schol, Bryn Mawr, Pennsylvania, and the Holton Arms School, Washington, D.C. In 1905 she married Philip Hichborn but in 1910 eloped with Horace Wylie, whom she married in 1916. The Wylies were divorced in 1923, and Elinor then married William Rose Benét, the poet and critic.

Apart from *Incidental Numbers*, which was published anonymously in 1912, Elinor Wylie's main work consists of nine books – four novels and five volumes of verse – in which she made wide use of the lore of history and literature. Well acquainted with the work of 17th-century English metaphysical poets, Wylie was also familiar with the earlier Scottish, Irish, and English ballads; she sang these – as well as her own verses – set to tunes that she made up herself. Her *Nets to Catch the Wind* (1921) is a collection of poems about animals and birds.

Wylie's first novel, *Jennifer Lorn* (1923), set in the 18th-century India of the English aristocracy, was immediately recognized as possessing a rare and delicate satire. Her collection of poems *Black Armor* appeared that same year. Her second novel, *The Venetian Glass Nephew* (1925), is a fable of the marriage of Christian art and pagan nature; while her third, *The Orphan Angel* (1926; British title *Mortal Image*, 1927), relates the fantasy that the poet Percy Bysshe Shelley was rescued by an American ship instead of drowning off the coast of Italy. Shelley's subsequent adventures on the rough American frontier give Wylie scope for witty and sensitive analysis of both the poet and the times. In *Mr. Hodge and Mr. Hazard* (1928) she describes England after the deaths of Shelley and Byron.

Wylie's final volumes of verse are *Trivial Breath* (1928), *Angels and Earthly Creatures* (1929), which was published after her death and includes the interesting sonnet sequence "One Person," and *Last Poems* (1943). She died in New York City. After her death her husband edited her *Collected Poems* (1932) and *Collected Prose* (1933) and wrote a brief critical study of her work, *The Poetry and Prose of Elinor Wylie* (1934).

Wylie, Ida Alexa Ross

(1885–1959)

BRITISH WRITER

Wylie's novels, with their mainly political themes, show her understanding of the national and social characteristics of her time.

Wylie was born in Melbourne, Australia, but soon afterward her family moved to England, where her mother died. From her tenth year she was accustomed to traveling unaccompanied through Europe at her father's expense; until the age of 14 she received no formal education, although she read widely. At the age of 19, after attending schools in Belgium and England, she continued her education in Germany, where she remained for eight years; it was here that her first stories were published. In 1911 she became active in the suffrage movement in England, and in 1917 she visited the United States, where she spent her later years. She never married.

Towards Morning (1920), Wylie's first mature novel, was based on her time in Germany as a young woman. *To the Vanquished* (1934) takes place during the rise of Nazism. After a visit to the USSR in 1934 she wrote *Furious Young Man* (1935), in which a young Englishman is converted to Communism. *Where No Birds Sing* (1947) is set in Germany under the American occupation after World War II. In *Candles for Thérèse* (1951) she explores the quest for revenge on the betrayer of Resistance fighters during World War II. Her last novel, *The Undefeated* (1957), tells of the efforts made by members of a guilt-ridden community in post-occupation Provence (France) to exonerate themselves. Wylie also wrote more than 200 short stories, some screenplays, and an amusing autobiography, *My Life with George* (1940), George being her unconscious mind. She died in Princeton, New Jersey.

Wynette, Tammy

(1942–)

AMERICAN COUNTRY SINGER

In her long and successful career Tammy Wynette has had many hits – 20 of her records have made it to the top of the charts – and she has been called "the First Lady in country music."

Born Virginia Wynette Pugh in Tupelo, Mississippi, she grew up on her grandparents' cotton farm in Alabama. She married her first husband in 1959 and had three children in the three years they spent together. After their separation she worked as a beautician to pay for her youngest daughter's medical treatment for spinal meningitis. Wynette had always wanted to become a singer and began performing on local radio and television to earn more money. In 1966 she made her first recording, "Apartment No. 9." Two hits followed in 1967 – "Your Good Girl's Gonna Go Bad" and "I Don't Wanna Play House" – and in 1968 she recorded one of her most famous songs, "D-I-V-O-R-C-E." The success of this record brought her the Country Music Association Award for Female Vocalist of the Year. Her next major hit, "Stand by Your Man" (1969), made her one of the best-selling female country singers of all time.

In 1969 Wynette married the country singer George Jones, but their relationship was a stormy one, and they divorced in 1975. Together they made a number of recordings in the early 1970s, including "Take Me" and "We're Gonna Hold On," and performed on stage at the Grand Ole Opry and elsewhere. In 1978 Wynette married the songwriter George Richey. She continued singing and recording through the 1980s, releasing hit singles, such as "Crying in the Rain" (1981) and "Sometimes When We Touch" (1985), and such albums as *Higher Ground* (1987). Her autobiography, *Stand By Your Man*, was filmed in 1982.

Xanthippe

(5th century BC)

GREEK MATRON

...in Xanthippe's society [I] shall learn to adapt myself to other persons.
—Socrates, quoted by Diogenes Laertius in *Lives and Opinions of Eminent Philosophers*

Xanthippe has become notorious as the nagging and scolding wife of Socrates.

The great Athenian philosopher made his wife famous by comparing her with a spirited horse. Socrates claimed that just as horsemen who have mastered difficult horses have no trouble with tamer ones, Xanthippe had taught him (Socrates) how to handle any person, good-natured or not.

Socrates himself was apparently unattractive, with a turned-up nose and a beer belly, but despite this Xanthippe bore him a son.

Yalow, Rosalyn Sussman

(1921–   )

AMERICAN PHYSICIST

Rosalyn Yalow shared the Nobel Prize for physiology or medicine in 1977 for her work in developing the technique of radioimmunoassay, which enables the detection of extremely small amounts of hormone.

Yalow was born in New York City and educated at Hunter College and at the University of Illinois, where she obtained her PhD in nuclear physics in 1945. Since 1947 she has worked at the Veterans Administration Hospital in the Bronx as a physicist and since 1968 she has also held the post of research professor at the Mount Sinai School of Medicine.

In the 1950s, working with Solomon Berson, Yalow developed radioimmunoassay. The technique involves taking a known amount of radioactively labeled hormone, together with a known amount of antibody against it, and mixing it with human serum containing an unknown amount of unlabeled hormone. The antibodies bind to both the radioactive and normal hormone in the proportions in which they are present in the mixture. It is then possible to calculate with great accuracy the amount of unlabeled hormone present in the original sample.

This technique enabled Roger Guillemin and Andrew Schally to detect hormones released from the part of the brain called the hypothalamus.

Yonge, Charlotte M(ary)

(1823–1901)

BRITISH NOVELIST

Yonge wrote about 160 novels and other books for children and adults. Reflecting her own Christian beliefs, her works reinforced the firm moral values of Victorian society.

Born in Otterbourne, in southern England, Yonge was educated at home by her father, a country gentleman. Under the influence of John Keble, vicar of the neighboring village of Hursley, she became interested in the "High Church" or "Anglo-Catholic" movement in the Church of England, which promoted a return to a more mystic and artistic style of worship, based on medieval practices. She remained in Otterbourne for the rest of her life.

As Yonge's talent as a writer developed, Keble encouraged her to focus on her religious views in her work. Her first full-length novel, *The Heir of Redclyffe* (1853), was immediately successful, partly because it was sentimental and somewhat pious. These qualities would not appeal today, but they moved readers at the time. Her other stories of contemporary life include *Heartsease*

(1854), *The Daisy Chain* (1856), and *The Clever Woman of the Family* (1865). Yonge branched out into historical romances with *The Lances of Lynwood* (1855), *The Prince and the Page* (1865), and *The Dove in the Eagle's Nest* (1866). She also wrote biographies, popular history, and Bible study material. From 1851 until 1890 she edited *The Monthly Packet*, a children's magazine.

Young, Ella

(1867–1956)

IRISH WRITER

Something of a recluse, Ella Young created a mysterious world of fantasy in much of her verse and prose. The writer George William Russell (pen name "AE") described her as "a druidess reincarnated."

Young was born in Fenagh, now in Northern Ireland. She moved to southern Ireland during her teens and later became involved with the Irish literary revival in Dublin as well as supporting the Irish Republican Army, which fought for the complete independence of a united Ireland. She published several volumes of verse, prose sketches, and tales based largely on Celtic mythology. The most famous of these is *The Unicorn with Silver Shoes* (1932).

In 1925 Young went to America and became a lecturer on Celtic literature and mythology, eventually at the University of California. She continued to live on the west coast and in 1945 published her autobiographical work *Flowering Dusk*. She died in Oceano, California.

Young, Ella Flagg

(1845–1918)

AMERICAN EDUCATOR

A believer in John Dewey's ideas concerning progressive education, Ella Flagg Young emphasized the importance of actual experience in the learning process. She stressed the value of giving students freedom but also of teaching them a sense of responsibility.

Born Ella Flagg in Buffalo, New York, she was educated at the Chicago Normal School and began a career as a teacher after leaving school in 1862. In 1868 she married William Young, but her husband died the following year.

Ella Young was appointed a district superintendent of schools in Chicago in 1887; in 1899 she became professor of education at the University of Chicago. Having studied under John Dewey, she received a PhD from the university in 1900. Over the next few years she published several well-received books on education – *Isolation in the School* (1900), *Ethics in the School* (1902), and *Some Types of Modern Educational Theory* (1902).

Young served as principal of the Chicago Normal School from 1905 to 1909 and then became superintendent of Chicago's public school system, retiring in 1915. In addition to her educational theories and writings, she was also active in social work, with Jane ADDAMS, and in the woman-suffrage movement. In 1910–11 she was the first woman president of the National Education Association. Ella Flagg Young died in Washington, D.C.

Young, Loretta

(1913–   )

AMERICAN FILM AND
TELEVISION ACTRESS

A glamorous leading lady, Loretta Young proved herself a capable actress and a highly successful movie star before giving up the screen for a TV career.

Loretta Young's real name was Gretchen Michaela Young. Born in Salt Lake City, Utah, she moved to Hollywood with her mother at the age of four after her parents' marriage broke up. With the help of an uncle she, her two sisters, and her brother found parts in silent movies when they were still young children. Later, when she was 14, Gretchen was given a part first offered to her sister (who was too busy) in the silent picture *Naughty but Nice* (1927). The movie company First National Studios put her under contract and changed her name to Loretta.

After this Young played leading roles in nearly 100 motion pictures with Warner Brothers (1927–34), with 20th Century-Fox (1934–40), and as a freelance star (from 1940). She received the Academy Award for Best Actress for her performance in *The Farmer's Daughter* (1947), a Cinderella tale in which Young played a Swedish servant who runs for her employer's Congressional seat. Later films included *Come to the Stable* (1949), in which she played a nun and earned an Oscar nomination, *Cause for Alarm* (1951), and *It Happens Every Thursday* (1953).

Young afterward became one of America's favorite television actresses in the *Loretta Young Show*, which won Emmy Awards in 1954, 1956, and 1959. Years later she won a Golden Globe Award for her work in the television movie *Christmas Eve* (1986). She also appeared on stage in *An Evening with Loretta Young* (1989). Married twice, Young had an illegitimate daughter by Clark Gable. Her autobiography, *The Things I Had to Learn*, was published in 1961.

Young, Rida

(*c.* 1875–1926)

AMERICAN PLAYWRIGHT AND LIBRETTIST

> Sure I love the dear silver that shines in your hair,
> And the brow that's all furrowed and wrinkled with care...
> Oh God bless you and keep you, Mother Machree.
>
> —"Mother Machree" (1911)

Rida Young is remembered for her successful plays, song lyrics, and librettos for musical comedy. Some of her work drew on European, especially Irish, tradition.

Born in Baltimore, Maryland, Young went to New York City as an aspiring young playwright. Having been a society beauty in Baltimore, she spent several years as a minor actress, as well as writing popular song lyrics for a music publisher, before completing her first satisfactory play, *Glorious Betsy*. Her first real success, *Brown of Harvard* (1906), gave an idealized view of a Harvard undergraduate. It was followed by *The Boys of Company B* (1907) and *The Lottery Man* (1909).

In 1910 Young prepared the book and lyrics for Victor Herbert's operetta *Naughty Marietta*. For the popular entertainer Chauncey Olcott she wrote the lyrics for the musical *Barry of Ballymore* (1911), including the words for the popular song "Mother Machree." This was followed by *Isle of Dreams* (1912) and *Shameen Dhu* (1913). Later Young undertook the dramatic adaptation for Sigmund Romberg's first great success, the musical *Maytime* (1917), the book and lyrics for Rudolf Friml's musical *Sometime* (1918), and other librettos. Her comedies *Captain Kidd Junior* and *Her Soldier Boy* were produced in 1916; *Little Old New York* was staged in 1920.

Yourcenar, Marguerite

(1903–1987)

BELGIAN-BORN FRENCH–AMERICAN WRITER

> She [Yourcenar] feels she is linked to everything, to the past as well as the present, to human beings but also to animals, landscapes, buildings.
> —Jacqueline Piatier in *Les Yeux ouverts* (1984; *With Open Eyes*)

In 1980 Marguerite Yourcenar became the first woman member of the French Academy. The winner of many awards who always wrote in French, this scholarly writer was not only a historical novelist but also a poet, essayist, playwright, and translator.

Yourcenar's real name was Marguerite de Crayencour. She was born in Brussels to a Belgian mother (who died a few days after her birth) and a French father. Educated at home, near Lille, she could read French, English, Latin, and Greek at an early age.

Displaced by World War I, Marguerite and her father settled in Paris. She wrote poetry from the age of 14, and in 1921–22 her father helped her publish two volumes under the name Yourcenar – a near anagram of her real name. When her father died in 1927, Yourcenar took comfort in travel and writing novels. Among her earliest were *Dénier du rêve* (1934; *A Coin in Nine Hands*, 1982) and *Coup de grâce* (1939; published in English in 1957).

After she visited the United States in 1937, Yourcenar decided to move there at the outbreak of World War II. Staying with her friend Grace Frick, she found a teaching job in Bronxville, New York, and in 1947 took U.S. citizenship. In 1950 Yourcenar and Frick set up home in Maine, and a year later Yourcenar's masterpiece, *Les Mémoires d'Hadrien* (1951; *Memoirs of Hadrian*, 1954), was published. Constructed as a letter written by the emperor Hadrian on his deathbed, it gives a remarkably full portrait of his character, including his homosexual love for a young man. Complex but less real was Zeno, the character at the center of Yourcenar's Renaissance novel *L'Oeuvre en noir* (1968; *The Abyss*, 1976).

In her two autobiographical volumes, *Souvenirs pieux* (1974; Pious Memories) and *Archives du nord* (1977; Northern Archives), Yourcenar brought her skills as a historical novelist to the task of describing the dramatic events of the 20th century.

Z

Zaharias, Babe Didrikson

(1914–1956)

AMERICAN ATHLETE

An all-round sportswoman, Zaharias was chosen by an Associated Press poll in 1950 as the outstanding woman athlete of the first half of the 20th century.

Mildred Ella (known as "Babe") Didrikson was born in Port Arthur, Texas, the daughter of Norwegian immigrants, and was raised in Beaumont, Texas. She began her sports career in basketball with an insurance company team and was named an all-American in 1930–32.

In 1932 Didrikson became famous when she won eight of ten events in the Amateur Athletic Union's national women's track and field championships, including the 80-meter hurdles, baseball throw, shotput, broad jump, and javelin throw. Later that year at the Olympic Games she set two world records – for the javelin throw (143 feet 4 inches, or 43.68 meters) and the 80-meter hurdles (11.7 seconds). After this Didrikson became a professional athlete and spent the next years playing basketball and baseball, as well as revealing her talent for billiards, swimming, diving, and other sports. In 1938 she married George Zaharias, a professional wrestler.

Zaharias started her championship record in golf in 1940 and won every available women's title at least once during the next decade. However, her career was tragically cut short when she was stricken with cancer in 1953. She died in Galveston, Texas, a year after the publication of her autobiography, *This Life I've Led* (1955).

Zakrzewska, Maria

(1829–1902)

GERMAN-BORN AMERICAN PHYSICIAN

At her hospital for women and children, which had an all-female staff, Maria Zakrzewska not only improved the healthcare available to women but also encouraged them to enter the medical profession. In addition, she was a defender of human rights, joining the campaign against slavery.

Zakrzewska was born in Berlin to a Polish father and a mother of gypsy descent. Her mother worked as a midwife to support the family, and Maria, who was the eldest child, followed in her footsteps. Maria Zakrzewska trained as a midwife at the charity hospital in Berlin and qualified as a teacher of midwives. In 1852 she became principal midwife at the hospital.

Women were not allowed to qualify as doctors in Berlin, and in 1853 Zakrzewska decided to emigrate to New York City with one of her sisters. Although she could speak very little English, she won the support of Elizabeth BLACKWELL and was accepted in a medical course at Cleveland Medical College, Ohio. Graduating in 1856, she joined Blackwell from 1857 in running the newly founded New York Infirmary for Women and Children. In 1859 she left to become professor of obstetrics at the New England Female Medical College, Boston.

There was no clinical hospital at the college in Boston, which Zakrzewska found frustrating. She therefore left after three years and in 1862 founded her own New England Hospital for Women and Children, initially with only ten beds, although it soon expanded after becoming highly successful. Running it with an all-female staff for nearly 40 years, Zakrzewska trained many women nurses and doctors. She also gave lectures and maintained a prestigious private practice.

Zasulich, Vera Ivanovna

(1851–1919)

RUSSIAN REVOLUTIONARY

A revolutionary activist from her teens, Zasulich was seen as a heroine by the oppressed Russians after she shot and wounded a general who had been cruel to a political prisoner.

Born in Mikhailovka, Smolensk, Russia, Zasulich belonged to a family of the lesser nobility. Her early revolutionary activities led to a two-year prison sentence when she was 18. In 1878 the military governor of St. Petersburg had a political prisoner flogged for no good reason, which created a great stir in revolutionary circles. On February 5 Vera Zasulich shot and seriously wounded the general in his office, making no attempt to escape. She was acquitted at her trial, and the people were delighted, unlike the authorities, who were alarmed and had the verdict set aside. Vera Zasulich escaped abroad and did not return to Russia until the amnesty of 1905.

In 1900 Zasulich joined Lenin and others in founding the Marxist newspaper *Iskra* (The Spark). When the Russian Social Democratic Party split into the Bolsheviks and Mensheviks in 1903, she became associated with the Menshevik wing. Because of this she opposed the October Revolution of 1917, in which the Bolsheviks seized power.

Zauditu

(1876–1930)

EMPRESS OF ETHIOPIA

Zauditu (whose name is a variant of Judith) had an eventful life during troubled times in Ethiopia.

Born in Addis Ababa, Zauditu was the daughter of Emperor Menelik II. Already a widow at the age of 12, she was widowed again in her twenties; she was married a third time, to Ras Gugsa Wolie, in 1902. Zauditu ascended the throne as "queen of kings" in 1917 after Menelik's grandson, Lij Yasu, was deposed and on condition that she renounce her third husband. At the same time, Ras Tafari Makonnen (later Haile Selassie) was made regent.

Zauditu came into conflict with Ras Tafari over his efforts to liberalize and modernize the country and to arrange its membership of the League of Nations (achieved in 1923). In 1928 he forced Zauditu to name him emperor. After this, in spite of an unsuccessful attempt by her former husband to restore her authority through a revolt, she had little political influence, although she kept her title until her death.

Zenobia

(late 3rd century)

QUEEN OF PALMYRA

Beautiful and ruthless by reputation, Zenobia was a powerful figure who for a short time ruled both Egypt and Asia Minor.

Septima Zenobia was probably of Arab descent. She married the Bedouin Odenathus, who was lord of the Syrian city of Palmyra, an outpost of the Roman Empire. In 264 her husband was given the title "governor of all the east," but three years later he and his son (Zenobia's stepson) were murdered. Zenobia's own son Wahballat became ruler of Palmyra, but she ruled for him as queen of Palmyra.

Ambitious to have an empire independent of Rome, Zenobia invaded and conquered Egypt and much of Asia Minor in 269. However, the Roman emperor Aurelian defeated her armies in 271 at Antioch (Turkey) and Emesa (Syria). After a siege Aurelian captured Palmyra and took Zenobia and Wahballat back to Rome as prisoners. When the people of Palmyra revolted again in 273, their city was completely destroyed.

Meanwhile Zenobia fared surprisingly well. With two of her other sons she joined Aurelian's triumphal procession in Rome in 274, subsequently marrying a Roman senator, at whose villa in the summer resort of Tivoli, in central Italy, she ended her days.

Zetkin, Clara

(1857–1933)

GERMAN COMMUNIST LEADER

Zetkin was one of the founders of the German Communist Party. She also wrote about women's issues and was well known as a passionate speaker.

Born Clara Eissner in Wiederau, Saxony, she began her career as a schoolteacher. After joining the German Social Democratic Party in 1881, she became its outstanding spokesperson on women's rights and edited the paper *Die Gleichheit* (Equality) from 1892 until 1916. Married to the revolutionary Ossip Zetkin from 1881, she led the revolutionary Spartacus movement with Rosa LUXEMBURG.

After World War I Zetkin was a joint founder of the Communist Party in Germany (1919). From 1920 to 1932 she was a Communist deputy in the Reichstag (German parliament), although during much of this period she had disagreements with the Soviet leadership.

From the early 1930s Zetkin lived in Russia. In addition to writing a number of books on women's problems, she wrote *Reminiscences of Lenin*, based on her experiences as a close friend of the first communist leader of Russia; it appeared in English translation in 1929.

Zetterling, Mai

(1925–1994)

SWEDISH ACTRESS AND
DIRECTOR

Although she began her career on stage and screen in Sweden, Zetterling was especially popular in movies made in Britain. From the 1960s she enjoyed success as the director of her own powerful and sensuous films – often about the position of women.

Zetterling was born in Vasteras, Sweden, into a poor family. Her first appearance on stage at 16 led to a place at the Royal Dramatic Theater School in Stockholm. She had her first major success on screen playing a schoolgirl harassed by a sadistic teacher in Alf Sjöberg's *Hets* (1944; *Torment*).

After this Zetterling was invited to Britain and appeared in numerous movies, including *Frieda* (1947), as the German wife of a British wartime airman; *Quarter* (1948); and *The Bad Lord Byron* (1949). She also appeared in films in Sweden and the United States. In the American movie *Knock on Wood* (1954) Zetterling played opposite Danny Kaye, and in *Only Two Can Play* (1961) she costarred with Peter Sellers. As a stage actress, she continued to act in works by Ibsen, Chekhov, and Anouilh.

Zetterling's first venture in directing came in 1963 when she and her second husband, David Hughes, wrote the documentary *The War Game*. The movie won her the Golden Lion at the Venice Film Festival. Zetterling's subsequent movies included *Loving Couples* (1964), a tale of sexual hypocrisy; *Night Games* (1966), based on a novel of her own; the exaggerated feminist movie *The Girls* (1969); and *Vincent the Dutchman* (1972), about the painter Van Gogh.

Returning to acting in 1989, Zetterling took the role of a grand-mother in *The Witches* (1990), a film based on a Roald Dahl children's story, and appeared in *Hidden Agenda* (1990), a controversial movie about Northern Ireland.

Zia, Khaleda

(1944/45–)

BANGLADESHI POLITICIAN

In 1991 Begum Khaleda Zia became the first woman president of Bangladesh, promising the country economic improvements.

The daughter of Iskander and Taiyaba Majumder, Khaleda Zia studied at Surendranath College, Dinajpur. In her teens she was married to Major General Ziaur Rahman, with whom she had two sons. Her husband became leader of the center-right Bangladesh Nationalist Party (BNP).

Zia was held captive for a time during the Bangladeshi civil war (1971), when Mujibur Rahman, leader of a party called the Awami League, established himself as the country's first prime minister. He was assassinated in 1975, and after the resulting struggles Zia's husband took control of the country; he served as president from 1977 until his own assassination in 1981. Khaleda Zia was persuaded to take over the deputy leadership (1982) and then the leadership (1984) of the BNP. For the next 16 years Bangladesh was ruled by President Ershad.

In 1990 Ershad was deposed because of charges of corruption, and elections were held in 1991. The BNP and Awami League each won 32% of the vote, but the BNP had many more seats and therefore set up a minority government with Khaleda Zia as prime minister. She was also responsible for information, energy, establishment, and mineral resources. The opposition was led by Mujibur Rahman's daughter, Hasina Wajed, of the Awami League.

Zia's period of office (1991–96) began badly with a disastrous cyclone, which killed 139,000 people and caused damage amounting to billions of dollars. Zia's opponents criticized her handling of the international aid offered. That same year Zia visited several Arab states, China, and Thailand. She also reformed the parliamentary system.

See also BANDARANAIKE, SIRIMAVO; BHUTTO, BENAZIR; BRUNDTLAND, GRO HARLEM; ÇILLER, TANSU; MEIR, GOLDA; THATCHER, MARGARET.

Zoë

(*c.* 978–1050)

BYZANTINE EMPRESS

Zoë was empress of the Eastern Roman Empire for over 30 years, sharing the throne at various times with her husbands, stepnephew, and sister.

A daughter of Emperor Constantine VIII, Zoë shared the throne after her father's death in 1028 with her husband Romanus III Argyrus, banishing her sister Theodora to a nunnery. When her husband began to neglect her, Zoë had an affair with her chamberlain, Michael the Paphlagonian. In 1034 Romanus died, probably poisoned by Zoë and her lover, and the couple then married and ruled jointly.

Michael (now Michael IV) died in 1041 and was succeeded as coruler by his nephew Michael V Calaphates, whom Zoë had adopted. Michael V imprisoned the empress and seized sole power, but he was deposed in a revolt in 1042. Zoë then reigned briefly with her sister Theodora. The same year she took another husband, who as Constantine IX Monomachus ruled the empire jointly with both sisters until Zoë's death. Constantine then ruled with Theodora alone until his own death in 1055.

Index of People

The first number given in a reference is the volume number, subsequent numbers give the pages. References in bold type refer to the main biography of the person.

Abakanowicz, Magdalena **1:1**
Abbott, Berenice **1:2**
Abbott, Edith **1:3**; 1:4
Abbott, Grace **1:4**; 1:3
Abbott, Maude (Elizabeth Seymour) **1:4**
Abelard, Peter 5:13, 14
Aberdeen, Lord 10:24
Abigail **1:5**
Abraham 8:151, 152
Abzug, Bella **1:6**
Achurch, Janet **1:7**
Ackland, Rodney 7:99
Acton, Eliza(beth) **1:8**
Adadnirari III 8:181
Adam, Robert 7:51
Adams, Abigail **1:9**
Adams, Charles Francis 1:11
Adams, Hannah **1:10**
Adams, Henry 1:11
Adams, John 1:9, 10
Adams, John Quincy 1:9, 10, 11
Adams, Louisa **1:11**
Adams, Maude **1:12**; 4:137
Adamson, Joy **1:13**; 7:1
Addams, Jane **1:14**; 1:4, 121; 5:154; 6:19; 8:94; 10:144
Adelaide, Saint **1:16**
Adelheid 1:16
Adler, Alfred 8:143
Aelgifu **1:17**
Aelst, Willem von 8:126
Ætheldreda 1:19
Aethelflaed **1:17**
Aethelred (II) "the Unready," 1:17, 18

Aethelthryth, Saint **1:18**
Aethling, Edgar 6:137
Afra 1:157
African-American women
Anderson, Marian 1:48; Angelou, Maya 1:51; Bailey, Pearl 1:115; Baker, Josephine 1:119; Battle, Kathleen 1:141; Bethune, Mary McLeod 1:184; Brooks, Gwendolyn 2:69; Bumbry, Grace (Melzia) 2:85; Chisholm, Shirley Anita St. Hill 2:186; Davis, Angela 3:82; Devers, Gail 3:108; Dunham, Katherine 3:139; Elders, Joycelyn 3:158; Fauset, Jessie Redmon 4:13; Fitzgerald, Ella 4:38; Franklin, Aretha 4:66; Gibson, Althea 4:106; Goldberg, Whoopi 4:127; Hansberry, Lorraine 4:182; Harris, Patricia Roberts 4:187; Holiday, Billie 5:39; Horne, Lena Calhoun 5:46; Horne, Marilyn 5:47; Houston, Whitney 5:51; Hurston, Zora Neale 5:62; Jackson, Mahalia 5:84; Jemison, Mae Carol 5:94; Jordan, Barbara Charline 5:121; King, Coretta Scott 5:169; Kitt, Eartha 5:174; Lewis, Edmonia 6:55; Morrison, Toni 7:72; Norman, Jessye 7:118; Parks, Rosa 7:167; Price, Leontyne 8:33; Rainey, Ma 8:49; Ross, Diana 8:110; Simone, Nina 9:15; Smith, Bessie 9:25; Terrell, Mary 9:138; Truth, Sojourner 9:173; Tubman, Harriet 9:175; Tyson, Cicely 9:190, Vaughan, Sarah 10:15; Walker, Alice 10:38; Warwick, Dionne 10:49;Waters, Ethel 10:51; Wheatley, Phillis 10:80; Winfrey, Oprah 10:108
Agassiz, Elizabeth **1:19**
Agassiz, Jean Louis 1:19
Agatha, Saint **1:20**; 6:92

Agnes, Saint **1:21**; 3:9
Agnesi, Maria **1:22**
Agnodice **1:23**
Agnon, Shmuel Yosef 8:134
Agoult, Marie, Countess d' **1:23**; 10:34
Agrippa, Marcus 1:24
Agrippina Major **1:24**; 1:25; 5:135
Agrippina Minor **1:25**; 1:24
Aguilar, Grace **1:26**
Ahab 1:97; 5:100
Aidan, St. 5:27
Aidoo, Ama Ata **1:27**
Aikin, John 1:128
Aikin, Lucy 1:128
Ailey, Alvin 5:92
Aimée, Anouk **1:28**
A'isha **1:29**; 4:12
Akhmadulina, Bella **1:30**
Akhmatova, Anna **1:30**
Akiko, Empress 7:80
Alacoque, Saint Margaret Mary **1:31**
Alain 10:60
Alarcón, Fabián 1:82
Alaric 4:85
Alba, Duke of 1:53; 6:140
Albee, Edward 6:190; 9:26
Albéniz, Isaac 1:73
Albert, Prince 1:39; 7:97; 10:23, 24, 25
Alboni, Marietta **1:32**
Albright, Madeleine Korbel **1:33**
Alcott, Louisa May **1:35**; 1:78
Alda, Frances **1:36**
Alden, Isabella Macdonald **1:37**
Aldington, Richard 3:127
Alexander I of Russia 5:126
Alexander I of Scotland 6:137
Alexander II 7:189
Alexander III of Russia 1:38; 6:159; 7:189
Alexander III, King of Scots 6:135
Alexander IV 7:141
Alexander, Jane **1:37**
Alexander the Great 1:169; 7:140, 141;
    8:72; 9:117, 143
Alexandra **1:38**; 1:134; 6:159
Alexandra Fyodorovna **1:39**
Alexis I 9:48
Alexius I 1:54
Alfonso V 5:129
Alfonso XII 2:107; 5:76
Alfonso d'Este 2:34
Alfonso of Aragon, Duke of Bisceglie 2:34
Alfred the Great 1:18
Ali 1:29
Allen, Elizabeth Akers **1:40**
Allen, Florence Ellinwood **1:40**
Allen, Gracie **1:41**
Allen, Walter 1:102
Allen, Woody 4:11; 5:148, 149
Allende, Isabel **1:42**
Allende, Salvador 1:42

Allison, Dorothy 5:63
Alvarez, Al 8:13
Amalsuntha **1:43**
American women
art: Bacon, Peggy 1:110; Beaux, Cecilia 1:154;
    Cassatt, Mary 2:135; Chicago, Judy 2:180;
    Eames, Ray 3:149; Fitzgerald, Zelda 4:39;
    Frankenthaler, Helen 4:64; Gardner,
    Isabella Stewart 4:92; Guggenheim, Peggy
    4:163; Hesse, Eva 5:26; Hoffman, Malvina
    5:37; Hosmer, Harriet Goodhue 5:50; Hoxie,
    Vinnie Ream 5:55; Krasner, Lee 5:184;
    Lewis, Edmonia 6:55; Lin, Maya 6:60;
    Millett, Kate 7:25; Moses, Grandma 7:73;
    Nevelson, Louise 7:102; O'Keeffe, Georgia
    7:136; Scott Brown, Denise 8:175; Stevens,
    May 9:78; Vanderbilt, Gloria 10:11;
    Whitney, Anne 10:86; Whitney, Gertrude
    Vanderbilt 10:87
aviation: Cochran, Jacqueline 3:22; Earhart,
    Amelia 3:150; Jemison, Mae Carol 5:94
business: Ayer, Harriet Hubbard 1:105; Green,
    Hetty 4:149; Lauder, Estée 6:20; Pinkham,
    Lydia Estes 8:8; Rubinstein, Helena 8:117
cooking: Child, Julia 2:181; Farmer, Fannie
    Merritt 4:5
dance: Baker, Josephine 1:119; Brown, Trisha
    2:74; Chase, Lucia 2:172; Clarke, Martha
    3:11; De Mille, Agnes 3:95; Duncan, Isadora
    3:138; Dunham, Katherine 3:139; Fuller,
    Loie 4:80; Graham, Martha 4:143; Gregory,
    Cynthia 4:153; Holm, Hanya 5:42;
    Humphrey, Doris 5:58; Jamison, Judith
    5:92; Kaye, Nora 5:147; McBride, Patricia
    6:184; Monk, Meredith 7:47; Rainer,
    Yvonne 8:48; St. Denis, Ruth 9:69; Tamiris,
    Helen 9:118; Tharp, Twyla 9:144
design: Chase, Edna Woolman 2:171; de Wolfe,
    Elsie 3:110; Eames, Ray 3:149; Head, Edith
    5:7; Karan, Donna 5:140
education: Agassiz, Elizabeth 1:19; Angelou,
    Maya 1:51; Bates, Katharine Lee 1:140;
    Beecher, Catharine Esther 1:155; Berry,
    Martha McChesney 1:181; Bethune, Mary
    McLeod 1:184; Blanding, Sarah Gibson 2:5;
    Blow, Susan Elizabeth 2:14; Clapp,
    Margaret 3:8; Crandall, Prudence 3:53;
    Dunham, Katherine 3:139; Felton, Rebecca
    Ann 4:17; Gildersleeve, Virginia Crocheron
    4:108; Hamilton, Edith 4:179; Kreps, Juanita
    Morris 5:186; Lyon, Mary 6:103; Macy,
    Anne Mansfield Sullivan 6:112; Model,
    Lisette 7:40; Morrison, Toni 7:72; Paglia,
    Camille 7:148; Peabody, Elizabeth Palmer
    7:179; Spencer, Anna Garlin 9:54; St. Denis,
    Ruth 9:69; Szold, Henrietta 9:111; Thomas,
    (Martha) Carey 9:155; Wiggin, Kate
    Douglas 10:88; Willard, Emma 10:97;
    Willard, Frances 10:98; Wood, Mary

Elizabeth 10:115; Woolley, Mary Emma 10:121; Young, Ella Flagg 10:144

espionage: Boyd, Belle 2:43; Rosenberg, Ethel 8:107

heroism: Corbin, Margaret 3:39; Dustin, Hannah 3:144

history: Beard, Mary Ritter 1:148; Hurston, Zora Neale 5:62; Tuchman, Barbara 9:177; Warren, Mercy Otis 10:48

journalism: Ayer, Harriet Hubbard 1:105; Bly, Nellie 2:16; Brown, Helen Gurley 2:72; Croly, Jane 3:59; Faludi, Susan 4:4; Fuller, Margaret 4:81; Hale, Sarah Josepha 4:174; Hopper, Hedda 5:45; Loeb, Sophie 6:76; Lowell, Amy 6:87; Luce, Clare Boothe 6:91; Parsons, Louella 7:171; Quindlen, Anna 8:42; Riding, Laura 8:84; Sontag, Susan 9:47; Thompson, Dorothy 9:156; Vreeland, Diana 10:31; Wells-Barnett, Ida Bell 10:64

law: Abzug, Bella 1:6; Allen, Florence Ellinwood 1:40; Clinton, Hillary Rodham 3:16; Ginsburg, Ruth Bader 4:111; Harris, Patricia Roberts 4:187; Lockwood, Belva Ann 6:73; O'Connor, Sandra Day 7:130; Reno, Janet 8:74; Willebrandt, Mabel 10:100

medicine: Baker, Josephine 1:119; Bickerdyke, Mary Ann 1:186; Blackwell, Elizabeth 2:2; Blackwell, Emily 2:3; Dick, Gladys Henry 3:114; Elders, Joycelyn 3:158; Elion, Gertrude Belle 3:163; Hamilton, Alice 4:178; Horney, Karen 5:48; Jacobi, Mary Putnam 5:85; Jemison, Mae Carol 5:94; Sabin, Florence Rena 8:131; Shaw, Anna Howard 8:191; Taussig, Helen Brooke 9:123; Thompson, Mary Harris 9:158; Walker, Mary Edwards 10:40; Wexler, Nancy 10:76; Zakrzewska, Maria 10:150

military: Corbin, Margaret 3:39; Hopper, Grace Murray 5:44; Molly Pitcher 7:46; Sampson, Deborah 8:143

music: Alda, Frances 1:36; Battle, Kathleen 1:141; Beach, Amy Marcy 1:146; Brico, Antonia 2:53; Bumbry, Grace (Melzia) 2:85; Caldwell, Sarah 2:108; Crawford Seeger, Ruth 3:57; Curtin, Phyllis 3:70; Eames, Emma 3:148; Farrar, Geraldine 4:8; Fremstad, Olive 4:72; Garden, Mary 4:90; Glanville-Hicks, Peggy 4:117; Hauck, Minnie 4:190; Hempel, Frieda 5:15; Horne, Marilyn 5:47; Lehmann, Lotte 6:41; Monk, Meredith 7:47; Nordica, Lillian 7:115; Norman, Jessye 7:118; Pons, Lily 8:21; Ponselle, Rosa 8:22; Price, Leontyne 8:33; Resnik, Regina 8:75; Salerno-Sonnenberg, Najda 8:139; Schumann, Elizabeth 8:168; Schumann-Heink, Ernestine 8:169; Sills, Beverly 9:11; Sumac, Yma 9:100; Young, Rida 10:146

performing arts: Adams, Maude 1:12; Alexander, Jane 1:37; Allen, Gracie 1:41;

Anderson, Marian 1:48; Anderson, Mary Antoinette 1:49; Angelou, Maya 1:51; Anglin, Margaret 1:52; Arzner, Dorothy 1:85; Astor, Mary 1:94; Bacall, Lauren 1:107; Baez, Joan 1:112; Bailey, Pearl 1:115; Baker, Josephine 1:119; Ball, Lucille 1:122; Bancroft, Anne 1:123; Bankhead, Tallulah Brockman 1:125; Bara, Theda 1:126; Barrymore, Ethel 1:134; Berg, Gertrude 1:170; Bergen, Candice 1:173; Bigelow, Kathryn 1:187; Bond, Carrie Jacobs 2:24; Bonstelle, Jessie 2:29; Booth, Shirley 2:31; Bow, Clara 2:39; Boyd, Belle 2:43; Brice, Fanny 2:52; Burnett, Carol 2:88; Carter, Mrs. Leslie 2:131; Channing, Carol 2:165; Cher 2:177; Clarke, Shirley 3:12; Cline, Patsy 3:15; Close, Glenn 3:18; Colbert, Claudette 3:25; Cornell, Katharine 3:45; Cowl, Jane 3:49; Crabtree, Lotta 3:50; Crawford, Cheryl 3:54; Crawford, Joan 3:56; Cushman, Charlotte (Saunders) 3:71; Davis, Bette 3:83; Day, Doris 3:85; de Wolfe, Elsie 3:110; Dietrich, Marlene 3:117; Draper, Ruth 3:129; Dressler, Marie 3:130; Farmer, Frances 4:6; Farrell, Eileen 4:9; Farrow, Mia 4:10; Ferguson, Elsie 4:22; Field, Sally 4:27; Fiske, Minnie Maddern 4:36; Fitzgerald, Ella 4:38; Flanagan, Hallie 4:44; Fonda, Jane 4:50; Fontanne, Lynn 4:53; Foster, Jodie 4:59; Franklin, Aretha 4:66; Gabor, Zsa Zsa 4:83; Garbo, Greta 4:89; Gardner, Ava 4:91; Garland, Judy 4:93; Gish, Dorothy 4:115; Gish, Lillian 4:115; Gluck, Alma 4:120; Goldberg, Whoopi 4:127; Gordon, Ruth 4:137; Grable, Betty 4:139; Hagen, Uta 4:171; Harlow, Jean 4:185; Harris, Julie 4:186; Hawn, Goldie 4:192; Hayes, Helen 5:2; Hayworth, Rita 5:5; Henie, Sonja 5:16; Hepburn, Audrey 5:19; Hepburn, Katharine 5:20; Holiday, Billie 5:39; Homer, Louise 5:43; Hopper, Hedda 5:45; Horne, Lena Calhoun 5:46; Houston, Whitney 5:51; Huston, Angelica 5:63; Jackson, Mahalia 5:48; Joplin, Janis 5:120; Kael, Pauline 5:137; Keaton, Diane 5:148; Keene, Laura 5:151; Kelly, Grace 5:155; Kitt, Eartha 5:174; Lange, Jessica 6:11; Lansbury, Angela 6:15; Lansing, Sherry 6:16; Lee, Gypsy Rose 6:34; Lombard, Carole 6:78; Loy, Myrna 6:89; Lupino, Ida 6:96; MacLaine, Shirley 6:109; Madonna 6:114; Malina, Judith 6:123; Marlowe, Julia 6:158; Marshall, Penny 6:160; Menken, Adah Isaacs 7:13; Merman, Ethel 7:15; Midler, Bette 7:19; Minnelli, Liza 7:26; Modjeska, Helena 7:43; Monroe, Marilyn 7:49; Moore, Demi 7:60; Moore, Grace 7:61; Moore, Mary Tyler 7:63; Neal, Patricia 7:95; Normand, Mabel 7:119; Novak, Kim 7:122; O'Hara, Maureen 7:135; Page, Geraldine

Barney, Alice Pike 1:131
Barney, Natalie **1:131**
Barnum, P. T. 6:63
Barr, Amelia Edith **1:132**
Barrett, Elizabeth 3:45
Barrie, J. M. 1:12
Barrow, Clyde 7:164, 165
Barry, Elizabeth **1:133**
Barry, Dr. James 9:95
Barrymore, Ethel **1:134**
Barrymore, John 1:95, 134
Barrymore, Maurice 1:134
Bartók, Béla 3:57; 6:110
Bartoli, Cecilia **1:135**
Barton, Clara **1:135**
Barton, Elizabeth **1:137**
Baryshnikov, Mikhail 4:153; 6:12; 9:145
Bascom, Florence **1:138**
Bashkirtseff, Marie **1:138**
Basie, Count 5:39
Bateman, Hester **1:139**
Bates, Katharine Lee **1:140**
Batten, Jean **1:140**
Battle, Kathleen **1:141**
Baucq, Philippe 2:154
Baudelaire 9:34
Baum, Vicki **1:143**
Bausch, Pina **1:144**
Bavaria, Jacoba of 5:87
Bavaria, John of 5:88
Bavière, Elisabeth de 5:77
Bayley, John 7:81
Baylis, Lilian **1:145**; 3:107; 8:125; 9:159, 160
Beach, Amy Marcy **1:146**
Beach, Mrs. H. H. A. 1:146
Beach, Sylvia Woodbridge **1:146**
Beale, Dorothea **1:147**; 3:81
Beard, Mary Ritter **1:148**
Beardsley, Aubrey 7:93; 8:142
Beaton, Cecil 3:73
Beatrice **1:149**
Beatrix **1:150**; 5:133
Beatty, Warren 6:109
Beaufort, Lady Margaret **1:151**
Beauharnais, Alexandre de 1:152
Beauharnais, Hortense de **1:152**; 5:125
Beaujeu, Anne of 1:64
Beauvoir, Simone de **1:153**; 7:149
Beaux, Cecilia **1:154**
Beck, Julian 6:123
Beckett, Samuel 4:164
Becquerel, Henri 3:67, 68
Beecher, Catharine Esther **1:155**; 9:86
Beerbohm, Max 2:121
Beery, Wallace 9:110
Beeton, Isabella Mary **1:156**
Behan, Brendan 6:65
Behn, Aphra **1:157**; 4:172
Belafonte, Harry 6:121

Belasco, David 2:132; 9:69
Belgioioso, Cristina, Princess of **1:158**
Belisarius 9:149
Bell, Clive 1:161; 10:119
Bell, Gertrude Margaret Lowthian **1:159**
Bell, Marie **1:160**
Bell, Vanessa **1:161**; 10:119
Bell Burnell, (Susan) Jocelyn **1:162**
Bellini 4:161
Belloc, Hilaire 6:88
Belmont, Alva Erskine Smith Vanderbilt **1:164**
Bembo, Pietro 2:35; 3:33
Benchley, Robert 7:166
Benedict, Ruth Fulton **1:165**; 7:4, 5
Benedict III 5:104, 105
Benét, William Rose 8:145; 10:136
Benetton, Giuliana **1:166**
Benjamin 8:45
Bennett, Arnold 3:129
Bennett, Constance 5:46
Bennett, Richard Rodney 7:84
Benoit, Joan 8:144
Bentley, Phyllis **1:167**
Benton, Thomas Hart 5:50
Berengaria **1:168**
Berenice **1:168**
Berenice I **1:169**; 1:79
Berenice II **1:170**
Berenson, Bernard 4:93
Berg, Alban 3:57
Berg, Gertrude **1:170**
Berg, Patty **1:171**
Berganza, Teresa **1:172**
Bergen, Candice **1:173**; 10:68
Berghof, Herbert 4:171
Bergman, Ingmar 10:5, 6
Bergman, Ingrid **1:174**; 1:44, 106
Beriosova, Svetlana **1:175**
Berlin, Irving 7:126
Berlioz, Hector 9:38, 39
Bern, Paul 4:185
Bernadette of Lourdes, Saint **1:176**
Bernadotte, Count 8:67
Bernal, John 6:80
Bernarde, St. Marie 1:176
Bernauer, Agnes **1:177**
Bernhardt, Sarah **1:178**; 2:131; 3:143; 7:43; 9:20
Bernstein, Leonard 5:12; 7:20
Berry, Agnes 3:74
Berry, Duchess de **1:180**
Berry, Martha McChesney **1:181**
Berry, Mary 3:74
Berson, Solomon 10:141
Besant, Annie **1:182**
Besford, Pat 4:68
Bethune, Mary McLeod **1:184**
Bevan, Aneurin 6:35, 36
Bhutto, Benazir **1:185**

Bridge, Ann **2:54**
Bridgeman, Richard 9:74
Bridget of Sweden, Saint **2:55**; 2:150
Bridgman, Laura Dewey **2:56**; 4:8
Brighouse, Harold 5:50
Bright Eyes **2:57**
Brightman, Sarah **2:58**
Brigid of Ireland, Saint **2:59**
Brion, Friederike Elisabeth **2:60**
Bristow, Gwen **2:61**
British women
art: Bateman, Hester 1:139; Bell, Vanessa 1:161;
    Butler, Elizabeth 2:96; Carrington, Dora
    2:127; Damer, Anne Seymour 3:73; Drew,
    Dame Jane 3:131; Frink, Dame Elisabeth
    4:76; Greenaway, Kate 4:150; Hepworth,
    Dame Barbara 5:22; John, Gwen 5:112;
    Knight, Dame Laura 5:177; Potter, (Helen)
    Beatrix 8:30; Rie, Dame Lucie 8:85; Riley,
    Bridget 8:89; Smithson, Alison 9:37
aviation: Johnson, Amy 5:113
cooking: Acton, Eliza(beth) 1:8; Beeton, Isabella
    Mary 1:156; David, Elizabeth 3:80; Smith,
    Delia 9:26; Spry, Constance 9:58
dance: Beriosova, Svetlana 1:175; Brightman,
    Sarah 2:58; de Valois, Dame Ninette 3:107;
    Fonteyn, Dame Margot 4:54; Genée, Dame
    Adeline 4:98; Grey, Dame Beryl 4:156;
    Markova, Dame Alicia 6:155; Montez, Lola
    7:56; Rambert, Dame Marie 8:51; Shearer,
    Moira 8:192; Sibley, Dame Antoinette 9:8;
    Torvill, Jayne 9:164
design: Ashley, Laura 1:88; Muir, Jean 7:77;
    Quant, Mary 8:41; Rhodes, Zandra 8:76;
    Westwood, Vivienne 10:74
economics: Robinson, Joan 8:95; Ward, Dame
    Barbara 10:43; Webb, Beatrice 10:54
education: Astell, Mary 1:93; Baden-Powell,
    Dame Olave 1:111; Beale, Dorothea 1:147;
    Beaufort, Lady Margaret 1:151; Buss,
    Frances 2:93; Carter, Elizabeth 2:130;
    Clough, Anne Jemima 3:20; Davies, (Sarah)
    Emily 3:81; Montagu, Elizabeth 7:50; Raine,
    Kathleen (Jessie) 8:47; Spurgeon, Caroline
    9:59; Stocks, Mary, Baroness 9:80; Trimmer,
    Sarah 9:168; Vaughan, Dame Janet 10:14
gardening: Jekyll, Gertrude 5:93; Sackville-West,
    Vita 8:135
medicine: Anderson, Elizabeth Garrett 1:45;
    Barnes, Dame Josephine 1:130; Cavell, Edith
    2:153; Freud, Anna 4:73; Jex-Blake, Sophia
    Louisa 5:99; Klein, Melanie 5:175; Marsden,
    Kate 6:159; Nightingale, Florence 7:106;
    Pye, Edith Mary 8:37; Stuart, Miranda 9:95;
    Stoppard, Miriam 9:84; Vaughan, Dame
    Janet 10:14
music: Baillie, Dame Isobel 1:116; Baker, Dame
    Janet Abbott 1:118; Butt, Dame Clara 2:99;
    Cross, Joan 3:62; du Pré, Jacqueline 3:141;
    Ferrier, Kathleen 4:24; Gipps, Ruth 4:113;

Hess, Dame Myra 5:25; LeFanu, Nicola
    6:37; Lutyens, Elisabeth 6:98; Lympany,
    Dame Moura 6:101; Maconchy, Dame
    Elizabeth 6:110; Musgrave, Thea 7:83; Patti,
    Adelina (Juana Maria) 7:174; Smyth, Dame
    Ethel Mary 9:40; Tate, Phyllis Margaret
    9:122; Teyte, Dame Maggie 9:142; Weir,
    Judith 10:61
performing arts: Achurch, Janet 1:7; Andrews,
    Julie 1:50; Armatrading, Joan 1:74;
    Ashcroft, Dame Peggy 1:87; Barry,
    Elizabeth 1:133; Baylis, Lilian 1:145; Bisset,
    Jacqueline 1:191; Bloom, Claire 2:11;
    Bonham Carter, Helena 2:26; Box, Muriel
    2:42; Bracegirdle, Anne 2:45; Brightman,
    Sarah 2:58; Bush, Kate 2:92; Campbell, Mrs.
    Patrick 2:114; Clark, Petula 3:10; Clive,
    Kitty 3:17; Collier, Constance 3:30; Collins,
    Joan 3:32; Cooper, Dame Gladys 3:38;
    Dench, Dame Judi 3:96; Evans, Dame Edith
    3:190; Faithfull, Marianne 4:3; Fenton,
    Lavinia 4:20; Fields, Dame Gracie 4:29;
    Gwyn, Nell 4:168; Hiller, Dame Wendy 5:30;
    Horniman, Annie 5:49; Inchbald, Elizabeth
    5:69; Jackson, Glenda 5:81; Johnson, Dame
    Celia 5:114; Jordan, Dorothy 5:122; Kemble,
    Frances 5:157; Kendal, Felicity 5:159; Kerr,
    Deborah 5:163; Laine, Dame Cleo 6:5;
    Langtry, Lillie 6:13; Lawrence, Gertrude
    6:26; Le Gallienne, Eva 6:38; Leigh, Vivien
    6:45; Lennox, Annie 6:48; Lillie, Beatrice
    6:59; Littlewood, Joan 6:65; Lloyd, Marie
    6:72; Lockwood, Margaret 6:74; Lumley,
    Joanna 6:94; Lynn, Dame Vera 6:102;
    McKenna, Siobhán 6:192; Matthews, Jessie
    6:179; Mirren, Helen 7:28; Neagle, Dame
    Anna 7:94; Neilson, (Lilian) Adelaide 7:100;
    Oberon, Merle 7:127; Paige, Elaine 7:150;
    Plowright, Joan 8:15; Redgrave, Lynn 8:68;
    Redgrave, Vanessa 8:69; Reid, Beryl 8:71;
    Richardson, Miranda 8:82; Rigg, Dame
    Diana 8:87; Robson, Dame Flora 8:97;
    Rutherford, Dame Margaret 8:124; Sade
    8:136; Saunders, Jennifer 8:157; Siddons,
    Sarah 9:9; Smith, Dame Maggie 9:31;
    Springfield, Dusty 9:55; Suzman, Janet
    9:108; Tempest, Dame Marie 9:131; Terry,
    Dame Ellen 9:140; Thompson, Emma 9:157;
    Thorndike, Dame Sybil 9:159; Tilley, Vesta
    9:161; Tutin, Dorothy 9:186; Ullman,
    Tracey 10:3; Vestris, Madame 10:20;
    Walters, Julie 10:42; Webster, Margaret
    10:57; Whitlock, Elizabeth Kemble 10:84;
    Wood, Victoria 10:116
philanthropy: Burdett-Coutts, Angela Georgina,
    Baroness 2:87; Carpenter, Mary 2:123;
    Saunders, Dame Cicely 8:156; Somerset,
    Lady Isabella Caroline 9:43
politics: Astor, Nancy, Viscountess 1:96; Besant,
    Annie 1:182; Bondfield, Margaret Grace

Morrell, Lady Ottoline 7:70; Morris, Jan
7:71; Murdoch, Dame Iris 7:81; Nesbit,
Edith 7:101; Oliphant, Margaret 7:138;
Orczy, Baroness 7:143; Ouida 7:144;
Pargeter, Edith Mary 7:163; Piozzi, Hester
Lynch 8:9; Pizzey, Erin 8:11; Porter, Jane
8:27; Potter, (Helen) Beatrix 8:30; Pym,
Barbara 8:38; Radcliffe, Ann 8:46; Raine,
Kathleen (Jessie) 8:47; Rayner, Claire
Berenice 8:64; Rendell, Ruth, Baroness 8:73;
Rhys, Jean 8:77; Richardson, Dorothy M.
8:80; Rossetti, Christina Georgina 8:111;
Sackville-West, Vita 8:135; Sayers, Dorothy
L(eigh) 8:159; Sewell, Anna 8:186; Shelley,
Mary Wollstonecraft Godwin 9:3; Sinclair,
May 9:16; Sitwell, Dame Edith 9:18; Smith,
Dodie 9:28; Smith, Stevie 9:36; Spark, Dame
Muriel 9:52; Stark, Dame Freya 9:67;
Taylor, Elizabeth 9:125; Thirkell, Angela
Margaret 9:154; Trollope, Frances 9:170;
Trollope, Joanna 9:171; Warner, Sylvia
Townsend 10:47; Webb, Mary 10:56;
Wedgwood, Dame Veronica 10:58; Weldon,
Fay 10:63; Wesley, Mary 10:69; West, Dame
Rebecca 10:72; White, Antonia 10:82;
Winchilsea, Anne Finch, Countess of 10:105;
Winterson, Jeanette 10:109; Wood, Mrs.
Henry 10:114; Woolf, Virginia 10:118;
Wordsworth, Dorothy 10:126; Wylie, Ida
Alexa Ross 10:138; Yonge, Charlotte M(ary)
10:142
Brittain, Vera (Mary) **2:61**; 10:103
Britten, Benjamin 3:62; 4:24, 25; 6:111
Brontë, Anne **2:62**; 2:64, 66
Brontë, Charlotte **2:64**; 2:63, 66; 4:96; 5:69;
7:128; 8:78
Brontë, Emily **2:66**; 2:62, 63, 64, 92
Brontë, Patrick 2:62
Brooke, Rupert 3:46
Brookner, Anita **2:67**
Brooks, Gwendolyn **2:69**
Brooks, Louise 9:97
Brooks, Maria Gowen **2:70**
Brooks, Mel 1:124
Brooks, Richard 9:13
Brough, Louise **2:71**; 3:37; 4:106
Brown, Capability 7:51
Brown, Helen Gurley **2:72**
Brown, John 9:175
Brown, Kenneth H. 6:123
Brown, Olympia **2:73**
Brown, Rita Mae 7:92
Brown, Trisha **2:74**; 8:48
Browning, Elizabeth Barrett **2:75**; 5:51;
7:17; 10:120
Browning, Robert 2:75, 76
Brownlow, Kevin 4:115
Brueghel, Jan 7:181
Brundtland, Gro Harlem **2:77**
Brunhilde **2:78**; 4:69

Bryher **2:79**
Buchan, John 10:56
Buck, Pearl S. **2:80**
Budd, Zola **2:81**; 3:88
Buddhism and Women **2:82–83**
Bueno, Maria **2:84**
Buffalo Bill 7:125
Bülow, Hans von 8:82; 10:34
Bulwer-Lytton, Edward 7:144
Bumbry, Grace (Melzia) **2:85**
Burbidge, Geoffrey 2:86
Burbidge, (Eleanor) Margaret **2:86**
Burdett, Sir Francis 2:87
Burdett-Coutts, Angela Georgina,
Baroness **2:87**
Burgess, Anthony 1:157
Burgess, Guy 10:73
Burke, Edmund 2:91; 4:125; 6:147
Burnett, Carol **2:88**
Burnett, Frances Hodgson **2:89**; 5:41
Burney, Dr. Charles 2:91
Burney, Fanny **2:90**; 4:172
Burns, George 1:41, 42
Burton, Richard 4:84; 9:126
Bush, George 5:45; 9:147
Bush, Kate **2:92**
business
    Arden, Elizabeth 1:70; Ashley, Laura 1:88;
    Ayer, Harriet Hubbard 1:105; Green, Hetty
    4:149; Lauder, Estée 6:20; Pinkham, Lydia
    Estes 8:8; Roddick, Anita 8:99; Rubinstein,
    Helena 8:117
Buss, Frances **2:93**; 1:147, 148; 3:81
Butler, Elizabeth **2:96**; 7:17
Butler, Frank E. 7:125
Butler, Josephine **2:98**; 4:15
Butt, Dame Clara **2:99**
Byatt, A(ntonia) S(usan) **2:100**; 3:128
Byns, Anna 1:188
Byron, Augusta Ada, Countess of
Lovelace **2:101**
Byron, Lord 2:9, 10; 101; 3:133; 5:14; 6:7;
7:13; 9:3
Caballé, Montserrat **2:103**
Caballero, Fernán **2:104**
Cabrini, Saint Frances Xavier **2:105**
Caedmon 5:27
Caesar, Julius 3:13, 13; 7:133
Caesarion (later Ptolemy XV) 3:13
Calamity Jane **2:106**; 8:120
Calderón de la Barca, Fanny **2:107**
Caldwell, Erskine 2:38
Caldwell, Sarah **2:108**
Caldwell, Taylor **2:109**
Caligula 1:24, 25; 5:23; 6:71; 7:134
Callaghan, James 9:146
Callas, Maria **2:110**; 8:176
Callendar, Newgate 8:73
Calvé, Emma **2:111**
Calvocoressi, Richard 5:22

Charles VII, Holy Roman Emperor 6:145
Charles VIII 1:61; 6:139
Charles IX 2:142
Charles X 1:180
Charles XIV 3:103
Charles, Dame (Mary) Eugenia **2:168**
Charles, Prince of Wales 3:111, 176; 9:130
Charles, Theodore 3:49
Charlotte, Grand Duchess **2:169**
Charlotte, Queen 2:91
Charrière, Isabelle Agnès Elisabeth de **2:170**
Chase, Alison 3:11
Chase, Edna Woolman **2:171**
Chase, Ilka 2:172
Chase, Lucia **2:172**
Chase, Mary Coyle **2:173**
Chase, Mary Ellen **2:174**
Châteaubriand 8:68
Châtelet, Emilie, Marquise du **2:175**
Chavannes, Puvis de 10:10
Chekhov 4:95
Cheney, Ednah Dow Littlehale **2:176**
Cher **2:177**; 7:191
Chesterton, G. K. 10:56
Chevalier, Maurice 5:155; 7:29; 8:3
Chevreuse, Duchess de **2:178**
Chiang, Mayling Soong **2:179**; 9:102
Chicago, Judy **2:180**
Chi-Ha, Kim 8:118
Child, Julia **2:181**
Child, Lydia Maria **2:182**; 3:121
Childeric 4:100
Chilperic 4:69
Chin, Ch'iu 8:40
Chinese women
   Chiang, Mayling Soong 2:179; Deng
   Yingchao 3:99; Ding Ling 3:120; Jiang Qing
   5:102; Jung Chang 5:136; Pan Chao 7:153;
   Qiu Jin 8:40; Sun Ch'ing-ling 9:102; Tz'u-hsi
   9:191; Wu Zhao 10:135
Ch'ing, Chiang 5:102
Chin Kieu **2:183**
Chisholm, Caroline **2:184**
Chisholm, Shirley Anita St. Hill **2:186**
Chitty, Susan 10:83
Chopin, Frédéric 8:145, 146
Chopin, Kate **2:187**
Christianity and Women **2:188–189**
Christian IX 1:38
Christie, Dame Agatha **2:190**; 4:11; 5:3;
   6:75; 8:73, 125
Christina **2:191**; 6:46
Christine de Pisan **3:1**
Chrysostom, John 3:187
Chuai, Emperor 5:104
Churchill, John 6:157
Churchill, Peter 4:177
Churchill, Winston 6:157; 7:36; 10:95
Chute, Marchette **3:2**

Cibber, Colley 3:17
Çiller, Tansu **3:3**
Cixi 9:191
Cixous, Hélène 7:40
Claflin, Tennessee **3:5**
Claflin, Victoria Woodhull **3:5**
Clairon, Mademoiselle **3:7**; 3:137
Clairvaux, St. Bernard of 5:29
Clapp, Margaret **3:8**
Clare, Saint **3:9**
Clark, Hilda 8:37
Clark, Petula **3:10**
Clark, William 8:134
Clarke, Martha **3:11**
Clarke, Shirley **3:12**
Claudius 1:25, 26; 7:16, 132
Clayburgh, Jill 6:79
Clement VII 2:21; 5:106
Cleopatra **3:13**; 1:127; 7:133, 134
Clerici, Gianni 4:134
Cleveland, President 6:59; 8:121
Clifford, Rosamond 3:160
Cline, Patsy **3:15**; 6:9
Clinton, Bill 1:52; 3:16; 4:24, 112; 8:74
Clinton, Hillary Rodham **3:16**
Clive, Kitty **3:17**
Close, Glenn **3:18**; 9:29
Clotilda, Saint **3:19**
Clough, Anne Jemima **3:20**
Clough, Arthur 3:20
Clovis I 3:19, 20
Clurman, Harold 3:54
Coatsworth, Elizabeth Jane **3:21**
Cochran, Jacqueline **3:22**
Cocteau, Jean 1:132
Cody, Lew 7:119
Coeur, Jacques 9:50
Cohen, Stanley 6:55
Coit, Margaret Louise **3:24**
Colbert, Claudette **3:25**; 1:85
Coleridge, Samuel Taylor 10:126
Colet, Louise **3:26**
Colette **3:27**; 1:132; 3:73; 5:19; 6:82; 10:83
Coligny, Gaspard de 6:46
Collett, Camilla **3:28**
Collier, Constance **3:30**
Collier, Jean 4:28
Collins, Jackie **3:31**; 3:32
Collins, Joan **3:32**; 3:31; 10:3
Colonna, Vittoria **3:33**
Columbus, Christopher 5:75
Compton-Burnett, Dame Ivy **3:34**; 5:115
Conboy, Sara Agnes McLaughlin **3:35**
Condé, Prince de 1:59; 7:58, 59; 8:177
Congreve, William 2:45
Connolly, Maureen **3:36**; 3:48
Cons, Emma 1:145
Constant, Benjamin 9:61
Constantine VI 5:71
Constantine VIII 10:157

Dante 1:149; 4:62; 8:159
Danton 8:103
d'Aragona, Tullia **3:76**
Dare, Virginia **3:77**
Darius I 9:117
Darling, Flora Adams **3:77**
Darling, Grace (Horsley) **3:78**
Darlington, W. A. 3:190
Darnley, Lord 6:141, 169, 170
Darwin, Charles 3:46
Dashkova, Yekaterina Romanovna **3:79**
Dassin, Jules 7:14
Davenport, Marcia 4:120
David 1:5; 8:123, 124
David I 6:137
David, Elizabeth **3:80**
David, Hal 10:49
David, Jacques Louis 6:24
Davies, Bette 3:57
Davies, (Sarah) Emily **3:81**; 2:93; 4:14
Daviot, Gordon 6:108
Davis, Angela **3:82**
Davis, Bette **3:83**; 1:95; 4:116; 7:49
Davis, Miles 9:191
Davis, Victor 4:192
Dawson, Jeannie 1:106
Day, Doris **3:85**
Day, Dorothy **3:86**
Day, Ingeborg 10:31
Dean, Christopher 9:164
Dean, James 3:140
Deborah **3:87**; 5:89
Debussy, Claude 4:90; 9:142
Decker, Mary **3:88**; 2:81
Degas, Edgar 2:135, 136; 10:10
Dekker, Thomas 4:78
Deland, Margaret Wade **3:89**
Delaney, Shelagh **3:90**; 6:65
Delaunay, Robert 3:91
Delaunay, Sonia **3:91**
Deledda, Grazia **3:92**
Delius, Frederick 6:101
de los Angeles, Victoria **3:93**
Demessieux, Jeanne-Marie-Madeleine **3:94**
De Mille, Agnes **3:95**; 2:173; 5:148
De Mille, Cecil B. 3:95; 9:109
De Morgan, Augustus 2:101, 102
Demy, Jacques 10:13, 14
Dench, Dame Judi **3:96**
Deneuve, Catherine **3:97**
Deng Yingchao **3:99**
Depp, Johnny 8:128
Derain, André 7:42
Desai, Anita **3:100**
Desbordes-Valmore, Marceline **3:101**
Descartes, René 2:192
Deshoulières, Antoinette **3:102**
design
    Ashley, Laura 1:88; Benetton, Giuliana
    1:166; Chanel, Coco 2:164; Chase, Edna

Woolman 2:171; de Wolfe, Elsie 3:110;
    Eames, Ray 3:149; Exter, Alexandra 3:192;
    Head, Edith 5:7; Jekyll, Gertrude 5:93;
    Karan, Donna 5:140; Laurencin, Marie 6:21;
    Muir, Jean 7:77; Onassis, Jacqueline
    Kennedy 7:141; Popova, Lyubov Sergeevna
    8:23; Quant, Mary 8:41; Rhodes, Zandra
    8:76; Schiaparelli, Elsa 8:161; Vionnet,
    Madeleine 10:28; Westwood, Vivienne 10:74
Désirée **3:103**
d'Este, Isabella **3:104**
Destinn, Emmy **3:105**
Deutsch, Helen **3:105**
de Valois, Dame Ninette **3:107**; 1:145;
    4:54, 156; 6:155
Devers, Gail **3:108**
Devi, Kanan **3:109**
Devlin, Bernadette 6:183
Dewey, John 10:144
de Wolfe, Elsie **3:110**
Diaghilev, Sergei 3:75; 4:131; 6:21, 155;
    7:109, 178; 9:165
Diana, Princess of Wales **3:111**; 2:133;
    8:76; 9:130
Diane de France **3:112**
Diane de Poitiers **3:113**; 2:133, 142
Dick, George 3:114
Dick, Gladys Henry **3:114**
Dick, Kay 9:36
Dickens, Charles 2:57, 87, 119, 185; 7:13,
    122; 9:185
Dickinson, Emily **3:115**; 4:120, 144, 187;
    5:83
Dickson, Barbara 7:151
Diderot 3:79, 183
Didion, Joan **3:116**
Dietrich, Marlene **3:117**
Digby, Jane **3:118**
Dilkes, Lady Emily 9:179
Dillinger, John 7:164
Dinesen, Isak **3:119**
Ding Ling **3:120**
Diocletian, Emperor 3:189; 6:92
diplomacy
    Anderson, Eugenie Moore 1:46; Bell,
    Gertrude Margaret Lowthian 1:159; Khan,
    Ra'ana Liaquat Ali 5:166; Kirkpatrick,
    Jeane 5:173; Kollontai, Aleksandra
    Mikhailovna 5:180; Mistral, Gabriela 7:30;
    Pandit, Vijaya Lakshmi 7:155; Temple,
    Shirley 9:132
Disraeli, Benjamin 10:25
Dix, Dorothea **3:121**
Dix, Dorothy **3:122**
Dodge, Grace Hoadley **3:123**
Dodge, Mary Elizabeth Mapes **3:124**
Doesburg, Theo van 5:36
Dole, Elizabeth Hanford **3:125**
Dolin, Anton 6:155, 156
Domingo, Placido 2:108

Domitian 3:126
Domitilia, Saint Flavia **3:126**
Doolittle, Hilda **3:127**
Dorleac, Françoise 3:98
Dorsey, Tommy 9:6
Dossi, Dosso 2:35
Douglas, Melvyn 2:29
Dowell, Anthony 9:8
Drabble, Margaret **3:128**; 2:100
Drake, Francis 3:173
Draper, Henry 6:181
Draper, Ruth **3:129**
Dreiser, Theodore 7:117
Dressler, Marie **3:130**; 7:119
Drew, Georgiana 1:134
Drew, Dame Jane **3:131**
Drexel, Katharine **3:132**
Droste-Hülshoff, Annette Elisabeth von
   3:133
Dryden, John 4:168; 9:143
du Barry, Countess **3:134**
Dubois, Cardinal 9:134
Dubois, William 4:13
Du Bois, W. E. B. 10:65
Dubos, René 10:44
Duchamp, Marcel 4:164; 5:139
du Deffand, Marquise **3:135**
Dumas the elder, Alexandre 7:13, 57; 9:39
du Maurier, Dame Daphne **3:136**; 5:114;
   8:88, 125
Dumesnil, Marie-Françoise **3:137**
Dunant, Jean Henri 1:136
Dunaway, Faye 7:165
Duncan, Isadora **3:138**; 4:143; 6:93; 9:118
Dunham, Katherine **3:139**; 5:174
Dunn, Kaye 3:140
du Pré, Jacqueline **3:141**
Durante, Jimmy 7:15
Duras, Marguerite **3:142**
Duse, Eleonora **3:143**; 1:179; 6:87, 93; 7:43
Dustin, Hannah **3:144**
Dutch women
   Beatrix 1:150; Blankers-Koen, Fanny 2:6;
   Juliana 5:133; Leyster, Judith 6:56; Margaret
   of Austria 6:139; Margaret of Parma 6:140;
   Mata Hari 6:176; Ruysch, Rachel 8:126;
   Wilhelmina 10:92
Dutt, Toru **3:145**
Dworkin, Andrea **3:146**
Dyer, Mary **3:147**; 5:65
Dylan, Bob 1:112, 113; 9:34, 35
Eames, Charles 3:149
Eames, Emma **3:148**
Eames, Ray **3:149**
Earhart, Amelia **3:150**; 1:140; 7:149
Eastman, Crystal **3:151**
Eberhardt, Isabelle **3:152**
Eckstine, Billy 10:16
economics

Çiller, Tansu 3:3; Kreps, Juanita Morris
   5:186; Robinson, Joan 8:95; Ward, Dame
   Barbara 10:43; Webb, Beatrice 10:54
Eddy, Mary Baker **3:153**
Ederle, Gertrude Caroline **3:154**; 2:160
Edgeworth, Maria **3:155**
Edinburgh, Duke of 3:175; 10:107
education
   Abbott, Maude (Elizabeth Seymour) 1:4;
   Agassiz, Elizabeth 1:19; Ashrawi, Hanan
   1:90; Baden-Powell, Dame Olave 1:111;
   Bates, Katharine Lee 1:140; Beale, Dorothea
   1:147; Beecher, Catharine Esther 1:155;
   Berry, Martha McChesney 1:181; Bethune,
   Mary McLeod 1:184; Blanding, Sarah
   Gibson 2:5; Blow, Susan Elizabeth 2:14;
   Bright Eyes 2:57; Buss, Frances 2:93; Carter,
   Elizabeth 2:130; Clapp, Margaret 3:8;
   Clough, Anne Jemima 3:20; Crandall,
   Prudence 3:53; Davies, (Sarah) Emily 3:81;
   du Deffand, Marquise 3:135; Dunham,
   Katherine 3:139; Felton, Rebecca Ann 4:17;
   Gildersleeve, Virginia Crocheron 4:108;
   Hamilton, Edith 4:179; Hildegard, Saint
   5:28; Juana Inés de la Cruz 5:128; Jung
   Chang 5:136; Krupskaya, Nadezhda
   Konstantinovna 5:188; Lyon, Mary 6:103;
   Macy, Anne Mansfield Sullivan 6:112;
   Model, Lisette 7:40; Montagu, Elizabeth
   7:50; Montessori, Maria 7:55; Paglia,
   Camille 7:148; Pan Chao 7:153; Peabody,
   Elizabeth Palmer 7:179; Ramabai, Pandita
   8:50; Spencer, Anna Garlin 9:54; Spurgeon,
   Caroline 9:59; Stocks, Mary, Baroness 9:80;
   Szold, Henrietta 9:111; Thomas, (Martha)
   Carey 9:155; Trimmer, Sarah 9:168;
   Vaughan, Dame Janet 10:14; Wiggin, Kate
   Douglas 10:88; Willard, Emma 10:97;
   Willard, Frances 10:98; Woolley, Mary
   Emma 10:121; Young, Ella Flagg 10:144
Education and Women **3:156–157**
Edward I 3:161; 5:162; 6:135
Edward II 5:73, 74; 6:135
Edward III 1:151; 5:73, 74, 162; 6:138; 8:1,
   2
Edward IV 1:151; 3:166; 6:138; 9:7
Edward VI 2:146; 3:171; 6:166; 8:190
Edward VII 1:38; 5:50; 6:13, 174; 7:108;
   10:23
Edward VIII 3:175, 177; 6:136, 174;
   10:106, 107
Edward, the Black Prince 5:162
Edward the Confessor 3:181
Edwards, Blake 1:51
Einstein, Albert 7:113, 114
Eisenhower, Dwight D. 5:34; 6:92
Elderling, Dr. Grace 5:160
Elders, Joycelyn **3:158**
Eleanor of Aquitaine **3:159**; 2:4
Eleanor of Castile **3:161**

Eleanor of Provence **3:162**
Elgar, Sir Edward 2:99, 100
Elion, Gertrude Belle **3:163**
Eliot, George **3:164**; 7:17
Eliot, T. S. 1:129, 132; 7:48, 63, 70; 10:119
Elizabeth, wife of Edward IV **3:166**; 9:7
Elizabeth, wife of Frederick I **3:167**
Elizabeth, empress of Russia **3:168**; 2:140
Elizabeth, wife of Francis Joseph I **3:169**; 2:133
Elizabeth, wife of Carol I **3:170**
Elizabeth I **3:171**; 2:20; 4:37, 157; 5:82; 6:166, 167, 169, 170; 7:169; 8:83, 97; 9:19; 9:94
Elizabeth II **3:175**; 1:58; 2:101; 3:177; 6:135, 175; 9:58, 136, 163; 10:33, 107
Elizabeth, St. 6:165
Elizabeth, the Queen Mother **3:177**; 3:175
Elizabeth Farnese **3:178**; 10:9
Elizabeth of Hungary, Saint **3:179**
Ellerman, Annie Winifred 2:79
Ellington, Duke 10:51
Elliott, Denholm 7:2
Ellis, Havelock 2:79; 4:176; 8:166
Ellis, Ruth 3:90; 8:82
Elssler, Fanny **3:180**; 2:159
Emerson, Ralph Waldo 1:35; 3:115; 4:82
Emma **3:181**; 1:17
Emma of Waldeck 10:92
Ender, Kornelia **3:182**; 4:68
Engels, Friedrich 5:154; 6:164
Epictetus 2:131
Epinay, Louise-Florence d' **3:183**
Erik II 6:135
Ernst, Max 4:164
Ershad, President 10:156
Ervine, St John 8:97
Esenin, Sergei 3:139
espionage
    Boyd, Belle 2:43; Hallowes, Odette 4:177; Mata Hari 6:176; Ricard, Marthe 8:78; Rosenberg, Ethel 8:107
Esquivel, Laura **3:184**
Estrées, Gabrielle d' **3:185**
Etheldreda 1:19
Ethelfleda 1:17
Eudocia **3:185**; 8:36
Eudocia Macrembolitissa **3:186**
Eudoxia **3:187**
Eugénie **3:188**; 2:28; 9:41
Eulalia, Saint **3:189**
Evans, Dame Edith **3:190**
Evans, Janet **3:191**
Evans, Maurice 10:57
Evelyn, John 1:18; 10:41
Evert, Christine Marie 6:71
Exter, Alexandra **3:192**; 4:131
Faber, Cecilia Böhl von 2:104
Fairbank, Janet Ayer **4:1**; 1:131
Fairbanks, Douglas 8:6

Faisal I 1:160
Faithfull, Emily **4:2**
Faithfull, Marianne **4:3**
Falla, Manuel de 1:73; 6:8, 18, 19
Faludi, Susan **4:4**
Farmer, Fannie Merritt **4:5**
Farmer, Frances **4:6**
Farnese, Alessandro 6:140
Farnham, Eliza Woodson Burhans **4:7**
Farnsworth, Rodney 7:135
Farrar, Geraldine **4:8**; 5:97; 6:41
Farrell, Eileen **4:9**
Farrow, Mia **4:10**; 4:137
Fassbinder, Rainer Werner 8:172
Fatimah **4:12**; 5:166
Fauset, Jessie Redmon **4:13**
Fawcett, Dame Millicent **4:14**; 1:46; 3:81; 7:159; 8:59; 9:88
Fay, Alice 4:140
Feinstein, Dianne **4:15**
Feinstein, Elaine 9:175
Fell, Dame Honor Bridget **4:16**
Fellini, Federico 6:175; 10:67
Felton, Rebecca Ann **4:17**
Feminism **4:18–19**
Fenton, Lavinia **4:20**
Ferber, Edna **4:21**; 6:39
Ferdinand I 5:107
Ferdinand II 2:145
Ferdinand III 7:58
Ferdinand VI 3:178
Ferdinand VII 5:76
Ferguson, Elsie **4:22**
Fermi, Enrico 7:11, 113
Ferraro, Geraldine (Anne) **4:23**
Ferrer, José 4:171
Ferrer, Mel 5:19
Ferrier, Kathleen **4:24**
Ferrier, Susan (Edmonstone) **4:25**
Feuillière, Edwige **4:26**
Feynman, Richard 10:134
Field, Nathan 4:78
Field, Sally **4:27**
Fielding, Henry 2:90; 4:28; 7:52
Fielding, Sarah **4:28**
Fields, Dame Gracie **4:29**
Figner, Vera **4:30**
Finch, Anne 10:105
Finley, Martha Farquharson **4:31**
Finnbogadóttir, Vigdís **4:32**
Finney, Albert 1:28
First, Ruth **4:34**
Fisher, Dorothy Canfield **4:35**
Fiske, Minnie Maddern **4:36**
Fitton, Mary **4:37**
Fitzgerald, Ella **4:38**; 10:52
Fitzgerald, F. Scott 4:39; 9:74
Fitzgerald, Zelda **4:39**
Fitzherbert, Maria **4:41**
Flagstad, Kirsten **4:42**

Flanagan, Hallie **4:44**
Flaubert, Gustave 3:27
Fleitz, Beverly 2:71
Fleming, Peggy **4:45**
Fleming, Peter 6:117
Fleming, Williamina Paton **4:46**
Fletcher, Alice Cunningham **4:47**
Floyd, Carlisle 3:70
Flynn, Elizabeth Gurley **4:48**
Fo, Dario 8:53, 54
Fokine, Michel 3:139; 5:147; 7:179; 9:118
Follett, Mary Parker **4:49**
Fonda, Henry 4:50; 9:97
Fonda, Jane **4:50**; 5:12; 7:173; 8:70
Fontaine, Jean de La 6:2
Fontana, Lavinia **4:52**
Fontanne, Lynn **4:53**; 4:171; 9:120
Fontenelle, Bernard le 9:134
Fonteyn, Dame Margot **4:54**
Forbes, Esther **4:55**
Ford, Ford Madox 8:77
Ford, John 7:135
Ford, President 9:133
Forkbeard, Sweyn 3:181
Forster, E. M. 4:176; 5:102; 9:158; 10:119
Fossey, Dian **4:56**; 10:53
Foster, Abigail Kelley **4:57**
Foster, Hannah Webster **4:57**
Foster, Jodie **4:59**; 6:17
Fowler, William 2:86
Fox, Charles James 2:154; 3:74
Fox, Margaret **4:60**
Fragonard, Honoré 7:69
Frame, Janet Paterson **4:61**; 2:115
Françoise Marie 7:54
France, Anatole 9:143
Francesca da Rimini **4:62**
Francis I, Holy Roman Emperor 6:146, 147
Francis I of Austria 6:151
Francis I of France 1:61; 3:33, 113; 6:139, 144
Francis II 2:142; 6:169
Francis Joseph I of Austria 2:118; 3:169
Franco, General 5:68; 10:60
Frank, Anne **4:63**
Frankenthaler, Helen **4:64**
Franklin, Aretha **4:66**; 5:51; 6:49
Franklin, Benjamin 9:184
Franklin, Rosalind Elsie **4:67**
Fraser, Dawn **4:68**; 3:182
Fredegund **4:69**; 2:78
Frederick, Pauline **4:70**
Frederick II of Norway and Denmark 1:63
Frederick II the Great 3:169
Frederick III 1:101
Frederick V 3:167
Frederick IX 6:142
Frederick William IV 1:79
Freeman, Mary E. Wilkins **4:71**

Fremstad, Olive **4:72**; 6:41
French, Dawn 8:157
French women
art: Bonheur, Rosa 2:27; Delaunay, Sonia 3:91; Goncharova, Natalia Sergeyevna 4:131; Kyo, Machiko 5:192; Laurencin, Marie 6:21; Morisot, Berthe 7:69; Valadon, Suzanne 10:10; Vigée-Lebrun, Marie Anne Elisabeth 10:27
dance: Camargo, Marie Anne de Cupis de 2:112; Caron, Leslie 2:122; Sallé, Marie 8:140; Toumanova, Tamara 9:165; Verdy, Violette 10:19
design: Chanel, Coco 2:164; Laurencin, Marie 6:21; Schiaparelli, Elsa 8:161; Vionnet, Madeleine 10:28
education: du Deffand, Marquise 3:135
espionage: Hallowes, Odette 4:177; Ricard, Marthe 8:78
heroism: Verchères, Marie Madeleine Jarret de 10:18
medicine: Irigaray, Luce 5:72; Kristeva, Julia 5:187; Pelletier, Madeleine 7:182
military: Joan of Arc, Saint 5:108
music: Boulanger, Nadia (Juliette) 2:36; Calvé, Emma 2:111; Chaminade, Cécile Louise Stéphanie 2:161; Demessieux, Jeanne-Marie-Madeleine 3:94; Malibran, Maria 6:122; Tailleferre, Germaine 9:116; Viardot-García, Pauline 10:21
noblewomen: Beauharnais, Hortense de 1:152; Berry, Duchess de 1:180; Chevreuse, Duchess de 2:178; Diane de France 3:112; Diane de Poitiers 3:113; du Barry, Countess 3:134; La Vallière, Louise, Duchess de 6:22; Longueville, Duchess de 6:79; Maintenon, Marquise de 6:118; Montespan, Marquise de 7:54; Rambouillet, Marquise de 8:52; Ursins, Princess des 10:8
performing arts: Aimée, Anouk 1:28; Arletty 1:73; Bardot, Brigitte 1:128; Bell, Marie 1:160; Bernhardt, Sarah 1:178; Caron, Leslie 2:122; Champmeslé, Marie 2:163; Clairon, Mademoiselle 3:7; Crespin, Régine 3:58; Deneuve, Catherine 3:97; Dumesnil, Marie-Françoise 3:137; Duras, Marguerite 3:142; Feuillère, Edwige 4:26; Guilbert, Yvette 4:165; Huppert, Isabelle 5:60; Lecouvreur, Adrienne 6:32; Mistinguett 7:29; Mnouchkine, Ariane 7:39; Moreau, Jeanne 7:67; Piaf, Edith 8:3; Rachel 8:45; Signoret, Simone 9:10; Varda, Agnès 10:13
philosophy: Beauvoir, Simone de 1:153; Irigaray, Luce 5:72; Kristeva, Julia 5:187; Weil, Simone 10:59
politics: Corday, Charlotte 3:40; Michel, Louise 7:18; Roland de la Platière, Marie-Jeanne 8:103; Tencin, Claudine-Alexandrine Guerin de 9:134; Tristan, Flora 9:169; Veil, Simone 10:17

Agnodice 1:23; Callas, Maria 2:110; Corinna 3:43; Hypatia 5:66; Mercouri, Melina 7:14; Olympias 7:140; Phryne 8:2; Sappho 8:150; Thaïs 9:143; Xanthippe 10:140

Green, Anna Katherine **4:148**
Green, Hetty **4:149**
Green, T. H. 10:45
Greenaway, Kate **4:150**
Greer, Germaine **4:151**
Gregory, Cynthia **4:153**
Gregory, Isabella Augusta, Lady **4:154**; 5:49
Gregory IX 3:179
Grevver, Frans Pieter de 6:56
Grey, Dame Beryl **4:156**
Grey, Earl 2:98
Grey, Lady Jane **4:157**; 2:26; 6:167
Griffith, D. W. 4:115; 6:82; 8:5
Grimké, Angelina Emily **4:158**; 2:167; 4:57
Grimké, Sarah Moore **4:158**
Grimm, Friedrich Melchior von 3:183
Grimshaw, Beatrice **4:159**
Grisi, Carlotta **4:160**; 2:159; 4:145, 161
Grisi, Giuditta 4:160, 161
Grisi, Giulia **4:161**; 4:160
Grosz, George 5:35
Grotius 2:192
Gruberová, Edita **4:162**
Grummt, Steffen 3:182
Guggenheim, Peggy **4:163**
Guilbert, Yvette **4:165**
Günderode, Karoline von 1:79
Gunhild 3:181
Gunnell, Sally **4:166**
Gusella, James 10:77
Gustav II Adolph 2:191
Gustav VI Adolf 6:142
Guyon, Jeanne-Marie **4:167**
Guzzo, Lou 8:63
Gwyn, Nell **4:168**; 9:131
Hadid, Zaha **4:170**
Hagar 8:151
Hagen, Uta **4:171**
Hahn, Emily **4:172**
Hahn, Otto 5:117; 7:11
Haldane, John Scott 7:34
Hale, Clara **4:173**
Hale, Nancy **4:174**
Hale, Sarah Josepha **4:174**
Hall, Sir Peter 2:123
Hall, (Marguerite) Radclyffe **4:175**
Hallowes, Odette **4:177**; 7:94
Hals, Frans 6:57
Hamilton, Alexander 1:98
Hamilton, Alice **4:178**
Hamilton, Edith **4:179**
Hamilton, Emma, Lady **4:180**; 10:27
Hammerstein, Oscar 6:27
Hammett, Dashiell 5:11, 12
Hammond, Dame Joan **4:181**

Hammond, John 5:39
Handel 3:18; 8:140, 141
Handel-Mazzetti, Enrica von **4:182**
Hansberry, Lorraine **4:182**
Harbach, Otto 7:23
Hard, Darlene Ruth **4:183**; 2:84, 85
Hardecanute 3:181
Hardy, Thomas 10:56
Harefoot, Harold 1:17; 3:181
Harkness, Rebekah **4:184**
Harlow, Jean **4:185**; 1:95
Harris, Julie **4:186**
Harris, Patricia Roberts **4:187**
Harrison, Rex 7:152, 153
Hart, Doris 3:37
Hart, Moss 1:50
Hasan 4:12
Haskell, Molly 7:49
Hassam, Childe 9:148
Hastings, Lady Flora 10:23
Hathaway, Anne **4:188**
Hatshepsut **4:189**
Hauck, Minnie **4:190**
Hauptmann, Gerhart 8:143
Hausmann, Raoul 5:35
Haward, Nancy 8:32
Hawkes, Jacquetta **4:191**
Hawkins, Sir John 3:173
Hawks, Howard 4:6
Hawn, Goldie **4:192**; 7:20
Hawthorne, Nathaniel 1:35
Hayden, Melissa **5:1**
Haydn 3:180
Hayes, Helen **5:2**
Hayward, Brooke 9:100
Haywood, Eliza **5:4**
Hayworth, Rita **5:5**; 7:123
Hazlitt, William 9:9
Head, Bessie **5:6**
Head, Edith **5:7**
Hearst, Patricia **5:8**
Hearst, William Randolph 5:8; 7:173, 174
Heartfield, John 5:35
Heath, Edward 9:146
Hebbel, Friedrich 1:177
Heck, Barbara Ruckle **5:9**
Heidegger, Martin 1:71, 109
Helena, Saint **5:10**
Hellman, Lillian **5:11**; 1:88, 126; 6:186; 9:126
Héloïse **5:13**
Hemans, Felicia Dorothea **5:14**
Hemingway, Ernest 3:117, 118; 9:74, 163
Hempel, Frieda **5:15**
Henderson, Fletcher 10:51
Henie, Sonja **5:16**; 8:100
Henrietta Anne, Duchess d'Orléans **5:17**; 6:22
Henrietta Maria **5:18**; 2:155; 5:17
Henry, Prince 3:111

Henry I 6:137, 177
Henry II 3:159; 6:178
Henry III of England 3:160, 161, 162; 5:29, 80; 6:149, 177
Henry III of France 2:142, 143; 3:112, 113; 6:143, 169
Henry IV, Holy Roman Emperor 6:178
Henry IV of Castile 5:75, 129
Henry IV of England 5:111, 111
Henry IV of France 3:113, 185; 5:18; 6:143, 145, 150; 8:53
Henry V, Holy Roman Emperor 6:177, 179
Henry V of England 2:151; 5:77, 111
Henry VI 2:151; 6:138
Henry VII 2:145, 151; 3:167, 171; 6:141, 167; 9:94
Henry VIII 1:62, 137; 2:21, 145; 3:171; 4:157; 5:52; 6:136, 141, 166, 169; 7:168, 169; 8:190
Hensley, Patsy 3:15
Henze, Hans Werner 1:109
Hepburn, Audrey **5:19**
Hepburn, Katharine **5:20**; 1:85; 4:51, 138
Hepworth, Dame Barbara **5:22**
Herod Agrippa I 1:168
Herod Agrippa II 1:168
Herodias **5:23**; 8:97, 141
Herodotus 1:83; 8:182; 9:117
heroism
  Abigail 1:5; Arundell, Blanche 1:84; Corbin, Margaret 3:39; Darling, Grace (Horsley) 3:78; Dustin, Hannah 3:144; Jael 5:89; Judith 5:132; MacDonald, Flora 6:106; Pocahontas 8:16; Seacole, Mary 8:178; Verchères, Marie Madeleine Jarret de 10:18
Herophilus 1:23
Herschel, Caroline Lucretia **5:24**
Herschel, Sir John **5:25**; 9:46
Herschel, Sir William 5:24
Hertzsprung, Ejnar 6:181
Hess, Dame Myra **5:25**
Hesse, Eva **5:26**
Hewish, Antony 1:162, 163
Heywood, Thomas 1:18
Hickok, James B. (Wild Bill) 2:106, 107
Highsmith, Patricia **5:26**
Hilda, Saint **5:27**
Hildegard, Saint **5:28**
Hill, Octavia **5:29**
Hill, Susan 10:118
Hiller, Dame Wendy **5:30**
Hilton, Conrad 4:84
Hindemith, Paul 4:144
Hinduism and Women **5:32–33**
Hines, Earl 10:15, 16
Hingis, Martina 4:141
Hippius, Zinaida Nikolayevna **5:31**
Hisano, Eiko 9:114
Hitchings, George H. 3:163

Hitler, Adolf 2:48; 8:86, 87; 9:156
Ho, Emperor 7:154
Hobby, Oveta Culp **5:34**
Höch, Hannah **5:35**
Hodgkin, Dorothy Crowfoot **5:36**; 6:80
Hoffman, Malvina **5:37**
Hofleit, Dorrit 4:46; 6:31
Hofmann, Hans 5:185
Hogg-Priestly, Helen Battles Sawyer **5:38**
Holiday, Billie **5:39**; 8:111
Holinshed 6:166
Holland, Agnieszka **5:40**; 2:90
Holm, Hanya **5:42**; 3:12
Holofernes 4:102; 5:132
Holroyd, Michael 3:128
Holst, Gustav 3:62
Homer, Louise **5:43**
Honegger 9:116
Honorius, Emperor 4:85
Hoover, Herbert 8:131
Hope, Francis 9:52
Hopper, Grace Murray **5:44**
Hopper, Hedda **5:45**
Horace 8:151
Horne, Lena Calhoun **5:46**
Horne, Marilyn **5:47**; 2:108
Horney, Karen **5:48**
Horniman, Annie **5:49**; 4:155; 9:159
Horst, Louis 3:11
Hosmer, Harriet Goodhue **5:50**; 6:56
Houssay, Bernardo 3:43
Houston, Cissy 10:49
Houston, Whitney **5:51**; 6:160; 7:173; 10:49, 50
Howard, Catherine **5:52**; 1:62; 3:171; 7:169
Howard, Trevor 5:114
Howe, Julia Ward **5:54**
Howells, Herbert 1:116
Hoxie, Vinnie Ream **5:55**
Hoyle, Fred 2:86
Hrosvitha **5:56**
Hsieng-feng 9:191
Hsi-Lin, Hsü 8:40, 41
Huch, Ricarda **5:57**
Huchra, John 4:97
Hudson, Rock 3:85
Hughes, Howard 8:120
Hughes, Langston 5:62
Hughes, Ted 8:12, 13
Hugo, Victor 9:39
Humboldt, Friedrich von 9:46
Hume, Rosemary 9:58
Humphrey, Doris **5:58**, 9:69
Humphrey, Duke of Gloucester 5:88
Humphrey, Hubert 1:46
Hunt, Holman 7:17
Hunt, Leigh 9:9
Hunter, Holly 2:115
Huntingdon, Selina Hastings, Countess of **5:59**

Huppert, Isabelle **5:60**
Hurst, Fannie **5:61**
Hurston, Zora Neale **5:62**
Husayn 4:12
Husserl, Edmund 1:71
Huston, Angelica **5:63**
Huston, John 5:63
Huston, Walter 5:63
Hutchinson, Anne **5:64**; 3:147
Huxley, Aldous 7:71; 10:46
Huxley, Julian 10:46
Hyde, Anne 6:168
Hyman, Libbie Henrietta **5:65**
Hypatia **5:66**
Ibarbourou, Juana de **5:67**
Ibárruri Gómez, Dolores **5:68**
Ibsen, Henrik 1:7; 4:36; 7:93; 8:93, 94
Idem, Dito 3:170
Imrie, Celia 10:116
Inchbald, Elizabeth **5:69**
Inchbald, Joseph 5:69
Indian women
performing arts: Devi, Kanan 3:109
politics: Gandhi, Indira 4:87; Naidu, Sarojini
   7:89; Pandit, Vijaya Lakshmi 7:155;
   Ramabai, Pandita 8:50
religion: Teresa, Mother 9:135
writing: Desai, Anita 3:100; Dutt, Toru 3:145;
   Jhabvala, Ruth Prawer 5:101; Naidu,
   Sarojini 7:89; Rama Rau, Santha 8:51
Ingelow, Jean **5:70**
Ingres 4:62
Ireland, John 6:101
Irene **5:71**; 1:54; 5:133
Irigaray, Luce **5:72**
Irish women
performing arts: Gonne, Maud 4:132; Gregory,
   Isabella Augusta, Lady 4:154; McKenna,
   Siobhán 6:192; O'Connor, Sinead 7:131;
   Smithson, Harriet (Constance) 9:38;
   Woffington, Peg 10:111
politics: Gonne, Maud 4:132; Markiewicz,
   Constance, Countess 6:153; Robinson, Mary
   8:96
religion: Brigid of Ireland, Saint 2:59
writing: Blessington, Countess of 2:9; Gregory,
   Isabella Augusta, Lady 4:154; Grimshaw,
   Beatrice 4:159; Lavin, Mary 6:23; O'Brien,
   Edna 7:128; Somerville, Edith Oenone 9:44;
   Young, Ella 10:143
Iron, Ralph 8:166
Ironside, Edmund 6:137
Irving, Henry 9:140
Isaac 8:44, 151, 152
Isabeau 5:77
Isabelita 7:188
Isabella **5:73**
Isabella I **5:74**; 2:145; 5:51, 107, 129
Isabella II **5:76**
Isabella of Bavaria **5:77**; 2:151

Isabel of Angoulême **5:80**
Iscariot, Judas 6:172
Isherwood, Christopher 9:29
Ishiguro, Kazuo 9:158
Ishmael 8:151
Islam and Women **5:78–79**
Italian women
art: Anguissola, Sofonisba 1:53; Carriera,
   Rosalba 2:126; Fontana, Lavinia 4:52;
   Gentileschi, Artemisia 4:101; Sirani,
   Elisabetta 9:17
dance: Cerrito, Fanny 2:159; Grisi, Carlotta
   4:160; Taglioni, Maria 9:115
design: Benetton, Giuliana 1:166
education: Montessori, Maria 7:55
music: Alboni, Marietta 1:32; Bartoli, Cecilia
   1:135; Galli-Curci, Amelita 4:86; Grisi,
   Giulia 4:161; Scotto, Renata 8:176; Tebaldi,
   Renata 9:129; Tetrazzini, Luisa 9:141
noblewomen: Beatrice 1:149; Borgia, Lucrezia
   2:34; Cenci, Beatrice 2:157; Francesca da
   Rimini 4:62
performing arts: Duse, Eleonora 3:143;
   Lollobrigida, Gina 6:77; Loren, Sophia 6:84;
   Magnani, Anna 6:115; Masina, Giulietta
   6:175; Rame, Franca 8:53; Wertmuller, Lina
   10:67
philanthropy: d'Este, Isabella 3:104
religion: Catherine de' Ricci, Saint 2:143;
   Catherine of Bologna, Saint 2:146;
   Catherine of Genoa, Saint 2:148; Catherine
   of Siena, Saint 2:149; Clare, Saint 3:9
rulers: Joanna I 5:105
science: Agnesi, Maria 1:22; Levi-Montalcini,
   Rita 6:54
writing: Belgioioso, Cristina, Princess of 1:158;
   Colonna, Vittoria 3:33; d'Aragona, Tullia
   3:76; Deledda, Grazia 3:92; Ginzburg,
   Natalia Levi 4:112; Morante, Elsa 7:64;
   Rame, Franca 8:53; Serao, Matilde 8:182
Ivan VI 1:56; 3:168
Ivan the Terrible 3:173
Ivory, James 2:26; 5:101; 9:158
Jackson, Glenda **5:81**; 7:95; 9:37
Jackson, Helen Hunt **5:83**; 9:161
Jackson, Mahalia **5:84**; 4:66
Jackson, Shirley **5:85**
Jacob 8:44, 45
Jacobi, Mary Putnam **5:85**
Jacobs, Helen Hull **5:86**; 6:132
Jacqueline of Bavaria **5:87**
Jacques-Dalcroze, Emile 5:42
Jael **5:89**; 3:87
Jaffe, Stanley R. 6:17
Jagger, Mick 4:3, 4
Jakubowska, Wanda **5:90**
James, Henry 4:118; 9:140; 10:46, 72, 79,
   80, 124
James, Jesse 9:68
James, P(hylis) D(orothy), Baroness **5:91**

Messiaen, Oliver 10:61
Meynell, Alice **7:17**; 2:96
Michael IV 10:157, 158
Michael V Calaphates 10:158
Michel, Louise **7:18**
Michel, Peggy 4:135
Michelangelo 1:53; 3:33; 4:102
Middleton, Thomas 4:78
Midler, Bette **7:19**; 4:192
Midori **7:20**
Milanov, Zinka **7:21**; 8:75
Miles, Sarah 6:8
military
    Corbin, Margaret 3:39; Hopper, Grace
    Murray 5:44; Joan of Arc, Saint 5:108;
    Sampson, Deborah 8:143
Mill, John Stuart 7:158; 9:43
Millay, Edna St. Vincent **7:22**
Miller, Alice Duer **7:23**
Miller, Arthur 7:50
Miller, Elizabeth Smith 2:12
Miller, Henry 7:112
Miller, Lee **7:24**
Miller, Rachel 10:95
Millett, Kate **7:25**
Minnelli, Liza **7:26**; 4:94
Minnelli, Vincente 4:94; 7:26
Mirren, Helen **7:28**
Mistinguett **7:29**
Mistral, Gabriela **7:30**
Mitchell, Ellen M. 5:54
Mitchell, Joni **7:31**
Mitchell, Margaret **7:32**
Mitchell, Maria **7:33**
Mitchison, Naomi **7:34**
Mitford, Jessica (Lucy) **7:35**; 7:38
Mitford, Mary Russell **7:37**
Mitford, Nancy **7:38**; 7:35
Mnouchkine, Ariane **7:39**
Model, Lisette **7:40**; 1:69
Modersohn-Becker, Paula **7:42**
Modjeska, Helena **7:43**
Modotti, Tina **7:44**
Moffit, Billie Jean 5:168
Mohammed 1:29; 4:12; 5:166
Moholy-Nagy, László 5:36
Molière 6:46; 8:53, 177
Molly Pitcher **7:46**; 3:40
Mondale, Walter 4:23
Mondrian 5:185
Monk, Meredith **7:47**
Monmouth, Duke of 10:41, 42
Monroe, Harriet **7:48**
Monroe, Marilyn **7:49**; 2:165; 4:140; 6:82;
    8:120; 9:19, 77
Montagu, Elizabeth **7:50**; 2:131; 7:65
Montagu, Lady Mary Wortley **7:52**
Montand, Yves 9:10, 11
Montespan, Marquise de **7:54**; 6:22; 118
Montesquieu, Baron de 2:140; 9:134

Montessori, Maria **7:55**; 4:36
Montez, Lola **7:56**; 3:50
Montgomery, L(ucy) M(aud) **7:57**
Montpensier, Duchess de **7:58**
Moodie, Susanna Strickland **7:59**
Moody, Helen Wills 10:104
Moore, Demi **7:60**
Moore, George 2:62; 7:17
Moore, Grace **7:61**
Moore, Henry 5:22
Moore, Sir John 9:63
Moore, Marianne (Craig) **7:62**; 1:189
Moore, Mary Tyler **7:63**
Morante, Elsa **7:64**
Moravia, Alberto 7:64
More, Hannah **7:65**
More, Sir Thomas 1:137; 9:7
Moreau, Gustave 8:142
Moreau, Jeanne **7:67**
Morgan, Margery 8:15
Morgan, Robin **7:68**
Morisot, Berthe **7:69**
Morrell, Lady Ottoline **7:70**
Morris, Jan **7:71**
Morris, William 7:101
Morrison, Toni **7:72**; 1:142; 5:62
Mortimer, Roger 5:73, 74
Morton, Jelly Roll 9:144
Moses, Grandma **7:73**
Motherhood **7:74–75**
Mott, Lucretia Coffin **7:76**; 9:64, 65
Muir, Jean **7:77**
Mumford, Lewis 7:117
Munro, Alice **7:78**
Münter, Gabriele **7:79**
Murasaki, Shikibu **7:80**
Murat, Joachim 2:22, 23
Murat, Marie 10:27
Murdoch, Dame Iris **7:81**; 2:100
Murfin, Jane 3:49
Musgrave, Thea **7:83**
music
    Alboni, Marietta 1:32; Alda, Frances 1:36;
    Anderson, Marian 1:48; Bacewicz, Grazyna
    1:108; Baillie, Dame Isobel 1:116; Baker,
    Dame Janet Abbott 1:118; Bartoli, Cecilia
    1:135; Battle, Kathleen 1:141; Beach, Amy
    Marcy 1:146; Berganza, Teresa 1:172; Bori,
    Lucrezia 2:35; Boulanger, Nadia (Juliette)
    2:36; Brico, Antonia 2:53; Bumbry, Grace
    (Melzia) 2:85; Caballé, Montserrat 2:103;
    Caldwell, Sarah 2:108; Callas, Maria 2:110;
    Calvé, Emma 2:111; Carreño, Maria Teresa
    2:125; Chaminade, Cécile Louise Stéphanie
    2:161; Chin Kieu 2:183; Crawford Seeger,
    Ruth 3:57; Cross, Joan 3:62; Curtin, Phyllis
    3:70; de los Angeles, Victoria 3:93;
    Demessieux, Jeanne-Marie-Madeleine 3:94;
    Destinn, Emmy 3:105; du Pré, Jacqueline
    3:141; Eames, Emma 3:148; Farrar,

pioneers and explorers

Bailey, Ann 1:114; Bishop, Isabella Bird 1:190; Calamity Jane 2:106; Dare, Virginia 3:77; Dustin, Hannah 3:144; Jemison, Mary 5:95; Kingsley, Mary 5:170; Rowlandson, Mary White 8:113; Workman, Fanny 10:127

Piozzi, Hester Lynch **8:9**

Pitt, William 9:63

Pitt-Rivers, Rosalind **8:10**

Pius VII 5:125

Pius XII 3:9; 6:165

Pizzey, Erin **8:11**

Planck, Max 7:10

Plath, Sylvia **8:12**; 8:187

Plato 7:82

Plisetskaya, Maya **8:14**

Plowright, Joan **8:15**

Plutarch the Younger 5:66

Pocahontas **8:16**; 10:90

Poe, Edgar Allan 10:85

Pogash, Carol 4:4

Polish women

Abakanowicz, Magdalena 1:1; Bacewicz, Grazyna 1:108; Curie, Marie (Skłodowska) 3:66; Holland, Agnieszka 5:40; Jakubowska, Wanda 5:90; Landowska, Wanda 6:8; Negri, Pola 7:99; Suchocka, Hanna 9:96; Szewinska, Irena 9:110; Szymborska, Wislawa 9:112

politics

Abzug, Bella 1:6; Albright, Madeleine Korbel 1:33; Aquino, Corazon 1:67; Arteaga, Rosalia 1:82; Ashrawi, Hanan 1:90; Astor, Nancy, Viscountess 1:96; Bandaranaike, Sirimavo Ratwatte Dias 1:124; Belgioioso, Cristina, Princess of 1:158; Bhutto, Benazir 1:185; Bondfield, Margaret Grace 2:25; Bonner, Yelena 2:28; Boxer, Barbara 2:42; Breshko-Breshkovskaya, Yekaterina 2:51; Brittain, Vera (Mary) 2:61; Brundtland, Gro Harlem 2:77; Caraway, Hattie Ophelia Wyatt 2:117; Chamorro, Violetta Barrios de 2:162; Charles, Dame (Mary) Eugenia 2:168; Chisholm, Shirley Anita St. Hill 2:186; Çiller, Tansu 3:3; Conboy, Sara Agnes McLaughlin 3:35; Davis, Angela 3:82; Deng Yingchao 3:99; Feinstein, Dianne 4:15; Felton, Rebecca Ann 4:17; Figner, Vera 4:30; Finnbogadóttir, Vigdís 4:32; First, Ruth 4:34; Flynn, Elizabeth Gurley 4:48; Gandhi, Indira 4:87; Gonne, Maud 4:132; Grasso, Ella 4:146; Harris, Patricia Roberts 4:187; Ibárruri Gómez, Dolores 5:68; Jackson, Glenda 5:81; Jiang Qing 5:102; Jones, Mary Harris 5:118; Jordan, Barbara Charline 5:121; Joseph, Helen 5:123; Kelly, Petra 5:156; Key, Ellen 5:165; Khan, Ra'ana Liaquat Ali 5:166; Kreps, Juanita Morris 5:186; Kumaratunge, Chandrika

Bandaranaike 5:189; Lease, Mary Elizabeth 6:30; Lee, Jennie 6:35; Luce, Clare Boothe 6:91; Luxemburg, Rosa 6:99; McAliskey, Bernadette 6:183; Macphail, Agnes Campbell 6:111; Makeba, Miriam 6:121; Mandela, Winnie 6:125; Marcos, Imelda (Romualdez) 6:132; Markiewicz, Constance, Countess 6:153; Marx, Eleanor 6:163; Meinhof, Ulrike Marie 7:8; Meir, Golda 7:9; Mercouri, Melina 7:14; Naidu, Sarojini 7:89; Olsen, Tillie 7:139; Pandit, Vijaya Lakshmi 7:155; Pankhurst, (Estelle) Sylvia 7:160; Perón, Eva 7:186; Perón, Isabel 7:188; Perovskaya, Sophie 7:189; Popp, Adelheid 8:24; Prichard, Katharine Susannah 8:34; Pye, Edith Mary 8:37; Qiu Jin 8:40; Rathbone, Eleanor Florence 8:59; Reno, Janet 8:74; Robinson, Mary 8:96; Roland de la Platière, Marie-Jeanne 8:103; Sauvé, Jeanne Benoit 8:158; Schneiderman, Rose 8:164; Schreiner, Olive 8:166; Smith, Margaret Chase 9:33; Suchocka, Hanna 9:96; Summerskill, Edith, Baroness 9:101; Sun Ch'ing-ling 9:102; Suttner, Bertha von 9:105; Suu Kyi, Aung San 9:106; Tencin, Claudine-Alexandrine Guerin de 9:134; Tereshkova, Valentina Vladimirovna 9:137; Thatcher, Margaret, Baroness 9:145; Tristan, Flora 9:169; Tuckwell, Gertrude 9:179; Veil, Simone 10:17; Webb, Beatrice 10:54; Wilkinson, Ellen 10:94; Williams, Shirley, Baroness 10:103; Zasulich, Vera Ivanovna 10:151; Zia, Khaleda 10:156

Politics and Women **8:18–19**

Polk, President 6:114

Pollock, Jackson 4:65, 164; 5:184; 5:185

Pompadour, Marquise de **8:20**; 4:86

Pompey 7:133

Pons, Lily **8:21**

Ponselle, Rosa **8:22**; 4:9

Pont, Margaret Osborne du 2:71

Ponti, Carlo 6:84

Pope, Alexander 2:158; 5:4; 7:52; 7:53; 10:106

Popieluszko, Jerzy 5:41

Popova, Lyubov Sergeevna **8:23**

Popp, Adelheid **8:24**

Popp, Lucia **8:25**

popular music *see* performing arts

Porete, Marguerite **8:26**

Porter, Anna Maria 8:27

Porter, Jane **8:27**

Porter, Katherine Anne **8:28**

Post, Emily **8:29**

Potter, (Helen) Beatrix **8:30**

Poulenc 9:116

Pound, Ezra 1:132; 3:46, 127; 6:87; 7:48

Powell, Dick 6:97

Powell, William 4:185; 6:89, 90

Power, Anna M. 10:85

Powhatan 8:16, 17
Praed, Mrs. Campbell 8:32
Praed, Rosa **8:32**
Praxiteles 1:84; 8:2
Previn, André 1:142; 4:11; 7:20
Price, Leontyne **8:33**
Prichard, Katharine Susannah **8:34**
Priestley, J. B. 1:87; 4:191; 7:82
Priestley, Joseph 6:88
Primus, Pearl **8:35**
Profumo, John 5:150
Ptolemy I 1:79, 169; 9:143
Ptolemy II 1:79, 82, 169
Ptolemy III 1:170
Ptolemy IV 1:170
Ptolemy VIII 3:44
Ptolemy XIII Philopater 3:13
Ptolemy XIV 3:13
Ptolemy XV 3:14
publishing
    Bates, Katharine Lee 1:140; Beach, Sylvia
    Woodbridge 1:146; Dodge, Mary Elizabeth
    Mapes 3:124; Faithfull, Emily 4:2; Monroe,
    Harriet 7:48; Rebuck, Gail 8:66; Steinem,
    Gloria 9:76
Pulcheria **8:36**; 3:185
Purviance, Edna 7:120
Pye, Edith Mary **8:37**
Pym, Barbara **8:38**
Qiu Jin **8:40**
Quaid, Dennis 8:127
Quant, Mary **8:41**
Quindlen, Anna **8:42**
Quirot, Ana **8:43**
Rachel (Old Testament) **8:44**
Rachel (actress) **8:45**
Rachmaninov 4:62
Racine 1:169; 2:163; 3:137; 6:46, 119; 7:54
Radcliffe, Ann **8:46**; 1:103
Raft, George 10:71
Rahman, Mujibur 10:156, 157
Raine, Kathleen (Jessie) **8:47**
Rainer, Yvonne **8:48**
Rainey, Ma **8:49**; 9:25
Rainier, Prince 5:155
Raleigh, Walter 3:173
Ramabai, Pandita **8:50**
Rama Rau, Santha **8:51**
Rambert, Dame Marie **8:51**
Rambouillet, Marquise de **8:52**; 8:132, 177
Rame, Franca **8:53**
Ramos, Fidel 1:68
Rand, Ayn **8:55**
Rank, Otto 7:111
Rankin, Jeannette **8:56**
Rankin, Judy **8:57**
Rantzen, Esther **8:58**; 10:116
Rashid, Ahmed 5:166
Rasputin 1:39
Rathbone, Eleanor Florence **8:59**; 9:80

Ratushinskaya, Irina Borisovna **8:60**
Ravel, Maurice 9:116
Rawlings, Marjorie Kinnan **8:62**
Rawsthorne, Alan 6:101
Ray, Dixy Lee **8:63**
Ray, Man 1:2; 7:24
Rayner, Claire Berenice **8:64**
Read, Herbert 4:164
Reagan, Nancy **8:65**
Reagan, Ronald 2:169; 3:116; 4:23, 173;
    5:173; 7:131; 8:65; 9:30, 147
Rebecca 8:44
Rebuck, Gail **8:66**
Récamier, Jeanne Françoise Julie Adelaide
    8:67; 1:105
Redgrave, Lynn **8:68**; 8:70
Redgrave, Vanessa **8:69**; 3:139; 8:68, 69
Reed, Rex 9:190
Reid, Beryl **8:71**
Reilly, Kate 10:28
religion
    Abigail 1:5; Aethelthryth, Saint 1:18;
    Agatha, Saint 1:20; Agnes, Saint 1:21; A'isha
    1:29; Alacoque, Saint Margaret Mary 1:31;
    Askew, Anne 1:91; Aylward, Gladys 1:106;
    Baldwin, Monica 1:122; Barton, Elizabeth
    1:137; Bernadette of Lourdes, Saint 1:176;
    Blavatsky, Helena Petrovna 2:8; Booth,
    Evangeline 2:30; Bourignon, Antoinette
    2:37; Bridget of Sweden, Saint 2:55; Brigid
    of Ireland, Saint 2:59; Cabrini, Saint Frances
    Xavier 2:105; Catherine de' Ricci, Saint
    2:143; Catherine of Alexandria, Saint 2:144;
    Catherine of Bologna, Saint 2:146;
    Catherine of Genoa, Saint 2:148; Catherine
    of Siena, Saint 2:149; Catherine of Sweden,
    Saint 2:150; Cecilia, Saint 2:156; Chantal,
    Saint Jane Frances de 2:166; Clare, Saint
    3:9; Deborah 3:87; Dyer, Mary 3:147; Eddy,
    Mary Baker 3:153; Elizabeth of Hungary,
    Saint 3:179; Eulalia, Saint 3:189; Fatimah
    4:12; Fox, Margaret 4:60; Frideswide, Saint
    4:74; Geneviève, Saint 4:99; Gertrude of
    Helfta, Saint 4:104; Guyon, Jeanne-Marie
    4:167; Heek, Barbara Ruckle 5:9; Helena,
    Saint 5:10; Héloïse 5:13; Hilda, Saint 5:27;
    Hildegard, Saint 5:28; Huntingdon, Selina
    Hastings, Countess of 5:59; Hutchinson,
    Anne 5:64; Jael 5:89; Juana Inés de la Cruz
    5:128; Judith 5:132; Julian of Norwich 5:134;
    Kempe, Margery 5:158; Khadijah 5:166;
    Lee, Ann 6:33; Lucy, Saint 6:92; McPherson,
    Aimée Semple 7:2; Mary 6:164; Mary
    Magdalene, Saint 6:171; Mary of Bethany
    6:173; O'Hair, Madalyn Murray 7:134;
    Porete, Marguerite 8:26; Rachel 8:44; Rose
    of Lima, Saint 8:108; Ruth 8:123; Sarah
    8:151; Seton, Saint Elizabeth Ann 8:183;
    Slessor, Mary (Mitchell) 9:22; Southcott,
    Joanna 9:51; Taylor, Annie 9:124; Teresa,

Schnitzler, Artur 8:143
Schoenberg, Arnold 6:99
Schreiner, Olive **8:166**
Schücking, Levin 3:133
Schuman, William 4:144
Schumann, Clara **8:167**; 9:40
Schumann, Elisabeth **8:168**
Schumann, Robert 8:167, 168
Schumann-Heink, Ernestine **8:169**
Schwarzenberg, Felix 3:118
Schwarzkopf, Dame Elisabeth **8:170**
Schwitters, Kurt 5:36
Schygulla, Hanna **8:172**
science
    Agassiz, Elizabeth 1:19; Agnesi, Maria 1:22;
    Anning, Mary 1:64; Arber, Agnes 1:68;
    Bascom, Florence 1:138; Bell, Gertrude
    Margaret Lowthian 1:159; Bell Burnell,
    (Susan) Jocelyn 1:162; Benedict, Ruth
    Fulton 1:165; Burbidge, (Eleanor) Margaret
    2:86; Byron, Augusta Ada, Countess of
    Lovelace 2:101; Cannon, Annie Jump 2:116;
    Carson, Rachel Louise 2:128; Châtelet,
    Emilie, Marquise du 2:175; Cori, Gerty
    Theresa Radnitz 3:42; Curie, Marie
    (Skłodowska) 3:66; Fleming, Williamina
    Paton 4:46; Fletcher, Alice Cunningham
    4:47; Fossey, Dian 4:56; Franklin, Rosalind
    Elsie 4:67; Geller, Margaret Joan 4:97;
    Germain, Sophie 4:103; Gimbutas, Marija
    4:110; Goodall, Jane 4:133; Hawkes,
    Jacquetta 4:191; Herschel, Caroline Lucretia
    5:24; Hodgkin, Dorothy Crowfoot 5:36;
    Hogg-Priestly, Helen Battles Sawyer 5:38;
    Hopper, Grace Murray 5:44; Hyman, Libbie
    Henrietta 5:65; Hypatia 5:66; Jemison, Mae
    Carol 5:94; Joliot-Curie, Irène 5:117; Karle,
    Isabella Helen 5:141; Kendrick, Pearl 5:160;
    Kenyon, Dame Kathleen 5:162; Kimura,
    Doreen 5:168; Kirch, Maria Margarethe
    5:172; Klumpke, Dorothea 5:176;
    Kovalevsky, Sonya Vasilievna 5:183;
    Lavoisier, Marie Anne Pierrette 6:24;
    Leakey, Mary 6:29; Leavitt, Henrietta Swan
    6:31; Lehmann, Inge 6:39; Lonsdale, Dame
    Kathleen 6:80; McClintock, Barbara 6:186;
    Manton, Sidnie Milana 6:130; Maury,
    Antonia Caetana de Paiva Pereira 6:181;
    Mayer, Maria Goeppert 6:182; Mead,
    Margaret 7:4; Meitner, Lise 7:10; Mitchell,
    Maria 7:33; Needham, Dorothy Mary
    Moyle 7:97; Nice, Margaret Morse 7:104;
    Noddack, Ida Eva Tacke 7:113; Noether,
    Amalie 7:113; Nüsslein-Volhard, Christiane
    7:123; Parsons, Elsie (Worthington) Clews
    7:170; Perey, Marguerite Catherine 7:184;
    Pitt-Rivers, Rosalind 8:10; Ray, Dixy Lee
    8:63; Ride, Sally 8:83; Rothschild, Miriam
    Louisa 8:112; Rubin, Vera Cooper 8:115;
    Scharrer, Berta 8:160; Somerville, Mary

9:45; Stevens, Nettie Maria 9:79; Wexler,
    Nancy 10:76; Wrinch, Dorothy 10:132; Wu,
    Chien-Shiung 10:134; Yalow, Rosalyn
    Sussman 10:141
Science and Women **8:173–174**
Scopas 1:84
Scott, Sir Walter 1:102, 104, 118; 3:133,
    155; 4:26; 5:15; 8:27; 10:56
Scott Brown, Denise **8:175**
Scott-James, Anne 1:70
Scotto, Renata **8:176**
Scovell, Jane 5:48
Scribe, Eugène 6:33; 8:46
Scribonia 5:135
Scudéry, Madeleine de **8:177**
Seacole, Mary **8:178**
Seaman, Elizabeth 2:16
Sedges, John 2:81
Seeger, Peggy 3:58
Seeger, Pete 9:14
Seghers, Anna **8:179**
Segrais, Jean Regnauld de 7:59
Selassie, Haile 10:152
Seles, Monica **8:180**; 4:141
Seleucus I Nicator 1:79
Selznick, David O. 1:174
Semiramis **8:181**
Seneca, Lucius Annaeus 7:132
Sennett, Mack 7:119
Serao, Matilde **8:182**
Sergeyevna, Galina 10:1
Seton, Saint Elizabeth Ann **8:183**
Sévigné, Marquise de **8:185**; 6:2; 8:132
Sewell, Anna **8:186**
Sewell, Mary Wright 8:186
Sexton, Anne **8:187**
Sexuality and Women **8:188–189**
Seyfert, Gabriele 4:45
Seymour, Jane **8:190**; 2:21; 7:169
Sforza, Giovanni 2:34
Shakespeare, William 4:37, 188; 9:7
Shalikashvili, Gen. John 1:33
Shamshi-Adad V 8:181
Sharif, Nawaz 1:186
Shaw, Anna Howard **8:191**
Shaw, Artie 4:92; 5:39
Shaw, Dinah 9:6
Shaw, George Bernard 1:7, 182, 183;
    2:114; 5:30, 50; 7:101; 9:140, 141, 160;
    10:22
Shawn, Ted 5:58; 9:69, 70
Shearer, Moira **8:192**
Shearer, Norma **9:1**
Sheba, Queen of **9:2**
Shelley, Mary Wollstonecraft Godwin **9:3**;
    4:126
Shelley, Percy Bysshe 2:157; 4:126; 5:14;
    9:3; 10:137
Shemiramat 8:181
Shephard, Sam 6:12

Stone, Lucy Blackwell 9:81; Stopes, Marie 9:82; Stowe, Emily Howard 9:85; Strachey, Ray 9:88; Terrell, Mary 9:138; Thomas, (Martha) Carey 9:155; Tristan, Flora 9:169; Truth, Sojourner 9:173; Tubman, Harriet 9:175; Tuckwell, Gertrude 9:179; Twining, Louisa 9:188; Wells-Barnett, Ida Bell 10:64; Willard, Frances 10:98; Wright, Frances 10:129

sociology
Chiang, Mayling Soong 2:179; Chisholm, Caroline 2:184; Follett, Mary Parker 4:49; Johnson, Virginia E(shelman) 5:116; Keller, Helen 5:152; Lathrop, Julia Clifford 6:19; Loeb, Sophie 6:76; Myrdal, Alva 7:87; Szold, Henrietta 9:111; Wald, Lillian D. 10:37; Ward, Mrs. Humphry 10:45; Wootton, Barbara, Baroness 10:124

Socrates 10:140
Söderström, Elisabeth Anna **9:42**
Sokolow, Anna 3:11
Solomon 9:2, 3
Somerset, Lady Isabella Caroline **9:43**
Somerville, Edith Oenone **9:44**
Somerville, Mary **9:45**; 2:101; 5:24
Sontag, Susan **9:47**
Sophia (Regent of Russia) **9:48**; 3:168, 169
Sophia (Electress of Hanover) **9:49**; 1:57
Sorel, Agnès **9:50**
Sothern, E. A. 5:151
Sothern, E. H. 6:158
South African women
Budd, Zola 2:81; First, Ruth 4:34; Gordimer, Nadine 4:135; Joseph, Helen 5:123; Makeba, Miriam 6:121; Mandela, Winnie 6:125; Ngoyi, Lilian Masediba 7:103; Renault, Mary 8:72; Schreiner, Olive 8:166; Suzman, Helen 9:107

Southcott, Joanna **9:51**
Southey, Robert 2:70
Spanish women
music: Berganza, Teresa 1:172; Bori, Lucrezia 2:35; Caballé, Montserrat 2:103; de los Angeles, Victoria 3:93; Larrocha, Alicia de 6:18

performing arts: Argentina, La 1:72; Casarès, Maria 2:133

politics: Ibárruri Gómez, Dolores 5:68

religion: Eulalia, Saint 3:189; Teresa of Avila, Saint 9:136

rulers: Isabella I 5:74; Isabella II 5:76; Joanna the Mad 5:106

writing: Avellaneda y Arteaga, Gertrudis Gómez de 1:104; Caballero, Fernán 2:104; Castro, Rosalía de 2:136; Matute (Ausejo), Ana Maria 6:180; Pardo Bazán, Emilia, Countess of 7:161

Spacek, Sissy 6:12
Spark, Dame Muriel **9:52**
Spence, Catherine Helen **9:53**

Spencer, Anna Garlin **9:54**
Spencer, Herbert 3:165
sport
Berg, Patty 1:171; Blankers-Koen, Fanny 2:6; Brough, Louise 2:71; Budd, Zola 2:81; Bueno, Maria 2:84; Chadwick, Florence 2:160; Connolly, Maureen 3:36; Court, Margaret Smith 3:48; d'Angeville, Henriette 3:74; Decker, Mary 3:88; Devers, Gail 3:108; Ederle, Gertrude Caroline 3:154; Ender, Kornelia 3:182; Evans, Janet 3:191; Fleming, Peggy 4:45; Fraser, Dawn 4:68; Gibson, Althea 4:106; Goolagong, Evonne 4:134; Graf, Steffi 4:141; Gunnell, Sally 4:166; Hard, Darlene Ruth 4:183; Jacobs, Helen Hull 5:86; King, Billie Jean 5:168; Koch, Marita 5:179; Korbut, Olga 5:182; Lenglen, Suzanne 6:47; Lloyd, Chris Evert 6:71; Lopez, Nancy 6:83; Loroupe, Tegla 6:85; McColgan, Liz 6:188; Maillart, Ella 6:116; Marble, Alice 6:131; Markham, Beryl 6:152; Navratilova, Martina 7:92; Peck, Annie Smith 7:180; Pérec, Marie-José 7:183; Peters, Mary 7:190; Quirot, Anna 8:43; Rankin, Judy 8:57; Sabatini, Gabriela 8:129; Samuelson, Joan Benoit 8:144; Seles, Monica 8:180; Smythe, Pat 9:41; Szewinska, Irena 9:110; Tabei, Junko 9:114; Turishcheva, Lyudmila Ivanovna 9:180; Wade, (Sarah) Virginia 10:33; Waitz, Grete 10:35; Whitbread, Fatima 10:81; Wightman, Hazel 10:89; Williams, Esther 10:102; Wills, Helen Newington 10:104; Workman, Fanny 10:127; Zaharias, Babe Didrikson 10:149

Sports and Women **9:56–57**
Springfield, Dusty **9:55**
Springsteen, Bruce 6:10
Spry, Constance **9:58**
Spurgeon, Caroline **9:59**
Spyri, Johanna **9:59**
Stabiner, Karen 3:184
Staël, Madame de **9:60**; 7:96; 8:67
Stafford, Jean **9:62**
Stalin 5:189; 6:127
Stancykowna 9:112
Standing Bear 9:160, 161
Stanhope, Lady Hester **9:63**
Stanislavsky, Konstantin 3:54; 7:39, 145
Stanton, Elizabeth Cady **9:64**; 1:65; 2:7, 12; 7:77
Stanwyck, Barbara **9:66**
Stark, Dame Freya **9:67**
Starr, Belle **9:68**
Starr, Ellen 1:14
St. Denis, Ruth **9:69**; 4:143; 5:58
Stead, Christina **9:71**
Steffens, Lincoln 9:121
Steiger, Rod 2:11
Stein, Charlotte von **9:72**
Stein, Edith **9:73**

Index of Works

Titles of Works Cited in the Biographies

Amazing Adventures of Letitia Carberry, The (Mary Roberts Rinehart) 8:90

Ambassador, The (Pearl Craigie) 3:51

American Beauty (Edna Ferber) 4:21

American Dances (Agnes De Mille) 3:95

American Document (Martha Graham) 4:143

American Exodus (Dorothea Lange) 6:10

American Portraits (Dorothy Fisher) 4:35

American Provincials (Martha Graham) 4:143

American Slavery as It Is (Sarah Moore Grimké) 4:158

American Songbag, The (Ruth Crawford Seeger) 3:57

American Way of Birth, The (Jessica Mitford) 7:35

American Way of Death, The (Jessica Mitford) 7:35

America's Paul Revere (Esther Forbes) 4:55

America the Beautiful (Katharine Lee Bates) 1:140

Amité (Marquise de Sablé) 8:132

Among the Cities (Jan Morris) 7:71

Among the Tibetans (Isabella Bird Bishop) 1:190

Among Young Russians (Ella Maillart) 6:116

Among You Taking Notes (Naomi Mitchison) 7:34

Amurath to Amurath (Gertrude Bell) 1:159

Ananya (Kanan Devi) 3:109

Anarchism and Other Essays (Emma Goldman) 4:128

Anatomy of Freedom, The (Robin Morgan) 7:68

Anatomy of Me (Fannie Hurst) 5:61

And a Voice to Sing With (Joan Baez) 1:112

And Keep Your Powder Dry (Margaret Mead) 7:4

Andrew Jackson (Margaret Louise Coit) 3:24

And They Shall Walk (Elizabeth Kenny) 5:161

Anecdotes of Destiny (Isak Dinesen) 3:119

Angel (Elizabeth Taylor) 9:125

Angel at My Table, An (Janet Frame) 4:61

Angelic Avengers, The (Isak Dinesen) 3:119

Angels and Earthly Creatures (Elinor Morton Wylie) 10:136

Angels and Insects (A. S. Byatt) 2:100

Angry Harvest (Agnieszka Holland) 5:40

Ankle Deep (Angela Margaret Thirkell) 9:154

Annals of a Publishing House (Margaret Oliphant) 7:138

Anna Svärd (Selma Lagerlöf) 6:3

Anne (Constance Fenimore Woolson) 10:123

Anne of Avonlea (L. M. Montgomery) 7:57

Anne of Green Gables (L. M. Montgomery) 7:57

Anne of the Island (L. M. Montgomery) 7:57

Anne of Windy Poplars (L. M. Montgomery) 7:57

Anne's House of Dreams (L. M. Montgomery) 7:57

Annie Allen (Gwendolyn Brooks) 2:69

Anno Domini MCMXXI (Anna Akhmatova) 1:30

Another Part of the Forest (Lillian Hellman) 5:11

Another Story: As in Falling (Trisha Brown) 2:74

Anowa (Ama Ata Aidoo) 1:27

Anthem (Ayn Rand) 8:55

Anthony Comstock (Margaret Leech) 6:36

Antikrists mirackler (Selma Lagerlöf) 6:3

Antiphon, The (Djuna Chappell Barnes) 1:129

Anti-Slavery Catechism (Lydia Maria Child) 2:182

Antiworld (Nicola LeFanu) 6:37

Any Day Now (Joan Baez) 1:112

Any Woman's Blues (Erica Jong) 5:119

Ape in Me, The (Cornelia Otis Skinner) 9:20

Appassionata (Fannie Hurst) 5:61

Appeal for the Indians, An (Lydia Maria Child) 2:182

Appeal in Favor of the Class of Americans Called Africans, An (Lydia Maria Child) 2:182

Appeal to the Christian Women of the South, An (Sarah Moore Grimké) 4:158

April Twilight (Willa Cather) 2:137

Aracoeli (Elsa Morante) 7:64

Archives du nord (Marguerite Yourcenar) 10:147

Arctic Fox, The (Marianne Moore) 7:62

Ardnamurchan Point (Judith Weir) 10:61

Arena (Hallie Flanagan) 4:44

Are You There, God? It's Me, Margaret (Judy Sussman Blume) 2:14

Ariane (Rosa Praed) 8:32

Ariel (Sylvia Plath) 8:12

Arm and the Darkness, The (Taylor Caldwell) 2:109

Armour Wherein He Trusted (Mary Webb) 10:56

Around and About (Marchette Chute) 3:2

Around Old Chester (Margaret Wade Deland) 3:89

Artamène (Madeleine de Scudéry) 8:177

Art and Eros (Dame Iris Murdoch) 7:81

Art and Lies (Jeanette Winterson) 10:109

Arthropoda, The (Sidnie Milana Manton) 6:130

Artist among the Missing (Olivia Manning) 6:128

Art Objects (Jeanette Winterson) 10:109

Arturo's Island (Elsa Morante) 7:64

Ashes (Grazia Deledda) 3:92

As Husbands Go (Rachel Crothers) 3:63

Aspects of Jews and Jewishness in the Work of Rembrandt (Anna Seghers) 8:179

Aspects of Modern Poetry (Edith Sitwell) 9:18

Aspirations of the World (Lydia Maria Child) 2:182

Assignation, The (Joyce Carol Oates) 7:126

Assignment in Brittany (Helen MacInnes) 6:107

Assumption of the Rogues and the Rascals, The (Elizabeth Smart) 9:23

At Fault (Kate Chopin) 2:187

Athelings, The (Margaret Oliphant) 7:138

Atherton (Mary Russell Mitford) 7:37

At Home and Abroad (Margaret Fuller) 4:81

Big House at Inver, The (Edith Somerville) 9:44

Bird in the Tree, The (Elizabeth Goudge) 4:138

Bird of Time, The (Sarojini Naidu) 7:89

Birds, The (Daphne du Maurier) 3:136

Birds (Judith Wright) 10:131

Birds' Christmas Carol, The (Kate Douglas Wiggin) 10:88

Birds Fall Down, The (Rebecca West) 10:72

Bird's Nest, The (Shirley Jackson) 5:85

Birds of America (Mary McCarthy) 6:185

Birds of Oklahoma, The (Margaret Morse Nice) 7:104

Bishop's Move, The (Pearl Craigie) 3:51

Bitch, The (Jackie Collins) 3:31

Black Armor (Elinor Morton Wylie) 10:136

Black Beauty (Anna Sewell) 8:186

Blackberry Winter (Margaret Mead) 7:4

Black Flower and Blue Larkspur (Georgia O'Keeffe) 7:136

Black Gold; The Mozambique Miner (Ruth First) 4:34

Black Iris (Georgia O'Keeffe) 7:136

Black Is My Truelove's Hair (Elizabeth Madox Roberts) 8:91

Black Lamb and Grey Falcon (Rebecca West) 10:72

Black Narcissus (Rumer Godden) 4:122

Black Opal (Katharine Susannah Prichard) 8:34

Black Oxen (Gertrude Atherton) 1:98

Black Prince, The (Shirley Ann Grau) 4:147

Black Prince, The (Iris Murdoch) 7:81

Black Sparta (Naomi Mitchison) 7:34

Black Spider, The (Judith Weir) 10:61

Black Venus (Angela Carter) 2:129

Blessing, The (Nancy Mitford) 7:38

Blind Girl and Other Poems, The (Fanny Crosby) 3:60

Bliss and Other Stories (Katherine Mansfield) 6:129

Blood of Others, The (Simone de Beauvoir) 1:153

Blood Shot (Sara Paretsky) 7:162

Bloody Chamber, The (Angela Carter) 2:129

Blubber (Judy Blume) 2:14

Blue (Joni Mitchell) 7:31

Bluebeard (Pina Bausch) 1:144

Blue Book of Social Usage (Emily Post) 8:29

Blue Lantern, The (Colette) 3:27

Blues, The (Emilia, Countess of Pardo Bazán) 7:161

Blue Sky, The (Shirley Ann Grau) 4:147

Blue Steel (Kathryn Bigelow) 1:187

Bluest Eye, The (Toni Morrison) 7:72

Boarding School (Hannah Webster Foster) 4:57

Boating for Beginners (Jeanette Winterson) 10:109

Boatswain's Mate, The (Dame Ethel Smyth) 9:40

Bodily Harm (Margaret Atwood) 1:99

Body Book, The (Claire Rayner) 8:64

Body Farm, The (Patricia Cornwell) 3:47

Body of Evidence (Patricia Cornwell) 3:47

Body of Waking (Muriel Rukeyser) 8:118

Bold Stroke for a Wife, A (Susanna Centlivre) 2:158

Bond of Wedlock, The (Rosa Praed) 8:32

Bonheur d'occasion (Gabrielle Roy) 8:114

Bonjour Tristesse (Françoise Sagan) 8:138

Bonus, A (Elizabeth Smart) 9:23

Book, A (Djuna Chappell Barnes) 1:129

Book and the Brotherhood, The (Iris Murdoch) 7:81

Book of Common Prayer, A (Joan Didion) 3:116

Book of Dance, The (Agnes De Mille) 3:95

Book of Folly, The (Anne Sexton) 8:187

Book of Foundations (Teresa of Avila) 9:136

Book of Margery Kempe, The (Margery Kempe) 5:158

Book of Repulsive Woman (Djuna Barnes) 1:129

Book of Small, The (Emily Carr) 2:124

Book of the City of Ladies, The (Christine de Pisan) 3:1

Book of the Three Virtues, The (Christine de Pisan) 3:1

Born Free (Joy Adamson) 1:13

Born of the Conquerors (Judith Wright) 10:131

Boston Adventure (Jean Stafford) 9:62

Bottom of the Sea (Loie Fuller) 4:80

Boys of Company B, The (Rida Young) 10:146

Brat Farrar (Elizabeth Mackintosh) 6:108

Breaking Out (Muriel Rukeyser) 8:118

Breakneck Hill (Esther Forbes) 4:55

Breathing Lessons (Anne Tyler) 9:189

Brewsie and Willie (Gertrude Stein) 9:74

Bridal Wreath, The (Sigrid Undset) 10:6

Bride Wore Red, The (Dorothy Arzner) 1:85

Bridge for Passing, A (Pearl S. Buck) 2:80

Bridges-Go-Round (Shirley Clarke) 3:12

Briefing for a Descent into Hell (Doris Lessing) 6:52

Brief Lives (Anita Brookner) 2:67

Bright Land, The (Janet Ayer Fairbank) 4:1

Brimstone Wedding, The (Ruth Rendell) 8:73

Britannia's Daughters: Women of the British Empire (Joanna Trollope) 9:171

British Synonymy (Hester Lynch Piozzi) 8:9

Broadway Album, The (Barbra Streisand) 9:92

Broken Column, The (Frida Kahlo) 5:138

Broken English (Marianne Faithfull) 4:3

Broken Wing, The (Sarojini Naidu) 7:89

Brontës of Haworth, The (Elizabeth Goudge) 4:138

Brother Carl (Susan Sontag) 9:47

Brothers and Sisters (Ivy Compton-Burnett) 3:34

Brown of Harvard (Rida Young) 10:146

Buccaneers, The (Edith Wharton) 10:78

Bullfight (Shirley Clarke) 3:12

Bull from the Sea, The (Mary Renault) 8:72

Burger's Daughter (Nadine Gordimer) 4:135

Buried Treasure, A (Elizabeth Madox Roberts) 8:91

Child Marriage (Eleanor Florence Rathbone) 8:59

Child of Light (Muriel Spark) 9:52

Child of the Hurricane (Katharine Susannah Prichard) 8:34

Child of Wrath (Sara Lidman) 6:57

Children, The (Alice Meynell) 7:17

Children, The (Edith Wharton) 10:78

Children Are Bored on Sunday (Jean Stafford) 9:62

Children Are People (Emily Post) 8:29

Children First (Christiane Rochefort) 8:98

Children of Heaven (Christiane Rochefort) 8:98

Children of Men, The (P. D., Baroness James) 5:91

Children of My Heart (Gabrielle Roy) 8:114

Children of the Albatross (Anaïs Nin) 7:111

Children of Violence (Doris Lessing) 6:52

Children's Hour, The (Lillian Hellman) 5:11

Child Star (Shirley Temple) 9:132

Chimpanzee, The (Jane Goodall) 4:133

Chimpanzees of Gombe (Jane Goodall) 4:133

Chinaberry Tree, The (Jessie Redmon Fauset) 4:13

China Fights Back (Agnes Smedley) 9:24

China Men (Maxine Hong Kingston) 5:171

China Shall Rise Again (Mayling Soong Chiang) 2:179

China to Me (Emily Hahn) 4:172

Chinese Destinies (Agnes Smedley) 9:24

Chinese Pictures (Isabella Bird Bishop) 1:190

Chinese Prime Minister, The (Enid Bagnold) 1:113

Chinese Puzzle (Rumer Godden) 4:122

Choice Not an Echo, A (Phyllis Schlafly) 8:162

Choices (Liv Ullmann) 10:5

Choir, The (Joanna Trollope) 9:171

Christian's Mistake (Dinah Maria Craik) 3:52

Christine Diamond, The (Marie Adelaide Belloc Lowndes) 6:88

Christine's Vision (Christine de Pisan) 3:1

Christopher Strong (Dorothy Arzner) 1:85

Chromosome Organization and Genic Expression (Barbara McClintock) 6:186

Chronicles of Carlingford (Margaret Oliphant) 7:138

Chrysanthemum and the Sword (Ruth Fulton Benedict) 1:165

Chunky (Victoria Wood) 10:116

Cimarron (Edna Ferber) 4:21

Circle Game, The (Margaret Atwood) 1:99

Circular Staircase, The (Mary Roberts Rinehart) 8:90

Citadels (Marguerite Ogden Wilkinson) 10:96

City Heiress, The (Aphra Behn) 1:157

City of Gems, The (Joanna Trollope) 9:171

City of the Mind (Penelope Lively) 6:68

Clara Morison (Catherine Helen Spence) 9:53

Claudine at School (Colette) 3:27

Clear Horizon (Dorothy M. Richardson) 8:80

Clear Light of Day (Anita Desai) 3:100

Clelia (Madeleine de Scudéry) 8:177

Clemencia (Fernán Caballero) 2:104

Cleo from 5 to 7 (Agnès Varda) 10:13

Cleopatra's People (Naomi Mitchison) 7:34

Cleopatra's Sister (Penelope Lively) 6:68

Clever Woman of the Family, The (Charlotte M. Yonge) 10:142

Clock without Hands (Carson McCullers) 6:189

Cloning of Joanna May, The (Fay Weldon) 10:63

Close Chaplet, The (Laura Riding) 8:84

Cloudberry Land (Sara Lidman) 6:57

Cloud Cuckoo Land (Naomi Mitchison) 7:34

Clouds (Joni Mitchell) 7:31

Clowns (Ariane Mnouchkine) 7:39

Cobras (Ruth St. Denis) 9:69

Cocktails with Mum (Mary Coyle Chase) 2:173

Coelebs in Search of a Wife (Hannah More) 7:65

Coin in Nine Hands, A (Marguerite Yourcenar) 10:147

Coin of Carthage, The (Bryher) 2:79

Collector of Treasures, The (Bessie Head) 5:6

Colored Woman in a White World, A (Mary Terrell) 9:138

Color Purple, The (Alice Walker) 10:38

Colors of Love (Wanda Jakubowska) 5:90

Colors of Vaud, The (Bryher) 2:79

Colossus, The (Sylvia Plath) 8:12

Colour of Life, The (Alice Meynell) 7:17

Columbia Falls (Nicola LeFanu) 6:37

Come and Find Me (Elizabeth Robins) 8:93

Come Dance with Me (Ninette de Valois) 3:107

Comedy: American Style (Jessie Redmon Fauset) 4:13

Come Out of the Kitchen (Alice Duer Miller) 7:23

Comforters, The (Muriel Spark) 9:52

Comic Artist, The (Susan Glaspell) 4:119

Coming of Age, The (Simone de Beauvoir) 1:153

Coming of Age in Samoa (Margaret Mead) 7:4

Common Reader, The (Virginia Woolf) 10:118

Common Sense Applied to Woman Suffrage (Mary Putnam Jacobi) 5:85

Company of Wolves, The (Angela Carter) 2:129

Company She Keeps, The (Mary McCarthy) 6:185

Compass Rose (Elizabeth Jane Coatsworth) 3:21

Complete Cookery Course (Delia Smith) 9:26

Concertante (Elisabeth Lutyens) 6:98

Condition of Women, The (Sarah Moore Grimké) 4:158

Condor Passes, The (Shirley Ann Grau) 4:147

Confessions of an Art Addict (Peggy Guggenheim) 4:163

Congenital Malformations of the Heart (Helen Brooke Taussig) 9:123

Congo Solo (Emily Hahn) 4:172

Connection, The (Shirley Clarke) 3:12

Conquered, The (Naomi Mitchison) 7:34

Conqueror, The (Gertrude Atherton) 1:98

Deadlock (Dorothy M. Richardson) 8:80
Deadlock (Sara Paretsky) 7:162
Dear and Glorious Physician (Taylor Caldwell) 2:109
Dear Octopus (Dodie Smith) 9:28
Dear Sarah Bernhardt (Françoise Sagan) 8:138
Death Comes for the Archbishop (Willa Cather) 2:137
Death Kit (Susan Sontag) 9:47
Death Notebooks, The (Anne Sexton) 8:187
Death of an Expert Witness (P. D. James) 5:91
Death of Cleopatra, The (Edmonia Lewis) 6:55
Death of the Heart, The (Elizabeth Bowen) 2:41
Deaths and Entrances (Martha Graham) 4:143
Death Seizing a Woman (Käthe Kollwitz) 5:181
Death Walks in Kashmir (M. M. Kaye) 5:146
Decision, The (Thea Musgrave) 7:83
Declaration of Conscience (Margaret Chase Smith) 9:33
Deeper into Movies (Pauline Kael) 5:137
Deephaven (Sarah Orne Jewett) 5:98
Degradation of Disenfranchisement, The (Elizabeth Cady Stanton) 9:64
Delia Blanchflower (Mrs. Humphry Ward) 10:45
Delphine (Madame de Staël) 9:60
Delta of Venus (Anaïs Nin) 7:111
Delta Wedding (Eudora Welty) 10:66
Democracy (Joan Didion) 3:116
Democracy and Social Ethics (Jane Addams) 1:14
De Monfort (Joanna Baillie) 1:117
Demon in My View, A (Ruth, Baroness Rendell) 8:73
Descendant, The (Ellen Glasgow) 4:118
Desert and the Sown, The (Gertrude Bell) 1:159
Desire in Language (Julia Kristeva) 5:187
Desolaçion (Gabriela Mistral) 7:30
Destiny (Susan Ferrier) 4:25
Destroy She Said (Marguerite Duras) 3:142
Deuce Coupe (Twyla Tharp) 9:144
Deva (Nicola LeFanu) 6:37
Devil's Motor, The (Marie Corelli) 3:41
Devil to Pay, The (Dorothy L. Sayers) 8:159
Dialogue (Saint Catherine of Siena) 2:149
Dialogues on the Soul and the Body (Saint Catherine of Genoa) 2:148
Diamond Cutters, The (Adrienne Rich) 8:79
Diamond Life (Sade) 8:136
Diamond Lil (Mae West) 10:70
Diamonds and Rust (Joan Baez) 1:112
Diana (Susan Bogert Warner) 10:46
Diary Without Dates (Enid Bagnold) 1:113
Dido, Queen of Hearts (Gertrude Atherton) 1:98
Dido (Charlotte von Stein) 9:72
Did She? (Elinor Glyn) 4:121
Different Days (Frances Cornford) 3:46
Digging up Jericho (Kathleen Kenyon) 5:162
Digging up Jerusalem (Kathleen Kenyon) 5:162
Dilemma of a Ghost, The (Ama Ata Aidoo) 1:27
Dimple Hill (Dorothy M. Richardson) 8:80

Dinner at the Homesick Restaurant (Anne Tyler) 9:189
Dinner Party, The (Judy Chicago) 2:180
Dirt Tracks in the Road (Zora Neale Hurston) 5:62
Disclosing the Past (Mary Leakey) 6:29
Dishonored Lady (Margaret Ayer Barnes) 1:131
Distant Mirror, A (Barbara Tuchman) 9:177
Divided Heaven (Christa Wolf) 10:113
Divine Fire, The (May Sinclair) 9:16
Divine Miss M, The (Bette Midler) 7:19
Divine Narcissus, The (Juana Inés de la Cruz) 5:128
Diving into the Wreck (Adrienne Rich) 8:79
Doctor, His Wife, and the Clock, The (Anna Katherine Green) 4:148
Does, The (Bronislava Nijinska) 7:108
Dog Eat Dog (Joni Mitchell) 7:31
Dog of Flanders, A (Ouida) 7:144
Doll's House, The (Rumer Godden) 4:122
Dolores (Dame Ivy Compton-Burnett) 3:34
Domenica (Marceline Desbordes-Valmore) 3:101
Dome of Many-Colored Glass, A (Amy Lowell) 6:87
Domestic Manners of the Americans (Frances Trollope) 9:170
Donald and Dorothy (Mary Elizabeth Mapes Dodge) 3:124
Don't Look Now (Daphne du Maurier) 3:136
Don't Tell Alfred (Nancy Mitford) 7:38
Don't Tell the Grown-ups (Alison Lurie) 6:97
Dorothy and Other Italian Stories (Constance Fenimore Woolson) 10:123
Double Image, The (Denise Levertov) 6:53
Double Tree, The (Judith Wright) 10:131
Dove in the Eagle's Nest, The (Charlotte M. Yonge) 10:142
Dove's Nest, The (Katherine Mansfield) 6:129
Down among the Women (Fay Weldon) 10:63
Down By the River (Edna O'Brien) 7:128
Downing Street Years 1979–1990, The (Margaret, Baroness Thatcher) 9:145
Drag (k d lang) 6:9
Dream, The (Caroline Norton) 7:121
Dream and the Business, The (Pearl Maria Theresa Craigie) 3:51
Dred (Harriet Beecher Stowe) 9:86
Drops of Water (Ella Wheeler Wilcox) 10:90
Dry Your Smile (Robin Morgan) 7:68
Dubious Legacy, A (Mary Wesley) 10:69
Duet for Cannibals (Susan Sontag) 9:47
Duke Christian of Lüneborg (Jane Porter) 8:27
Duke's Daughter, The (Angela Margaret Thirkell) 9:154
Dulcitius (Hrosvitha) 5:56
Dusty Answer (Rosamond Lehmann) 6:42
Dusty in Memphis (Dusty Springfield) 9:55
Dynamic Administration (Mary Parker Follett) 4:49
Dynamo (Hallie Flanagan) 4:44

Faithfull (Marianne Faithfull) 4:3

Faithful Wife, The (Sigrid Undset) 10:6

Falker (Mary Shelley) 9:3

Fallen into the Pit (Edith Mary Pargeter) 7:163

Fall Flight (Eleanor Medill Patterson) 7:173

Fall River Legend (Agnes De Mille) 3:95

False Dawn (Edith Wharton) 10:78

Famiglia (Natalia Levi Ginzburg) 4:112

Family (Natalia Levi Ginzburg) 4:112

Family and Its Members, The (Anna Garlin Spencer) 9:54

Family Feelings (Claire Rayner) 8:64

Family Gathering (Kathleen Thompson Norris) 7:120

Family Likeness, A (Mary Lavin) 6:23

Family Limitations (Margaret Sanger) 8:148

Family Sayings (Natalia Levi Ginzburg) 4:112

Famous Five, The (Enid Blyton) 2:17

Fanchon the Cricket (George Sand) 8:145

Fanfare for Elizabeth (Dame Edith Sitwell) 9:18

Fanny (Erica Jong) 5:119

Fantasio (Dame Ethel Mary Smyth) 9:40

Fantasy (Matilde Serao) 8:182

Farmer Boy (Laura Ingalls Wilder) 10:91

Far Pavilions, The (M. M. Kaye) 5:146

Fashions for Women (Dorothy Arzner) 1:85

Fatal Falsehood, The (Hannah More) 7:65

Fatal Inversion, A (Ruth Rendell) 8:73

Father and His Fate, A (Ivy Compton-Burnett) 3:34

Fatigue and Efficiency (Josephine Goldmark) 4:130

Fatigue Study (Lillian Moller Gilbreth) 4:107

Fat Woman's Joke, The (Fay Weldon) 10:63

Fear of Fifty (Erica Jong) 5:119

Fear of Flying (Erica Jong) 5:119

Fear That Walks by Noonday, The (Dorothy Canfield Fisher) 4:35

Feathered Nest, The (Margaret Kernochan Leech) 6:36

Feeling and Form (Susanne K. Langer) 6:12

Felix Holt, the Radical (George Eliot) 3:164

Female Eunuch, The (Germaine Greer) 4:151

Female Friends (Fay Weldon) 10:63

Female Parts (Franca Rame) 8:53

Female Quixote, The (Charlotte Lennox) 6:49

Female Reader, The (Mary Wollstonecraft Godwin) 4:125

Feminine Mystique, The (Betty Friedan) 4:75

Feminist Education of Girls, The (Madeleine Pelletier) 7:182

Fenitschka (Lou Andreas Salomé) 8:142

Festival Jubilate (Amy Marcy Beach) 1:146

Fever, The (Agnieszka Holland) 5:40

Few Figs from Thistles, A (Edna St. Vincent Millay) 7:22

Few Friends and How They Amused Themselves, A (Mary Elizabeth Mapes Dodge) 3:124

Field of Forty Footsteps, The (Jane Porter) 8:27

Fifteen-Thirty (Helen Newington Wills) 10:104

Fifth Child, The (Doris Lessing) 6:52

Fight for Union, The (Margaret Louise Coit) 3:24

Filigree Ball, The (Anna Katherine Green) 4:148

Final Burning of Boats, A (Ethel Smyth) 9:40

Fine Old Conflict, A (Jessica Mitford) 7:35

Fire and the Sun, The (Dame Iris Murdoch) 7:81

Firefall (Mona Van Duyn) 10:12

Fire from Heaven (Mary Renault) 8:72

Fire on the Mountain (Anita Desai) 3:100

Fireworks (Angela Carter) 2:129

First Comes Courage (Dorothy Arzner) 1:85

First Four Years, The (Laura Ingalls Wilder) 10:91

First Lady (Erin Pizzey) 8:11

First Liberty, The (Marchette Chute) 3:2

First Salute, The (Barbara Tuchman) 9:177

Fisher's Face (Jan Morris) 7:71

Five and Ten (Fannie Hurst) 5:61

Five Ideas That Change the World (Dame Barbara Ward) 10:43

Flight from the Enchanter, The (Iris Murdoch) 7:81

Flight of the Falcon (Daphne du Maurier) 3:136

Flint Anchor, The (Sylvia Townsend Warner) 10:47

Flora Lyndsay (Susanna Moodie) 7:59

Flower and the Nettle, The (Anne Morrow Lindbergh) 6:64

Flower Fables (Louisa May Alcott) 1:35

Flowering Dusk (Ella Young) 10:143

Flowering Judas (Katherine Anne Porter) 8:28

Flush (Virginia Woolf) 10:118

Flute Player, The (Judith Leyster) 6:56

Flying (Kate Millett) 7:25

Folle-Farine (Ouida) 7:144

Forbidden Journey (Ella Maillart) 6:116

Forc'd Marriage, The (Aphra Behn) 1:157

Force of Circumstance (Simone de Beauvoir) 1:153

Foreign Affairs (Alison Lurie) 6:97

Foreman and Manpower Management, The (Lillian Moller Gilbreth) 4:107

Forerunner, The (Charlotte Perkins Gilman) 4:109

Forest and Game-law Tales (Harriet Martineau) 6:162

Forest Buds (Elizabeth Akers Allen) 1:40

Forest Sanctuary, The (Felicia Hemans) 5:14

Forever (Judy Sussman Blume) 2:14

Forever Darling (Helen Deutsch) 3:105

For God So Loved the World (Elizabeth Goudge) 4:138

For the New Intellectual (Ayn Rand) 8:55

Fortunes of Richard Mahony, The (Henry Handel Richardson) 8:81

45 Mercy Street (Anne Sexton) 8:187

Foscari (Mary Russell Mitford) 7:37

Fountainhead, The (Ayn Rand) 8:55

Fountain of Life, The (Betty Friedan) 4:75

Fountain Overflows, The (Rebecca West) 10:72

Four-Chambered Heart, The (Anaïs Nin) 7:111

Gods and Goddesses of Old Europe, 7000–3500 BC (Marija Gimbutas) 4:110

Gods Arrive, The (Edith Wharton) 10:78

God's Good Man (Marie Corelli) 3:41

Goethe's Correspondence with a Child (Bettina von Arnim) 1:78

Going Back (Penelope Lively) 6:68

Going Steady (Pauline Kael) 5:137

Going to Iran (Kate Millett) 7:25

Going Within (Shirley MacLaine) 6:109

Goldbergs, The (Gertrude Berg) 1:170

Gold Coast Customs (Dame Edith Sitwell) 9:18

Golden Apples, The (Eudora Welty) 10:66

Golden Apples (Marjorie Kinnan Rawlings) 8:62

Golden Arrow, The (Mary Webb) 10:56

Golden Fruits, The (Nathalie Sarraute) 8:153

Golden Gate Country (Gertrude Atherton) 1:98

Golden Miles (Katharine Prichard) 8:34

Golden Notebook, The (Doris Lessing) 6:52

Golden Slipper and Other Problems for Violet Strange, The (Anna Katherine Green) 4:148

Golden Threshold, The (Sarojini Naidu) 7:89

Goldfish Bowl, A (Elisabeth Lutyens) 6:98

Gone Again (Patti Smith) 9:34

Gone to Earth (Mary Webb) 10:56

Gone with the Wind (Margaret Mitchell) 7:32

Good American Witch, The (Peggy Bacon) 1:110

Good Apprentice, The (Dame Iris Murdoch) 7:81

Good Earth, The (Pearl S. Buck) 2:80

Good Fight, The (Shirley Anita St. Hill Chisholm) 2:186

Goodly Fellowship, A (Mary Ellen Chase) 2:174

Goodly Heritage, A (Mary Ellen Chase) 2:174

Good Man Is Hard to Find, A (Flannery O'Connor) 7:129

Good Morning, Midnight (Jean Rhys) 8:77

Goodness Had Nothing to Do with It (Mae West) 10:70

Goodnight, Willie, I'll See You in the Morning (Alice Walker) 10:38

Good Terrorist, The (Doris Lessing) 6:52

Good Time Was Had by All, A (Stevie Smith) 9:36

Good Wives (Louisa May Alcott) 1:35

Goose over the Jungle (Monica Baldwin) 1:122

Gorillas in the Mist (Dian Fossey) 4:56

Gospel According to Woman, The (Saint Teresa of Avila) 9:136

Gospel Oak (Sinead O'Connor) 7:131

Gösta Berlings saga (Selma Lagerlöf) 6:3

Governess, The (Sarah Fielding) 4:28

Gowns for Roberta (Alice Duer Miller) 7:23

Grace Had an English Heart (Jessica Mitford) 7:35

Gracias a la Vida (Joan Baez) 1:112

Graf Reichard (Enrica von Handel-Mazzetti) 4:182

Graham Hamilton (Lady Caroline Lamb) 6:7

Gramineae, The (Agnes Arber) 1:68

Grand Hotel (Vicki Baum) 1:143

Grand Pas de Deux (Twyla Tharp) 9:144

Grania (Isabella Augusta, Lady Gregory) 4:154

Grannarne (Fredrika Bremer) 2:49

Grapefruit (Yoko Ono) 7:142

Grasmere Journal (Dorothy Wordsworth) 10:126

Grass Is Singing, The (Doris Lessing) 6:52

Gravity and Grace (Simone Weil) 10:59

Gray Is the Color of Hope (Irina Ratushinskaya) 8:60

Great Dream, The (Marguerite O. Wilkinson) 10:96

Greater Inclination, The (Edith Wharton) 10:78

Great Fortune, The (Olivia Manning) 6:128

Great Grandfather's House (Rumer Godden) 4:122

Great Meadow, The (Elizabeth Madox Roberts) 8:91

Great Society, The (Barbara C. Jordan) 5:121

Greek Way, The (Edith Hamilton) 4:179

Green Dolphin Country (Elizabeth Goudge) 4:138

Green Knight, The (Dame Iris Murdoch) 7:81

Green Nautch (Ruth St. Denis) 9:69

Green Wave, The (Muriel Rukeyser) 8:118

Greuze (Anita Brookner) 2:67

Grim Glory (Lee Miller) 7:24

Gritli (Johanna Spyri) 9:59

Group, The (Mary Therese McCarthy) 6:185

Group, The (Mercy Otis Warren) 10:48

Groves of Academe, The (Mary McCarthy) 6:185

Growing Pains (Daphne du Maurier) 3:136

Growing Pains (Emily Carr) 2:124

Growing Up (Angela Margaret Thirkell) 9:154

Growing Up (Olivia Manning) 6:128

Growing Up in New Guinea (Margaret Mead) 7:4

Growing Years, The (Margaret Coit) 3:24

G-String Murders, The (Gypsy Rose Lee) 6:34

Guest of Honour, A (Nadine Gordimer) 4:135

Guide to Better Photography, A (Berenice Abbott) 1:2

Gulbadan (Rumer Godden) 4:122

Gulf Winds (Joan Baez) 1:112

Gunhild (Dorothy Canfield Fisher) 4:35

Guns of August, The (Barbara Tuchman) 9:177

Gut Symmetries (Jeanette Winterson) 10:109

Gypsy (Gypsy Rose Lee) 6:34

Gypsy's Baby, The (Rosamond Lehmann) 6:42

Habit of Being, The (Flannery O'Connor) 7:129

Habonok (Lydia Maria Child) 2:182

Hagar in the Wilderness (Edmonia Lewis) 6:55

Halbtier (Helene Böhlau) 2:19

Halcyon (Elinor Glyn) 4:121

Half-Lives (Erica Jong) 5:119

Halfway to Freedom (Margaret Bourke-White) 2:38

Handmaid's Tale, The (Margaret Atwood) 1:99

Hands Full of Love (Kathleen T. Norris) 7:120

Handsome Road, The (Gwen Bristow) 2:61

Hangsaman (Shirley Jackson) 5:85

Hans Brinker (Mary Dodge) 3:124

Hans Christian Andersen (Rumer Godden) 4:122

History of England (Catherine Macaulay) 6:104

History of England During the Thirty Years' Peace (Harriet Martineau) 6:162

History of Henrietta, The (Charlotte Ramsay Lennox) 6:49

History of Jemmy and Jenny Jessamy, The (Eliza Haywood) 5:4

History of Lady Sophia Sternheim, The (Sophie von La Roche) 6:17

History of Maria Kittle, The (Ann Eliza Bleecker) 2:9

History of Mary Prina, a West Indian Slave, The (Susanna Strickland Moodie) 7:59

History of Miss Betty Thoughtless, The (Eliza Haywood) 5:4

History of Ophelia, The (Sarah Fielding) 4:28

History of the Bell Street Chapel Movement (Anna Garlin Spencer) 9:54

History of the Condition of Women in Various Ages and Nations, The (Lydia Child) 2:182

History of the Former Han Dynasty (Pan Chao) 7:153

History of the Jews, A (Hannah Adams) 1:10

History of the Rise, Progress, and Termination of the American Revolution (Mercy Otis Warren) 10:48

History of the Standard Oil Company (Ida Minerva Tarbell) 9:121

History of the Women's Club Movement in America (Jane Croly) 3:59

History of Trade Unionism (Beatrice Webb) 10:54

History of Woman Suffrage (Susan B. Anthony) 1:65; (Elizabeth Cady Stanton) 9:64

Holiday, The (Stevie Smith) 9:36

Hollow Hill, The (Kathleen Raine) 8:47

Hollywood Husbands (Jackie Collins) 3:31

Hollywood Kids (Jackie Collins) 3:31

Hollywood Zoo, The (Jackie Collins) 3:31

Holy Family with the Sleeping Christ (Lavinia Fontana) 4:52

Homage to the World (Louise Nevelson) 7:102

Home (Janet Ayer Fairbank) 4:1

Home (Kathleen Thompson Norris) 7:120

Home, The (Fredrika Bremer) 2:49

Home for the Holidays (Jodie Foster) 4:59

Home Influence (Grace Aguilar) 1:26

Home-Maker, The (Dorothy Canfield Fisher) 4:35

Homes of the London Poor (Octavia Hill) 5:29

Homes of the New World (Fredrika Bremer) 2:49

Home to India (Santha Rama Rau) 8:51

Homosexuality in Perspective (Virginia E. Johnson) 5:116

Honeycomb (Dorothy M. Richardson) 8:80

Hong Kong (Jan Morris) 7:71

Honor Among Lovers (Dorothy Arzner) 1:85

Honours Board, The (Pamela Hansford Johnson) 5:115

Hope Abandoned (Nadezhda Mandelstam) 6:127

Hope against Hope (Nadezhda Mandelstam) 6:127

Horace Chase (Constance F. Woolson) 10:123

Horizon (Helen MacInnes) 6:107

Hornet's Nest (Patricia Cornwell) 3:47

Horn of Life, The (Gertrude Atherton) 1:98

Horse Fair, The (Rosa Bonheur) 2:27

Horses (Patti Smith) 9:34

Horses Make a Landscape More Beautiful (Alice Walker) 10:38

Hospice and Palliative Care (Dame Cicely Saunders) 8:156

Hospital Sketches (Louisa May Alcott) 1:35

Hotel, The (Elizabeth Bowen) 2:41

Hotel Berlin (Vicki Baum) 1:143

Hôtel du Lac (Anita Brookner) 2:67

Hot Line, The (Wanda Jakubowska) 5:90

Hound and the Falcon, The (Antonia White) 10:82

Hounds of Love (Kate Bush) 2:92

Hour of Gold, Hour of Lead (Anne Morrow Lindbergh) 6:64

Hours of Life, and Other Poems (Sarah Helen Power Whitman) 10:85

House and Its Head, A (Dame Ivy Compton-Burnett) 3:34

House Divided, A (Pearl S. Buck) 2:80

House in Clewe Street, The (Mary Lavin) 6:23

House in Dormer Forest, The (Mary Webb) 10:56

House in Good Taste, The (Elsie de Wolfe) 3:110

House in Paris, The (Elizabeth Bowen) 2:41

House of All Nations (Christina Stead) 9:71

House of All Sorts, The (Emily Carr) 2:124

House of Hospitality (Dorothy Day) 3:86

House of Incest, The (Anaïs Nin) 7:111

House of Liars (Elsa Morante) 7:64

House of Lies (Françoise Mallet-Joris) 6:124

House of Mirth, The (Edith Wharton) 10:78

House of Splendid Isolation (Edna O'Brien) 7:128

House of the Spirits, The (Isabel Allende) 1:42

House of the Whispering Pines, The (Anna Katherine Green) 4:148

House on Coliseum Street, The (Shirley Ann Grau) 4:147

House on Henry Street, The (Lillian D. Wald) 10:37

How I Grew (Mary Therese McCarthy) 6:185

How the Casual Labourer Lives (Eleanor Rathbone) 8:59

How to Behave Though a Debutante (Emily Post) 8:29

How to Cheat at Cooking (Delia Smith) 9:26

How to Get a Man, How to Keep a Man (Zsa Zsa Gabor) 4:83

How to Hold a Husband (Dorothy Dix) 3:122

How to Save Your Own Life (Erica Jong) 5:119

How to Sing (Luisa Tetrazzini) 9:141

How to Win (Emma Willard) 10:97

Hudson River Bracketed (Edith Wharton) 10:78

Letters on the Laws of Man's Social Nature and Development (Harriet Martineau) 6:162

Letters to a Friend (Rose Macaulay) 6:105

Letter to Myself, A (Françoise Mallet-Joris) 6:124

Letter to the World (Martha Graham) 4:143

Libya, the Elusive Revolution (Ruth First) 4:34

Life among the Savages (Shirley Jackson) 5:85

Life and Adventures of Jonathan Jefferson Whitlaw, The (Frances Trollope) 9:170

Life and Death of Harriet Frean, The (May Sinclair) 9:16

Life and Loves of a She-Devil, The (Fay Weldon) 10:63

Life for a Life, A (Dinah Maria Craik) 3:52

Life in Mexico (Fanny Calderón de la Barca) 2:107

Life in Prairie Land (Eliza Farnham) 4:7

Life in the Clearings versus the Bush (Susanna Strickland Moodie) 7:59

Life in the Studio, The (Nancy Hale) 4:174

Life of Abraham Lincoln, The (Ida Minerva Tarbell) 9:121

Life of Charlotte Brontë, The (Elizabeth Gaskell) 4:96

Life of Emmeline Pankhurst, The (Sylvia Pankhurst) 7:160

Life of Harriet Stuart, The (Charlotte Ramsay Lennox) 6:49

Life of Queen Victoria (Millicent Fawcett) 4:14

Life of the Bee, The (Doris Humphrey) 5:58

Life of the Mind, The (Hannah Arendt) 1:71

Life of the Mother Teresa of Jesus (Saint Teresa of Avila) 9:136

Life Promise Pride Love (Sade) 8:136

Life Story (Dame Elizabeth Maconchy) 6:110

Life Story of an Ugly Duckling, The (Marie Dressler) 3:130

Life Without and Life Within (Margaret Fuller) 4:81

Lifted Masks (Susan Glaspell) 4:119

Light for Fools, A (Natalia Levi Ginzburg) 4:112

Light Up the Cave (Denise Levertov) 6:53

Like Water for Chocolate (Laura Esquivel) 3:184

Lili (Helen Deutsch) 3:105

Links in the Chain of Life (Baroness Orczy) 7:143

Linnets and Valerians (Elizabeth Goudge) 4:138

Lion and the Cobra, The (Sinead O'Connor) 7:131

Lion and the Rose, The (May Sarton) 8:154

Lion and the Throne, The (Catherine Drinker Bowen) 2:40

Lionheart (Kate Bush) 2:92

Lion-Hearted Kitten, The (Peggy Bacon) 1:110

Lion in Love, The (Shelagh Delaney) 3:90

Lion's Den, The (Janet Ayer Fairbank) 4:1

Lions Love (Agnès Varda) 10:13

Listen! the Wind (Anne Morrow Lindbergh) 6:64

Literary History of England 1790–1825 (Margaret Oliphant) 7:138

Little Birds (Anaïs Nin) 7:111

Little Disturbances of Man, The (Grace Goodside Paley) 7:151

Little Foxes, The (Lillian Hellman) 5:11

Little Horses of Tarquinia (Marguerite Duras) 3:142

Little House in the Big Woods (Laura Ingalls Wilder) 10:91

Little House on the Prairie (Laura Ingalls Wilder) 10:91

Little Lord Fauntleroy (Frances Hodgson Burnett) 2:89

Little Man Tate (Jodie Foster) 4:59

Little Men (Louisa May Alcott) 1:35

Little Ocean Star (Laura Esquivel) 3:184

Little Old New York (Rida Young) 10:146

Little Tea, A Little Chat, A (Christina Stead) 9:71

Little White Horse, The (Elizabeth Goudge) 4:138

Little Women (Louisa May Alcott) 1:77

Live Flesh (Ruth, Baroness Rendell) 8:73

Live or Die (Anne Sexton) 8:187

Lives of Girls and Women (Alice Munro) 7:78

Living Free (Joy Adamson) 1:13

Living in the Manioto (Janet Frame) 4:61

Living My Life (Emma Goldman) 4:128

Living Out Loud (Anna Quindlen) 8:42

Living with the Dying (Cicely Saunders) 8:156

Lizards, The (Lina Wertmuller) 10:67

Loaves and Fishes (Dorothy Day) 3:86

Lodger, The (Marie Belloc Lowndes) 6:88

Lodger, The (Phyllis Margaret Tate) 9:122

Lodore (Mary Shelley) 9:3

Lolly Willowes (Sylvia Townsend Warner) 10:47

Lonely but Not Alone (Wilhelmina) 10:92

Lonely Girl, The (Edna O'Brien) 7:128

Lonely Woman, The (Agnieszka Holland) 5:40

Long Walks and Intimate Talks (Grace Goodside Paley) 7:151

Long Winter (Laura Ingalls Wilder) 10:91

Look at Me (Anita Brookner) 2:67

Loony Bin Trip, The (Kate Millett) 7:25

Lorenzo in Taos (Mabel Dodge Luhan) 6:93

Los hijos muertos (Ana Maria Matute) 6:180

Losing Battles (Eudora Welty) 10:66

Lost and Saved (Caroline Norton) 7:121

Lost Children, The (Ana Maria Matute) 6:180

Lost Country, The (Kathleen Raine) 8:47

Lost Honor of Katherina Blum, The (Margarethe von Trotta) 10:30

Lost Lady, A (Willa Cather) 2:137

Lost Traveller, The (Antonia White) 10:82

Lottery Man, The (Rida Young) 10:146

Lottie Dundass (Enid Bagnold) 1:113

Louisiana Blackbirds (Ma Rainey) 8:49

Love Again (Doris Lessing) 6:52

Love and Anarchy (Lina Wertmuller) 10:67

Love and Desire and Hate (Joan Collins) 3:32

Love and Friendship (Alison Lurie) 6:97
Love and Trouble (Alice Walker) 10:38
Love at a Venture (Susanna Centlivre) 2:158
Love Conquers Nothing (Emily Hahn) 4:172
Loved and Envied, The (Enid Bagnold) 1:113
Love Deluxe (Sade) 8:136
Love in a Cold Climate (Nancy Mitford) 7:38
Loveless, The (Kathryn Bigelow) 1:187
Love Poems (Anne Sexton) 8:187
Lover, The (Marguerite Duras) 3:142
Loveroot (Erica Jong) 5:119
Lovers and Gamblers (Jackie Collins) 3:31
Love Songs (Sara Teasdale) 9:128
Loving Couples (Mai Zetterling) 10:155
Loving Spirit, The (Daphne du Maurier) 3:136
Löwensköldska ringen (Selma Lagerlöf) 6:3
Lucidities (Elizabeth Jennings) 5:96
Lucie (Amalie Skram) 9:21
Lucky (Jackie Collins) 3:31
Lui (Louise Colet) 3:26
Lummox (Fannie Hurst) 5:61
L'Union ouvrière (Flora Tristan) 9:169
Lying Days, The (Nadine Gordimer) 4:135
Machina Carnis (Dorothy Needham) 7:97
Mackinac Island (Constance Woolson) 10:123
McLuhan and the Future of Literature (Rebecca West) 10:72
Madame De Fleury (Maria Edgeworth) 3:155
Madame de Pompadour (Nancy Mitford) 7:38
Madame de Treymes (Edith Wharton) 10:78
Madame Dorthea (Sigrid Undset) 10:6
Madam Höjer's Tenants (Amalie Skram) 9:21
Mademoiselle de la Quintinie (George Sand) 8:145
Madrigal (Cécile Chaminade) 2:161
Mad World, My Masters, A (Aphra Behn) 1:157
Magic for Marigold (L. M. Montgomery) 7:57
Magic of Sex, The (Miriam Stoppard) 9:84
Magic Touch (Peggy Bacon) 1:110
Magic Toyshop, The (Angela Carter) 2:129
Magic Wreath (Grace Aguilar) 1:26
Magnolia Blossom (Imogen Cunningham) 3:64
Maid of Maiden Lane, The (Amelia Barr) 1:132
Making of Americans, The (Gertrude Stein) 9:74
Male and Female (Margaret Mead) 7:4
Management of Terminal Disease, The (Cicely Saunders) 8:156
Man Born to Be King, The (Dorothy L. Sayers) 8:159
Mandarins, The (Simone de Beauvoir) 1:153
Mandelbaum Gate, The (Muriel Spark) 9:52
Manhattan '45 (Jan Morris) 7:71
Man in Lower Ten, The (Mary Roberts Rinehart) 8:90
Man in the Queue, The (E. Mackintosh) 6:108
Man-Made World (Charlotte Perkins Gilman) 4:109
Man of His Time, A (Phyllis Bentley) 1:167
Manors of Ulloa, The (Emilia, Countess of Pardo Bazán) 7:161
Mansfield Park (Jane Austen) 1:102

Man's World, A (Rachel Crothers) 3:63
Manual of the Mother Church (Mary Baker Eddy) 3:153
Man Who Loved Children, The (Christina Stead) 9:71
Many a Good Crusade (Virginia Gildersleeve) 4:108
Manzoni Family, The (Natalia Ginzburg) 4:112
Marcella (Mrs. Humphry Ward) 10:45
Märchen einer Königin (Elizabeth) 3:170
March of Folly, The (Barbara Tuchman) 9:177
March of the Women, The (Ethel Smyth) 9:40
Margaret Fuller (Julia Ward Howe) 5:54
Margin for Error (Clare Boothe Luce) 6:91
Maria Concepción (Katherine Anne Porter) 8:28
Marigold Garden, The (Kate Greenaway) 4:150
Marilyn (Gloria Steinem) 9:76
Marne, The (Edith Wharton) 10:78
Marriage (Susan Ferrier) 4:25
Married Love (Marie Stopes) 9:82
Marsh Island, A (Sarah Orne Jewett) 5:98
Martereau (Nathalie Sarraute) 8:153
Maru (Bessie Head) 5:6
Mary, Queen of Scots (Thea Musgrave) 7:83
Mary (A Fiction) (Mary Wollstonecraft Godwin) 4:125
Mary Barton (Elizabeth Cleghorn Gaskell) 4:96
Mary Christmas (Mary Ellen Chase) 2:174
Mary O'Grady (Mary Lavin) 6:23
Mary Olivier: A Life (May Sinclair) 9:16
Mary Peters (Mary Ellen Chase) 2:174
Mary Poppins (P. L. Travers) 9:167
Mask of Apollo, The (Mary Renault) 8:72
Mask of State, The (Mary McCarthy) 6:185
Masque of the Wild Man, The (Peggy Glanville-Hicks) 4:117
Massachusetts (Margaret Louise Coit) 3:24
Mass in D (Ethel Smyth) 9:40
Master Christian, The (Marie Corelli) 3:41
Mastering the Art of French Cooking (Julia Child) 2:181
Master of Hestviken (Sigrid Undset) 10:6
Matisse Stories, The (A. S. Byatt) 2:100
Matter of Gravity, A (Enid Bagnold) 1:113
Matter of Wales, The (Jan Morris) 7:71
Maud Martha (Gwendolyn Brooks) 2:69
Mauprat (George Sand) 8:145
Maurice Guest (Henry Handel Richardson) 8:81
Ma Vie (Edith Piaf) 8:3
Maximes (Marquise de Sablé) 8:132
Maybe (Lillian Hellman) 5:11
Me, Myself, and I (Joan Armatrading) 1:74
Me and Molly (Gertrude Berg) 1:170
Meaning of Treason, The (Rebecca West) 10:72
Mechanism of the Heavens, The (Mary Somerville) 9:45
Medea (Birgit Cullberg) 3:63
Mediterranean Food (Elizabeth David) 3:80
Medusa (Annie Lennox) 6:48
Mein Leben (Cosima Wagner) 10:34

Member of the Wedding, The (Carson McCullers) 6:189

Memento Mori (Dame Muriel Spark) 9:52

Mémoires à l'emporte pièce (Germaine Tailleferre) 9:116

Memoires de la cour de France (Madame de La Fayette) 6:2

Mémoires et réflexions sur l'art dramatique (Mademoiselle Clairon) 3:7

Memoirs of a Certain Island Adjacent to Utopia (Eliza Haywood) 5:4

Memoirs of a Dutiful Daughter (Simone de Beauvoir) 1:153

Memoirs of a Revolutionist (Vera Figner) 4:30

Memoirs of a Spacewoman (Naomi Mitchison) 7:34

Memoirs of Hadrian (Marguerite Yourcenar) 10:147

Memoirs of the Count of Comminges (Claudine-Alexandrine Guerin de Tencin) 9:134

Memorabilia and Apologia (Sarah Fielding) 4:28

Memories and Impressions (Helena Modjeska) 7:43

Memory and Other Stories, A (Mary Lavin) 6:23

Men, Women, and Tenors (Frances Alda) 1:36

Men, Women, and Ghosts (Amy Lowell) 6:87

Men and the Girls, The (Joanna Trollope) 9:171

Men and Wives (Ivy Compton-Burnett) 3:34

Menopause, The (Miriam Stoppard) 9:84

Men's Piece, The (Twyla Tharp) 9:144

Mens Sana in Thingummy Doodah (Victoria Wood) 10:116

Menstruation Bathroom (Judy Chicago) 2:180

Menzogna e sortilegio (Elsa Morante) 7:64

Mephisto (Ariane Mnouchkine) 7:39

Mercy (Andrea Dworkin) 3:146

Mercy Philbrick's Choice (Helen Hunt Jackson) 5:83

Meridian (Alice Walker) 10:38

Message to the Planet, The (Iris Murdoch) 7:81

Metaphysics as a Guide to Morals (Iris Murdoch) 7:81

Metropolitan Daily (Hanya Holm) 5:42

Metropolitan Opera Murders, The (Helen Traubel) 9:166

Michael Unger (Ricarda Huch) 5:57

Mickey (Mabel Normand) 7:119

Middle Ground, The (Margaret Drabble) 3:128

Middlemarch (George Eliot) 3:164

Midgie Purvis (Mary Coyle Chase) 2:173

Midler Madness (Bette Midler) 7:19

Midstream (Helen Keller) 5:152

Mighty and Their Fall, The (Ivy Compton-Burnett) 3:34

Migrant Mother (Dorothea Lange) 6:10

Mill on the Floss, The (George Eliot) 3:164

Millstone, The (Margaret Drabble) 3:128

Mince Pie and Mistletoe (Phyllis McGinley) 6:191

Mind: An Essay on Human Feeling (Susanne K. Langer) 6:12

Mind Has Mountains, The (Elizabeth Jennings) 5:96

Mind of the Maker, The (Dorothy L. Sayers) 8:159

Mine (Sara Lidman) 6:57

Mine the Harvest (Edna St. Vincent Millay) 7:22

Mingus (Joni Mitchell) 7:31

Minister's Wooing, The (Harriet Beecher Stowe) 9:86

Miracle at Philadelphia (Catherine D. Bowen) 2:40

Miracles of Antichrist, The (Selma Lagerlöf) 6:3

Mirror for Witches, A (Esther Forbes) 4:55

Mirror of Simple Souls, The (Marguerite Porete) 8:26

Mirror of the Sinning Soul, The (Marguerite of Navarre) 6:144

Misalliance, A (Anita Brookner) 2:67

Miscellaneous Pieces of Prose (Anna Barbauld) 1:127

Misfortunes of Love (Claudine-Alexandrine Guerin de Tencin) 9:134

Miss Happiness and Miss Flower (Rumer Godden) 4:122

Miss Herbert (Christina Stead) 9:71

Missing (Elizabeth Butler) 2:96

Miss Julie (Birgit Cullberg) 3:63

Miss Marjoribanks (Margaret Oliphant) 7:138

Miss Marvel (Esther Forbes) 4:55

Miss Pym Disposes (Elizabeth Mackintosh) 6:108

Miss Sophie's Diary (Ding Ling) 3:120

Mistaken Virtues (Joanna Trollope) 9:171

Mistress of Husaby, The (Sigrid Undset) 10:6

Mitla: Town of the Souls (Elsie Clews Parsons) 7:170

Mlle. de Clermont (Countess de Genlis) 4:100

Model Childhood, A (Christa Wolf) 10:113

Modern Cookery (Eliza Acton) 1:8

Modern Industry (Florence Kelley) 5:154

Modern Mephistopheles, A (Louisa May Alcott) 1:35

Modern Rake's Progress, The (Dame Rebecca West) 10:72

Modern Tragedy, A (Phyllis Bentley) 1:167

Mod Strommen (Camilla Collett) 3:28

Moment and Other Essays, The (Virginia Woolf) 10:118

Moment in Love, A (Shirley Clarke) 3:12

Moments of Grace (Elizabeth Jennings) 5:96

Monday or Tuesday (Virginia Woolf) 10:118

Monocotyledons (Agnes Arber) 1:68

Monster (Robin Morgan) 7:68

Montessori Method, The (Maria Montessori) 7:55

Montessori Mother, The (Dorothy Fisher) 4:35

Monuments to Interruption (Eudora Welty) 10:66

Monument to the Unknown Political Prisoner (Dame Elisabeth Frink) 4:76

Moods (Louisa May Alcott) 1:35

National Velvet (Enid Bagnold) 1:113
Natural Curiosity, A (Margaret Drabble) 3:128
Nature and Art (Elizabeth Inchbald) 5:69
Nature of Love, The (Judith Wright) 10:131
Naughty Marietta (Rida Young) 10:146
Nausicaa (Peggy Glanville-Hicks) 4:117
Near Dark (Kathryn Bigelow) 1:187
Near Johannesburg Boy, The (Gwendolyn Brooks) 2:69
Necessary Secrets (Elizabeth Smart) 9:23
Necessities of Life (Adrienne Rich) 8:79
Need for Roots, The (Simone Weil) 10:59
Needle's Eye, The (Margaret Drabble) 3:128
Negro Slavery Described by a Negro (Susanna Strickland Moodie) 7:59
Negro Speaks of Rivers, The (Pearl Primus) 8:35
Nélida (Marie, Countess d' Agoult) 1:23
Nelken (Pina Bausch) 1:144
Nets to Catch the Wind (Elinor M. Wylie) 10:136
Neurosis and Human Growth (Karen Horney) 5:48
Neurotic Personality of Our Time, The (Karen Horney) 5:48
Never-Ending Wrong, The (Katherine Anne Porter) 8:28
Never Forever (Kate Bush) 2:92
Never Must You Ask Me (Natalia Ginzburg) 4:112
Never Sing Louder than Lovely (Dame Isobel Baillie) 1:116
New Book of Cookery, A (Fannie Merritt Farmer) 4:5
New Canto, A (Lady Caroline Lamb) 6:7
New Dance (Doris Humphrey) 5:58
New England Discovery (Nancy Hale) 4:174
New England Girlhood, A (Nancy Hale) 4:174
New England Nun, A (Mary E. Wilkins Freeman) 4:71
New England Woman, A (Cecilia Beaux) 1:154
New Girl Friend, The (Ruth Rendell) 8:73
New Left, The (Ayn Rand) 8:55
New New Guinea, The (Beatrice Grimshaw) 4:159
New Russia, The (Dorothy Thompson) 9:156
New State, The (Mary Parker Follett) 4:49
New Ways in Psychoanalysis (Karen Horney) 5:48
New Woman, The (Robin Morgan) 7:68
New Woman's Broken Heart, The (Andrea Dworkin) 3:146
New Year's Bargain, The (Sarah Chauncey Woolsey) 10:122
New Year's Day (Edith Wharton) 10:78
New York in the Thirties (Berenice Abbott) 1:2
Next of Kin (Joanna Trollope) 9:171
Nice and the Good, The (Iris Murdoch) 7:81
Nice People (Rachel Crothers) 3:63
Night and Day (Virginia Woolf) 10:118
Night and Silence, Who is Here (Pamela Hansford Johnson) 5:115

Night and the Cat (Elizabeth Coatsworth) 3:21
Night at the Chinese Opera, A (Judith Weir) 10:61
Night Games (Mai Zetterling) 10:155
Night in Acadie, A (Kate Chopin) 2:187
Night Journey (Martha Graham) 4:143
Nights at the Circus (Angela Carter) 2:129
Night They Drove Old Dixie Down, The (Joan Baez) 1:112
Nightwood (Djuna Chappell Barnes) 1:129
Nine Magic Wishes (Shirley Jackson) 5:85
Nine Tailors, The (Dorothy L. Sayers) 8:159
Nineteen Beautiful Years (Emma Willard) 10:97
Nine Women (Shirley Ann Grau) 4:147
No, I'm Not Afraid (Irina Ratushinskaya) 8:60
Noblesse Oblige (Nancy Mitford) 7:38
Nobody (Susan Bogert Warner) 10:46
Nocturnes (Elisabeth Lutyens) 6:98
Noddy (Enid Blyton) 2:17
Noli me tangere (Lavinia Fontana) 4:52
None to Accompany Me (Nadine Gordimer) 4:135
Nonsense of Common-Sense (Mary Wortley Montagu) 7:52
Norma Ashe (Susan Glaspell) 4:119
Normality and Pathology in Childhood (Anna Freud) 4:73
North and South (Elizabeth Bishop) 1:188
North and South (Elizabeth Gaskell) 4:96
Northanger Abbey (Jane Austen) 1:102
North of the Danube (Margaret Bourke-White) 2:38
North to the Orient (Anne M. Lindbergh) 6:64
Northwood, a Tale of New England (Sarah Josepha Hale) 4:174
No Signposts in the Sea (Vita Sackville-West) 8:135
Nostalgia Isn't What It Used to Be (Simone Signoret) 9:10
No Sweetness Here (Ama Ata Aidoo) 1:27
Not By Strange Gods (Elizabeth Madox Roberts) 8:91
Notebooks (Simone Weil) 10:59
Notes de route; Maroc, Algérie, Tunisie (Isabelle Eberhardt) 3:152
Notes on Nursing (Florence Nightingale) 7:106
Nothing Ever Breaks Except the Heart (Kay Boyle) 2:44
Nothing Sacred (Angela Carter) 2:129
Not I, but the Wind (Frieda Lawrence) 6:25
Not So Deep as a Well (Dorothy Parker) 7:166
Not Waving But Drowning (Stevie Smith) 9:36
Novelle (Matilde Serao) 8:182
Novel of the Future, The (Anaïs Nin) 7:111
Novel on Yellow Paper (Stevie Smith) 9:36
Nowhere City, The (Alison Lurie) 6:97
Now Is the Time (Lillian Smith) 9:30
Now to My Mother (Antonia White) 10:82
Now You've Done It (Mary Coyle Chase) 2:173
Nuba (Leni Riefenstahl) 8:86
Nulma (Rosa Praed) 8:32

Osler Catalogue of the Circulatory System (Maude Abbott) 1:4

O the Chimneys (Nelly Sachs) 8:134

Other, The (Agnes De Mille) 3:95

Other Half, The (Judith Wright) 10:131

Other Half of the Sky: A China Memoir, The (Shirley MacLaine) 6:109

O To Be a Dragon (Marianne Moore) 7:62

Our Common Land (Octavia Hill) 5:29

Our Faces, Our Words (Lillian Smith) 9:30

Our Hearts Were Young and Gay (Cornelia Otis Skinner) 9:20

Our Human Conflicts (Karen Horney) 5:48

Our Independence (Dorothy Canfield Fisher) 4:35

Our Irish Theatre: A Chapter of Autobiography (Isabella Augusta, Lady Gregory) 4:154

Our Partnership (Beatrice Webb) 10:54

Our Sister Killjoy (Ama Ata Aidoo) 1:27

Our Village (Mary Russell Mitford) 7:37

Our Village Life (Lady Isabella Somerset) 9:43

Out Blood (Andrea Dworkin) 3:146

Outcast, The (Dame Edith Sitwell) 9:18

Outlaw and Lawmaker (Rosa Praed) 8:32

Out of Africa (Isak Dinesen) 3:119

Out of India (Ruth Prawer Jhabvala) 5:101

Out of the Air (Judith Weir) 10:61

Out of this Century (Peggy Guggenheim) 4:163

Out on a Limb (Shirley MacLaine) 6:109

Outrageous Acts and Everyday Rebellions (Gloria Steinem) 9:76

Over at the Crowleys (Kathleen T. Norris) 7:120

Over the Frontier (Stevie Smith) 9:36

Over Twenty-One (Ruth Gordon) 4:137

Owls Do Cry (Janet Paterson Frame) 4:61

Oxford Book of Oxford, The (Jan Morris) 7:71

O Ye Tongues (Anne Sexton) 8:187

Pack of Cards (Penelope Lively) 6:68

Pafnutius (Hrosvitha) 5:56

Pagan Place, A (Edna O'Brien) 7:128

Painted Lady, The (Françoise Sagan) 8:138

Palace and Mosque of Ukhaidir, The (Gertrude Bell) 1:159

Pale Horse, Pale Rider (Katherine Porter) 8:28

Palestine Awake (Sophie Loeb) 6:76

Palimpsest (Hilda Doolittle) 3:127

Pan (Gertrude Vanderbilt Whitney) 10:87

Parents and Children (Ivy Compton-Burnett) 3:34

Paris and the Parisians (Frances Trollope) 9:170

Paris Parks (Shirley Clarke) 3:12

Parson Harding's Daughter (Joanna Trollope) 9:171

Particularly Cats (Doris Lessing) 6:52

Part of the Furniture (Mary Wesley) 10:69

Passenger to Teheran (Vita Sackville-West) 8:135

Passing Show, The (Harriet Monroe) 7:48

Passion, The (Jeanette Winterson) 10:109

Passion Flowers (Julia Ward Howe) 5:54

Passionless Moments (Jane Campion) 2:115

Passion of New Eve, The (Angela Carter) 2:129

Passions of the Mind (A. S. Byatt) 2:100

Pastel (Marie Adelaide Belloc Lowndes) 6:88

Pastors and Masters (Dame Ivy Compton-Burnett) 3:34

Pastor's Fireside, The (Jane Porter) 8:27

Pat and Margaret (Victoria Wood) 10:116

Path to Power, The (Margaret Thatcher) 9:145

Patterns of Culture (Ruth F. Benedict) 1:165

Paula (Isabel Allende) 1:42

Paul Revere and the World He Lived In (Esther Forbes) 4:55

Paura e amore (Margarethe von Trotta) 10:30

Pause: a Sketch Book (Emily Carr) 2:124

Pauvres fleurs (Marceline Desbordes-Valmore) 3:101

Pavlova Impressions (Margot Fonteyn) 4:54

Pax Britannica (Jan Morris) 7:71

Peacock, The (Anita Desai) 3:100

Peacock Spring, The (Rumer Godden) 4:122

Peaks and Glaciers of Nun Kun (Fanny Workman) 10:127

Pearl (Janis Joplin) 5:120

Pearl of Orr's Island, The (Harriet Beecher Stowe) 9:86

Peasants' War, The (Käthe Kollwitz) 5:181

Peculiar Treasure, A (Edna Ferber) 4:21

Peguche, Canton of Otavalo (Elsie Clews Parsons) 7:170

Peking Picnic (Ann Bridge) 2:54

Pembroke (Mary E. Wilkins Freeman) 4:71

Pentimento (Lillian Hellman) 5:11

People in Love (Claire Berenice Rayner) 8:64

Pepita (Vita Sackville-West) 8:135

Percy (Hannah More) 7:65

Perdita (Juana de Ibarbourou) 5:67

Pérégrinations d'une paria (Flora Tristan) 9:169

Perfect Happiness (Penelope Lively) 6:68

Performers, The (Claire Berenice Rayner) 8:64

Perjured Husband, The (Susanna Centlivre) 2:158

Persian Boy, The (Mary Renault) 8:72

Persian Pictures (Gertrude M. L. Bell) 1:159

Personal History (Katharine M. Graham) 4:142

Personality of a House, The (Emily Post) 8:29

Persuasion (Jane Austen) 1:102

Peter Stuyvesant Memorial (Gertrude Vanderbilt Whitney) 10:87

Phaedra (Martha Graham) 4:143

Phases of an Inferior Planet (Ellen Glasgow) 4:118

Philip II (Sofonisba Anguissola) 1:53

Philosopher's Pupil, The (Iris Murdoch) 7:81

Philosophical Fancies (Margaret Cavendish) 2:155

Philosophy of Love, The (Elinor Glyn) 4:121

Philosophy: Who Needs It? (Ayn Rand) 8:55

Philosophy in a New Key (Susanne K. Langer) 6:12

Philothea (Lydia Maria Child) 2:182

Physical Geography (Mary Somerville) 9:45

Progress of Love, The (Alice Munro) 7:78
Progress of Religious Ideas, A (Lydia Child) 2:182
Promenades dans Londres (Flora Tristan) 9:169
Promise (Sade) 8:136
Promised Lands (Susan Sontag) 9:47
Promise of Love (Mary Renault) 8:72
Prone to Violence (Erin Pizzey) 8:11
Prophets for the Common Reader, The (Mary Ellen Chase) 2:174
Proposition, The (Judith Leyster) 6:56
Propositiones philosophicae (Maria Agnesi) 1:22
Prospect Before Us, The (Ninette de Valois) 3:107
Prospects of Industrial Civilization, The (Dora Russell) 8:119
Prostitution Papers, The (Kate Millett) 7:25
Providence (Anita Brookner) 2:67
Province of the Heart, The (Phyllis McGinley) 6:191
Provincial Actors (Agnieszka Holland) 5:40
Psychoanalysis of Children, The (Melanie Klein) 5:175
Psychology of Management, The (Lillian M. Gilbreth) 4:107
Ptomaine Canary, The (Helen Traubel) 9:166
Pueblo Indian Religion (Elsie C. Parsons) 7:170
Puffball (Fay Weldon) 10:63
Purgatory of St. Patric, The (Marie de France) 6:149
Pursuit of Love, The (Nancy Mitford) 7:38
Push Comes to Shove (Twyla Tharp) 9:144
Quarry (Meredith Monk) 7:47
Quartet in Autumn (Barbara Pym) 8:38
Quasi-Stellar Objects (Margaret Burbidge) 2:86
Quatre Bras (Elizabeth Butler) 2:96
Queechy (Susan Bogert Warner) 10:46
Queens and the Hive, The (Edith Sitwell) 9:18
Quest for Christa T., The (Christa Wolf) 10:113
Question of Power, A (Bessie Head) 5:6
Questions of Travel (Elizabeth Bishop) 1:188
Quicksilver (Dame Marie Rambert) 8:51
Quiver of Love, The (Kate Greenaway) 4:150
Race: Science and Politics (Ruth F. Benedict) 1:165
Radha (Ruth St. Denis) 9:69
Radiant Motherhood (Marie Stopes) 9:82
Radiant Way, The (Margaret Drabble) 3:128
Radio Ethiopia (Patti Smith) 9:34
Railway Children, The (Edith Nesbit) 7:101
Rainbird, The (Sara Lidman) 6:57
Rainbow (Thea Musgrave) 7:83
Rainbow Gold (Sara Teasdale) 9:128
Rainbow on the Road (Esther Forbes) 4:55
Rainer Maria Rilke (Lou A. Salomé) 8:142
Raising Demons (Shirley Jackson) 5:85
Raisin in the Sun (Lorraine Hansberry) 4:182
Raíz salvaje (Juana de Ibarbourou) 5:67
Rake's Progress, The (Ninette de Valois) 3:107
Rambles in Germany and Italy (Mary Wollstonecraft Godwin Shelley) 9:3

Ramona (Helen Hunt Jackson) 5:83
Rape (Franca Rame) 8:53
Raven's Wing (Joyce Carol Oates) 7:126
Raymonda (Alexandra Danilova) 3:75
Reader and the Writer, The (Christa Wolf) 10:113
Reality and Dreams (Dame Muriel Spark) 9:52
Real People (Alison Lurie) 6:97
Real Queen's Fairy Book, A (Elizabeth) 3:170
Rebecca (Dame Daphne du Maurier) 3:136
Rebecca of Sunnybrook Farm (Kate Douglas Wiggin) 10:88
Rebels (Lydia Maria Child) 2:182
Recherches sur la théorie des surfaces élastiques (Sophie Germain) 4:103
Recollections of a Literary Life (Mary Russell Mitford) 7:37
Recollections of a Tour Made in Scotland (Dorothy Wordsworth) 10:126
Recollections of Life and Work (Louisa Twining) 9:188
Recollections of Ludolf Ursleu the Younger (Ricarda Huch) 5:57
Record of a School (Elizabeth P. Peabody) 7:179
Records of Women (Felicia D. Hemans) 5:14
Recoveries (Elizabeth Jennings) 5:96
Rector's Wife, The (Joanna Trollope) 9:171
Red and the Green, The (Iris Murdoch) 7:81
Red Gods Call, The (Beatrice Grimshaw) 4:159
Red Roses for Bronze (Hilda Doolittle) 3:127
Red Shoes, The (Kate Bush) 2:92
Red Wine in Green Glasses (Birgit Cullberg) 3:63
Reed Shaken With the Wind; A Love Story, A (Emily Faithfull) 4:2
Reef, The (Edith Wharton) 10:78
Reflections in a Golden Eye (Carson McCullers) 6:189
Reflections Upon the Education of Children in Charity Schools (Sarah Trimmer) 9:168
Réflexions sur le divorce (Suzanne Necker) 7:96
Regina (Laura Esquivel) 3:184
Rehearsal, The (Marie Laurencin) 6:21
Relation du voyage d'Espagne (Countess d'Aulnoy) 1:101
Remains of the Day, The (Ruth Prawer Jhabvala) 5:101
Reminiscences of Lenin (Clara Zetkin) 10:154
Remodeling Her Husband (Lillian Gish) 4:115
Renaissance Man (Penny Marshall) 6:160
Renascence and Other Poems (Edna St. Vincent Millay) 7:22
Reply to Sister Filotea de la Cruz (Juana Inés de la Cruz) 5:128
Répons pour le temps de Pâques (Jeanne-Marie-Madeleine Demessieux) 3:94
Republic of Childhood, The (Kate D. Wiggin) 10:88
Requiem (Anna Akhmatova) 1:30
Reservations for Two (Dionne Warwick) 10:49
Reservoir and Other Stories, The (Janet Frame) 4:61

Testimony of Two Men (Taylor Caldwell) 2:109
Testing of Diana Mallory, The (Mrs. Humphry Ward) 10:45
Thaddeus of Warsaw (Jane Porter) 8:27
That Lass o'Lowries (Frances Hodgson Burnett) 2:89
Theater Piece (Doris Humphrey) 5:58
Théâtre d'éducation (Countess de Genlis) 4:100
Their Eyes Were Watching God (Zora N. Hurston) 5:62
Theme for Ballet (Vicki Baum) 1:143
Then Again, Maybe I Won't (Judy Blume) 2:14
Theory of Flight (Muriel Rukeyser) 8:118
There is Confusion (Jessie Redmon Fauset) 4:13
These Happy Golden Years (Laura Ingalls Wilder) 10:91
They Shall Not Pass (Dolores Ibárruri Gómez) 5:68
They Stooped to Folly (Ellen Glasgow) 4:118
They Went to Portugal (Rose Macaulay) 6:105
Things I Had to Learn, The (Loretta Young) 10:145
Thinking (Hannah Arendt) 1:71
Thinking Out Loud (Anna Quindlen) 8:42
Thinking Reed, The (Dame Rebecca West) 10:72
Third Eye, The (Elinor Glyn) 4:121
Third Life of Grange Copeland, The (Alice Walker) 10:38
Thirty Years' War, The (Dame Veronica Wedgwood) 10:58
This Bed Thy Centre (Pamela H. Johnson) 5:115
This England (Mary Ellen Chase) 2:174
This I Remember (Eleanor Roosevelt) 8:104
This Is India (Santha Rama Rau) 8:51
This Is Living (Lynn Redgrave) 8:68
This Is My Story (Eleanor Roosevelt) 8:104
This Is Our China (Mayling Soong Chiang) 2:179
This Is That (Aimée Semple McPherson) 7:2
This Life I've Led (Babe Didrikson Zaharias) 10:149
This 'N That (Bette Davis) 3:83
This Sex Which Is Not One (Luce Irigaray) 5:72
This Side of Glory (Gwen Bristow) 2:61
This Side of Peace (Hanan Ashrawi) 1:90
This Was the Old Chief's Country (Doris Lessing) 6:52
Thomas Hardy from Serial to Novel (Mary Ellen Chase) 2:174
Thoughts of a Queen (Elizabeth) 3:170
Thoughts on Some Questions Relating to Women (Emily Davies) 3:81
Thousand and One Churches, The (Gertrude Margaret Lowthian Bell) 1:159
Thousand Indias, The (Gloria Steinem) 9:76
Thrashing the Planet (Dixy Lee Ray) 8:63
Thread! (Judith Weir) 10:61
Three Arrows, The (Dame Iris Murdoch) 7:81
Three Greek Plays (Edith Hamilton) 4:179
Three Guineas (Virginia Woolf) 10:118
Three Lives (Gertrude Stein) 9:74

Three Lives (Kate Millett) 7:25
Three of Us, The (Rachel Crothers) 3:63
Three Sisters, The (May Sinclair) 9:16
Three Sisters Playing Chess (Sofonisba Anguissola) 1:53
Three Songs (Ruth Crawford Seeger) 3:57
Three Visits to America (Emily Faithfull) 4:2
Three Weeks (Elinor Glyn) 4:121
Three Women (Sylvia Plath) 8:12
Through a Window (Jane Goodall) 4:133
Through One Administration (Frances Hodgson Burnett) 2:89
Through the Black Curtain (Maxine Hong Kingston) 5:171
Through the Flower (Judy Chicago) 2:180
Through Town and Jungle (Fanny Workman) 10:127
Thy Servant Heareth (Sara Lidman) 6:57
Time of Bees, A (Mona Van Duyn) 10:12
Time of Man , The (Elizabeth M. Roberts) 8:91
Time of the Angels, The (Iris Murdoch) 7:81
Times Three (Phyllis McGinley) 6:191
Time to Dance, No Time to Weep, A (Rumer Godden) 4:122
Timothy's Quest (Kate Douglas Wiggin) 10:88
Tin Flute, The (Gabrielle Roy) 8:114
Tin Wedding (Margaret Kernochan Leech) 6:36
Tiny Garments (Cornelia Otis Skinner) 9:20
Tish (Mary Roberts Rinehart) 8:90
Titanic Memorial (Gertrude Vanderbilt Whitney) 10:87
To Bedlam and Part Way Back (Anne Sexton) 8:187
To Be Young, Gifted and Black (Lorraine Hansberry) 4:182
To Hell With Dying (Alice Walker) 10:38
Told by an Idiot (Dame Rose Macaulay) 6:105
To Love and Be Wise (Elizabeth Mackintosh) 6:108
Tomorrow Is a New Day (Jennie Lee) 6:35
Tongues (Shirley Clarke) 3:12
Too Damn Famous (Joan Collins) 3:32
Too Much Business (Mary Coyle Chase) 2:173
Tory Lover, The (Sarah Orne Jewett) 5:98
To See, To Take (Mona Van Duyn) 10:12
Total Eclipse (Agnieszka Holland) 5:40
To the Island (Janet Paterson Frame) 4:61
To the Lighthouse (Virginia Woolf) 10:118
To the Vanquished (Ida A. R. Wylie) 10:138
Touch (Annie Lennox) 6:48
Touch of Innocence (Katherine Dunham) 3:139
Towards a Better World (Evangeline Booth) 2:30
Towards Morning (Ida A. R. Wylie) 10:138
Towers of Trebizond, The (Dame Rose Macaulay) 6:105
To Whom She Will (Ruth Prawer Jhabvala) 5:101
Town That Was Murdered, The (Ellen Wilkinson) 10:94
Toys in the Attic (Lillian Hellman) 5:11

Women, The (Clare Boothe Luce) 6:91
Women and Economics (Charlotte Perkins Gilman) 4:109
Women and Ghosts (Alison Lurie) 6:97
Women at The Hague (Emily G. Balch) 1:121
Women in Industry (Edith Abbott) 1:3
Women in Industry (Gertrude Tuckwell) 9:179
Women in the American Economy (Juanita Morris Kreps) 5:186
Women in the Nineteenth Century (Margaret Fuller) 4:81
Women in the War (Elizabeth Gurley Flynn) 4:48
Women of Israel, The (Grace Aguilar) 1:26
Women's Place in the Fight for a Better World (Elizabeth Gurley Flynn) 4:48
Women's Record (Sarah Josepha Hale) 4:174
Women's Share in Social Culture (Anna Garlin Spencer) 9:54
Women's Suffrage (Dame Millicent Fawcett) 4:14
Women's Victory and After (Dame Millicent Fawcett) 4:14
Women Workers and Industrial Poisons (Alice Hamilton) 4:178
Wonder! A Woman Keeps a Secret, The (Susanna Centlivre) 2:158
Wonderful Adventures of Mrs. Seacole in Many Lands, The (Mary Seacole) 8:178
Wonderful Adventures of Nils, The (Selma Lagerlöf) 6:3
Wonderful Clouds, The (Françoise Sagan) 8:138
Wonderful Man, The (Sara Lidman) 6:57
Wood and Garden (Gertrude Jekyll) 5:93
Woods and Blue Sky (Emily Carr) 2:124
Word Child, A (Dame Iris Murdoch) 7:81
Words for the Hour (Julia Ward Howe) 5:54
Work, Accidents and the Law (Crystal Eastman) 3:151
Work: A Story of Experience (Louisa May Alcott) 1:35
Workhouses and Pauperism (Louisa Twining) 9:188
Workhouses and Women's Work (Louisa Twining) 9:188
Workhouse Ward, The (Lady Gregory) 4:154
Working Bullocks (Katharine Prichard) 8:34
World and I, The (Ella Wheeler Wilcox) 10:90
World Is Full of Divorced Women, The (Jackie Collins) 3:31
World Is Full of Married Men, The (Jackie Collins) 3:31
World My Wilderness, The (Dame Rose Macaulay) 6:105
World of Love, A (Elizabeth Bowen) 2:41
World of Strangers, A (Nadine Gordimer) 4:135

World Over, The (Edith Wharton) 10:78
Worry Week, The (Anne M. Lindbergh) 6:64
Wouldn't Take Nothing for My Journey Now (Maya Angelou) 1:51
Wreckers, The (Dame Ethel Mary Smyth) 9:40
Writer's Britain, A (Margaret Drabble) 3:128
Writer's Eye, A (Eudora Welty) 10:66
Writer's Recollections, A (Mrs. H. Ward) 10:45
Writing of Fiction, The (Edith Wharton) 10:78
Writing on the Wall, The (Mary McCarthy) 6:185
Writings of E. M. Forster, The (Dame Rose Macaulay) 6:105
Written on the Body (Jeanette Winterson) 10:109
Wuthering Heights (Emily Brontë) 2:66
Xingu and Other Stories (Edith Wharton) 10:78
Yankee From Olympus (Catherine D. Bowen) 2:40
Yearling, The (Marjorie Kinnan Rawlings) 8:62
Years, The (Virginia Woolf) 10:118
Years of Grace (Margaret Ayer Barnes) 1:131
Years of Opportunity, The (Dame Barbara Cartland) 2:132
Yellow Wall Paper, The (Charlotte Perkins Gilman) 4:109
Yonnondio (Tillie Olsen) 7:139
You and I (Harriet Monroe) 7:48
You Are Happy (Margaret Atwood) 1:99
You Are Now Entering the Human Heart (Janet Frame) 4:61
You Can Get There from Here (Shirley MacLaine) 6:109
You Can't Keep a Good Woman Down (Alice Walker) 10:38
You Have Seen Their Faces (Margaret Bourke-White) 2:38
You May Well Ask (Naomi Mitchison) 7:34
Young Children in Wartime (Anna Freud) 4:73
Young Cosima (Henry Handel Richardson) 8:81
Young Die Good, The (Nancy Hale) 4:174
Young Mrs. Jardine (Dinah Maria Craik) 3:52
Young Wisdom (Rachel Crothers) 3:63
Young Woman in Ball Dress (Berthe Morisot) 7:69
Your Baby (Miriam Stoppard) 9:84
Your Growing Child (Miriam Stoppard) 9:84
Zaïde (Madame de La Fayette) 6:2
Zaphorie (Françoise Sagan) 8:138
Zeal of Thy House, The (Dorothy L. Sayers) 8:159
Zimmermann Telegram, The (Barbara Tuchman) 9:177
Zóphiël (Maria Gowen Brooks) 2:70
Zsa Zsa's Complete Guide to Men (Zsa Zsa Gabor) 4:83
Zuñi Mythology (Ruth Fulton Benedict) 1:165